Lectures on Urban Economics

MW00534749

Lectures on Urban Economics

Jan K. Brueckner

The MIT Press
Cambridge, Massachusetts
London, England

© 2011 Massachusetts Institute of Technology

All rights reserved. No part of this book may be reproduced in any form by any electronic or mechanical means (including photocopying, recording, or information storage and retrieval) without permission in writing from the publisher.

For information on special quantity discounts, email special_sales@mitpress.mit.edu.

Set in Palatino by Toppan Best-set Premedia Limited. Printed and bound in the United States of America.

Library of Congress Cataloging-in-Publication Data

Brueckner, Jan K.
Lectures on urban economics / Jan K. Brueckner.
    p.   cm.
Includes bibliographical references and index.
ISBN 978-0-262-01636-0 (pbk. : alk. paper)
1. Urban economics. I. Title.
HT321.B78   2011
330.09173'2—dc22

2011006524

10   9   8   7

Contents

Preface

This book offers a rigorous but nontechnical treatment of major topics in urban economics. The book is directed toward several potential audiences. It could be used as a main textbook, or possibly a supplementary book, in an undergraduate or master's-level urban economics course. It could be used as background reading in a PhD-level course in which students would also read technical journal articles. It could also be read by economists or researchers in other fields seeking to learn what urban economics is about.

To make the book accessible to a broad group of readers, the analysis is mostly diagrammatic. A few chapters make use of some simple formulas and a bit of algebra, but calculus is almost absent. Even though the treatment is nontechnical, the analysis of urban topics attempts to rely on rigorous economic reasoning. The orientation is conceptual, with each chapter presenting and analyzing economic models that are relevant to the issue at hand. In contrast to the cursory theoretical development often found in undergraduate textbooks, the various chapters offer thorough and exhaustive treatments of the relevant models, with the goal of exposing the logic of economic reasoning and teaching urban economics at the same time. Because of its conceptual orientation, the book contains very little purely descriptive or factual material of the kind usually found in textbooks. Instructors wishing to expose students to such material could supplement the book with other readings. Some topics not associated with sharply defined models, such as urban poverty, receive no coverage.

Exercises are presented at the back of the book, for possible use when it is employed as an undergraduate text. They develop numerical examples based on the models presented in the chapters. Footnotes throughout the chapters point to exercises that are relevant to the current discussion.

In view of the nature of the book, the list of references is not particularly extensive. No attempt is made to provide exhaustive citations of the literature on each topic. Instead, one or two representative citations might be given as part of the discussion of standard material that is well accepted among urban economists. However, when a specific idea advanced by a particular author is discussed, the appropriate citation is included. Although the citations are not exhaustive, readers seeking more exposure to a topic can always find references to the literature in the works that are cited.

Since the book has grown out of my own research on a variety of topics in urban economics, the references include an unavoidably large number of my own papers. Other researchers should recognize that this pattern does not reflect an opinion about relative contributions to the field. Again reflecting my own interests within urban economics, the book contains less material on the New Economic Geography, an area of active research in the field since the early 1990s, than would a book written by an NEG researcher. The material relevant to NEG is confined to chapter 1.

The book's suitability as a text for an undergraduate course in urban economics, or for a series of such courses, would depend on the length of the course(s). All the chapters can be covered in the undergraduate urban sequence at UC Irvine, which runs for two quarters of 10 weeks each. In a semester-length course of 15 weeks, some of the chapters would have to be dropped, and only about half of the book could be covered in single-quarter course.

This book has grown out of 30 years of teaching urban economics to undergraduates and PhD students, and I'm grateful to all my students for the opportunity to refine my views on the subject. As for assistance with the book itself, I'm indebted to Nilopa Shah, one of my PhD students at UC Irvine, for her expert work in preparing the figures. I also thank various reviewers for helpful suggestions that improved the book in many places.

1   Why Cities Exist

1.1   Introduction

In most countries, the population is highly concentrated in a spatial sense. For example, cities occupy only about 2 percent of the land area of the United States, with the rest vacant or inhabited at very low population densities. Even in countries that lack America's wide-open spaces, spatial concentration of the population can be substantial, with much of the land vacant. This chapter identifies some forces that lead to the spatial concentration of population. Thus, it identifies forces that help to explain the existence of cities.

Depending on their orientation, different social scientists would point to different explanations for the existence of cities. A military historian, for example, might say that, unless populations are concentrated in cities (perhaps contained within high walls), defense against attack would be difficult. A sociologist might point out that people like to interact socially, and that they must be spatially concentrated in cities in order to do so. In contrast, economic explanations for the existence of cities focus on jobs and the location of employment. Economists argue that certain economic forces cause employment to be concentrated in space. Concentrations of jobs lead to concentrations of residences as people locate near their worksites. The result is a city.

The two main forces identified by economists that lead to spatial concentration of jobs are scale economies and agglomeration economies. With scale economies, also known as "economies of scale" or "increasing returns to scale," business enterprises become more efficient at large scales of operation, producing more output per unit of input than at smaller scales. Scale economies thus favor the formation of large enterprises. Since scale economies apply to a single business establishment (say, a factory), they favor the creation of large factories, and thus they favor spatial concentrations of employment.[1]

Whereas scale economies operate within a firm, without regard to the external environment, agglomeration economies are external to a firm. Agglomeration economies capture the benefits enjoyed by a firm when it locates amid other business enterprises. These benefits include potential savings in input costs, which may be lower when many firms are present, as well as productivity gains. A productivity effect arises because inputs (particularly labor) may be more productive when a firm locates amid other business enterprises rather than in an isolated spot. The mechanisms underlying these effects will be explained later in the chapter.

Transportation costs also influence where a firm locates, and they can lead to, or reinforce, spatial concentration of jobs. This chapter explains several different ways in which transportation costs affect the formation of cities. The last section explores a special kind of agglomeration force: the kind that causes the clustering of retail establishments and the creation of shopping malls.

1.2   Scale Economies

The role of scale economies in the formation of cities can be illustrated with a simple example. Consider an island economy that produces only one good: woven baskets. The baskets are exported, and sold to buyers outside the island. The inputs to the basket-weaving process are labor and reeds. With reeds growing everywhere on the island, the basket-weaving factories and their workers can locate anywhere without losing access to the raw-material input.

The basket-weaving production process exhibits scale economies. Output per worker is higher when a basket-weaving factory has many workers than when it has only a few. The reason is the common one underlying scale economies: division of labor. When a factory has many workers, each can efficiently focus on a single task in the production process, rather than carrying out all the steps himself. One worker can gather the reeds, another can prepare the reeds for weaving, yet another can do the actual weaving, and still another can prepare the finished baskets for shipment.

---

1. When used with "scale" or "agglomeration," the word "economies" means "savings" or "benefits."

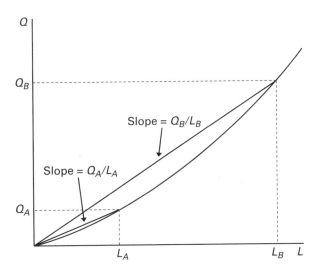

Figure 1.1
Scale economies.

The production function for the basket-weaving process is plotted in figure 1.1. The factory's output, Q, is represented on the vertical axis, and the number of workers, L, on the horizontal axis. Since the reed input is available as needed, it does not have to be shown separately in the diagram. Because the curve shows basket output increasing at an increasing rate as L rises, scale economies are present in basket weaving. This fact can be verified by considering output per worker, which is measured by the slope of a line connecting the origin to a point on the production function. For example, the lower line segment in the figure (call it A) has a slope of Q_A/L_A, equal to the rise (Q_A) along the line divided by the run (L_A). The higher line segment (call it B), which corresponds to a factory with more workers (L_B as opposed to L_A), has slope Q_B/L_B, equal to output per worker in the larger factory. Since line B is steeper than line A, output per worker is higher in the larger factory, a consequence of a finer division of labor.

Using this information, consider the organization of basket weaving on the island economy. If 100 workers are available, the question is how these workers should be grouped into factories. Consider two possibilities: the formation of one large 100-worker factory and the formation of 100 single-worker factories (involving "backyard" production of baskets). The natural decision criterion is the island's total output of baskets, with the preferred arrangement yielding the highest output.

Table 1.1
Basket output of the island economy.

Production arrangement	Number of factories (a)	Workers per factory (b)	Output per worker (c)	Output per factory ($b \times c$)	Total output ($a \times b \times c$)
Backyard factories	100	1	α	1α	$100 \times 1\alpha$ $= 100\alpha$
One large factory	1	100	β	100β	$1 \times 100\beta$ $= 100\beta$

The answer should be clear: given the greater efficiency of workers in large factories, the 100-worker factory will produce more output than the collection of 100 backyard factories.

But it is useful to verify this conclusion in a more systematic fashion. Let α be output per worker in a factory of size 1, equal to the slope of a line like A in figure 1.1 with $L_A = 1$. Let β be output per worker in a factory of size 100, equal to the slope of a line like B with $L_B = 100$. From the figure, it is clear that $\beta > \alpha$. Now consider table 1.1.

The island economy's total output of baskets equals (number of factories) × (workers per factory) × (output per worker). Table 1.1 shows that this output expression is largest with one large factory. It equals 100β, which is larger than the total output of 100α from the collection of backyard factories, given $\beta > \alpha$.

Since the island economy gains by having one large basket factory, the economy would presumably be pushed toward this arrangement, either by market forces or by central planning (if it is a command economy). But once one large factory has been formed, the basket workers will live near it, which will lead to the formation of a city.

This story is highly stylized, but it captures the essential link between scale economies and city formation, which will also be present in more complicated and realistic settings. But something is missing from the story. It can explain the formation of "company towns," but it cannot explain how truly large urban agglomerations arise.

To see this point, consider a more realistic example in which the production process is automobile assembly. This process clearly exhibits scale economies, since assembly plants tend to be large, typically employing 2,000 workers or more. Thus, an assembly plant will lead to a spatial concentration of employment, and these auto workers (and their families) will in turn attract other establishments designed to serve their personal needs—grocery stores, gas stations, doctor's offices, and so on. The result will be a "company town" with the auto plant at its center. But how large will this town be? In the absence of any other large employer, its population may be limited in size, say to 25,000. The upshot is that, while scale economies by themselves can generate a city, it will not be as large as, say, Chicago or Houston. In order to generate such a metropolis, many firms must locate together in close proximity. For this outcome to occur, *agglomeration economies* must be present.

1.3 Agglomeration Economies

Agglomeration economies can be either pecuniary or technological. Pecuniary agglomeration economies lead to a reduction in the cost of a firm's inputs without affecting the productivity of the inputs. Technological agglomeration economies raise the productivity of the inputs without lowering their cost. Simply stated, pecuniary economies make some inputs cheaper in large cities than in small ones, while technological economies make inputs more productive in large cities than in small ones.

1.3.1 Pecuniary agglomeration economies
The labor market offers examples of pecuniary agglomeration econo-mies. Consider a big city, with a large concentration of jobs and thus a large labor market, where many workers offer their labor services to employers. Suppose a firm is trying to hire a specialized type of worker, with skills that are rare among the working population. With its large labor market, a few such workers might reside in a big city, and one presumably could be hired with a modest advertising effort and modest interviewing costs. However, the labor market of a small city probably would contain no workers of the desired type. This absence would force the employer to conduct a more costly search in other cities, and to bring job candidates from afar for interviewing. The firm might also have to pay relocation costs for a hired worker, adding to its already high hiring costs. Thus, by locating in a big city, a firm may lower its cost of hiring specialized labor. The existing employment concentration in the big city thus attracts even more jobs as firms locate there to reduce their hiring costs. The big city then becomes even bigger as a result of this agglomeration effect.

Locating in a big city could also reduce the cost of inputs supplied by other firms (as opposed to labor inputs supplied by individual workers). For example, the large market for commercial security services in a big city would support many suppliers of security guards. These suppliers would compete among one another, driving down prices and thus lowering the cost of security services used in protecting office buildings or factories. Big-city competition could also reduce the prices of other business services—legal and advertising services, commercial cleaning and groundskeeping, and so on. The same effect could also arise in the context of locally supplied physical inputs, such as ball bearings for a production process or food inputs for the company cafeteria, where competition among big-city suppliers would reduce input costs. As in the case of hiring costs, the job concentration in a big city is self-reinforcing: once jobs become concentrated, even more firms will want to locate in the big city to take advantage of the lower input costs it offers.

In some cases, a small-town location might mean that a particular business service is entirely unavailable locally, just like the specialized worker discussed above. For example, a firm might require specialized legal services (help with an antitrust issue, for example), and there might be no local law firm with such expertise. The firm would then have to pay high-priced lawyers to travel to its headquarters from their big-city offices, or else would have to develop the required expertise "in house" at high cost. In this case, higher input costs arise from the sheer local unavailability of the service in the small city rather than from the low degree of competition among local suppliers. → No supply w/ high demand = premium price Tag, /small Town

Firms also purchase transportation services, which are used in shipping output to the market and in shipping inputs to the production site. A firm can reduce its output shipping costs by locating near its market, and it can reduce its input shipping costs by locating near its suppliers. A big city, with its many households, is a likely market for output, and it may also host many of a firm's input suppliers. In this situation, the firm can minimize its shipping costs for both output and inputs by also locating in the big city. Note that the resulting pecuniary agglomeration benefit is slightly different from those discussed above. Instead of facing a lower unit price of transportation services in the big city (a lower cost per ton-mile), the firm benefits from being able to purchase *less* of these services because of its proximity to the market and to suppliers.[2]

P oI

---

2. Paying high-priced big-city lawyers to travel to a firm's small-city location fits into this scenario. The firm is transporting its legal input, an outcome that could be avoided by locating in the big city.

NB- Move to a small Town w/ a large Need for specialized services. To Raise value/Income. Premium p- Inane.

Another observation is that this scenario "stacks the deck" in favor of the transportation-cost argument for a big-city location. Suppose instead that input suppliers are in a different location, while the market is still in the big city. Then, locating there will save on output shipping costs, but the inputs will have to come from afar. In this case, the location with the lowest total transport cost may not be in the big city, so that transport-related agglomeration economies may not be operative. This case is discussed in detail later in the chapter.

1.3.2 Technological agglomeration economies

Technological agglomeration economies arise when a firm's inputs are more productive if it locates in a big city, amid a large concentration of employment, than if it locates in a small city. To understand how such an effect can arise, suppose that a high-technology firm spends substantial sums on research and development. This spending leads to new technologies and products, which the firm can then patent, allowing it to earn revenue from licensing its discoveries. Suppose for simplicity that the firm's output is measured by the number of patents it generates per year, and that the only input is labor, measured by the number of engineers the firm employs.

The production function is plotted in figure 1.2, with the output (patents) again on the vertical axis and the input (engineers) on the

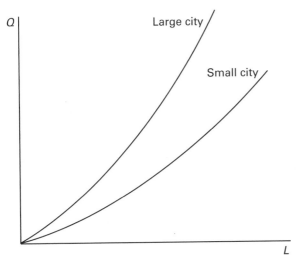

Figure 1.2
Technological agglomeration economies.

NB- Theoretically, you can move to a small town, charge a premium, pay less in Taxes, and housing. while increasing my chance of getting a job.

horizontal axis. The figure shows that research and development exhibits scale economies, although this feature isn't crucial to the story. The figure also shows two different production functions, which apply in different situations. The lower curve is relevant when the firm locates in a small city where few other high-tech firms are present. The upper curve is relevant when the firm locates in a big city amid a large number of other high-tech firms. The greater height of the upper curve indicates that the firm produces more patents, for any given number of engineers, when it locates in a big city. Thus, engineers are more productive, generating more patentable ideas, in the big city.

This beneficial effect could be a result of "knowledge spillovers", across high-tech firms, which are a type of externality. While engineers within a given firm collaborate intensively in producing patentable ideas, spillovers arise when contact between engineers in *different firms* also stimulates this productive process. For example, engineers from different high-tech firms might socialize together, sharing a pitcher of beer at a Friday "happy hour." Although the engineers wouldn't want to divulge their company's particular secrets, the happy-hour discussion might cover more general ideas, and it might get the engineers thinking in new directions. At work the following week, this stimulation may start a process that eventually leads to patents that wouldn't have been generated otherwise. Thus, the engineers end up being more productive because the large high-tech employment concentration allows them to interact with peers doing similar work in other companies.

Although a big city is likely to have a concentration of high-tech employment, allowing knowledge spillovers to occur, some big cities may not have many high-tech firms. Thus, the big city/small city distinction may be less relevant for knowledge spillovers than it was for pecuniary agglomeration economies. Instead, what may matter is the extent of the city's employment concentration in the industry in which such spillovers occur. If a small or medium-size city happens to have a big employment concentration in the relevant industry, it will offer strong technological agglomeration economies for industry firms despite its limited size.

Might some kinds of knowledge spillovers occur across different industries, so that a city where many different industries are represented is also is capable of generating technological agglomeration economies? For example, might knowledge spillovers arise between manufacturers of medical equipment and producers of computer software? This type of linkage seems possible, and to the extent that it exists, the overall employment level in a city (rather than employment in a firm's own industry) might be the source of technological agglomeration economies. City size may then capture the extent of such economies, as in the case of pecuniary agglomeration economies.

As will be discussed further below, empirical research on agglomeration effects sometimes finds evidence of such a link between and worker productivity and total employment (and thus city size). "Urbanization economies" is a name sometimes given to this effect. But the empirical evidence for a link between productivity and own-industry employment in a city is much stronger (this effect is referred to as "localization economies"). Thus, technological agglomeration economies appear to operate more strongly within industries than across industries.

In addition to knowledge spillovers, several other channels for such an agglomeration effect can be envisioned. When a city's employment in a particular industry is large, the existence of a large labor pool makes replacement of workers easy. As a result, unproductive workers can be fired with little disruption to the firm, since they can be immediately replaced. Recognizing this possibility, employees will work hard, achieving higher productivity than in an environment in which shirking on the job is harder to punish with dismissal.

The large labor pool also gives employers a broad range of choice in hiring decisions, which may make it harder for any individual to secure a first job in the industry. Workers may then have an incentive to improve their credentials via additional education and training, and these efforts would lead to higher productivity. Thus, the existence of a large labor pool may raise productivity for workers trying to get a job as well as for those worried about losing one.

A third channel could arise through the phenomenon of "keeping up with the Joneses." In a city with high employment in a particular industry, workers may be likely to socialize with employees working for other firms in their industry, as was noted above. In addition to making comparisons within their own firm, workers may then judge their achievements against those of friends in other firms. This comparison may spur harder work as employees try to "look good" in the eyes of a broader social set. Thus, in addition to being driven by knowledge spillovers, the higher worker productivity associated with technological agglomeration economies could arise from these three other sources.

A vast empirical literature tests for the existence of agglomeration economies. For a survey, see Rosenthal and Strange 2004. Early work investigated the connection between worker productivity and both own-industry and total employment in a city (see Henderson 1986, 2003). As was noted earlier, such studies often find evidence of an own-industry effect for knowledge-intensive industries, in which spillovers are likely to occur, without finding much evidence of a total-employment effect. Another empirical approach relates worker productivity to employment density in a city (Ciccone and Hall 1996). Yet another approach links the birth of new firms to own-industry employment, on the belief that business startups are more likely to occur in areas offering agglomeration economies (Rosenthal and Strange 2003). A similar approach relates employment growth to own-industry employment and other agglomeration factors (Glaeser et al. 1992). Other research focuses more explicitly on knowledge spillovers by considering patent activity. A patent application must cite earlier related patents, and some work shows that cited patents tend to be from the same city as the patent application, indicating local knowledge spillovers (Jaffe, Trajtenberg, and Henderson 1993). Other research relates the level of patenting activity to a city's employment density (Carlino, Chatterjee, and Hunt 2007). This literature offers an overwhelming body of evidence showing the existence of agglomeration economies, mostly of the technological type.

1.4   Transport Costs and Firm Location

As was seen above, transportation-cost savings can be viewed as a type of pecuniary agglomeration effect, which may draw firms to a large city when both its market and suppliers are located there. However, when the market and suppliers are far apart, the firm's location decision is less clear. To analyze this case, consider a situation in which a firm sells its output to a single market, presumably located in a city, and acquires its input from a single location distant from the market. Viewing the input as a raw material, let the input source be referred to as the "mine." Moreover, suppose that the mine and the market are connected by a road that can be used for shipments (see figure 1.3), and that the firm's factory can be located anywhere along this road, including at the market or at the mine. The mine and the market are D miles apart.

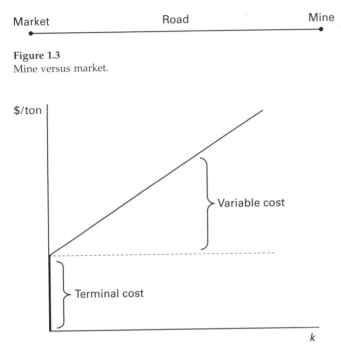

Market   Road   Mine

Figure 1.3
Mine versus market.

Figure 1.4
Transport costs.

Shipping costs exhibit "economies of distance" in the sense that the cost per mile of shipping a ton of material declines with the distance shipped. Figure 1.4 illustrates such a relationship, with the vertical axis representing cost per ton and the horizontal axis representing shipping distance (denoted by k). The figure shows shipping cost as having two components. The first is "terminal cost," which must be incurred regardless of shipping distance. This is the cost of loading the shipment onto a truck or a train, and it is represented by the vertical intercept of the line. The second component is variable cost, which equals the product of the fixed incremental cost per mile (equal to the slope of the line) and the distance shipped. Variable cost is thus the height of the line above its intercept. The presence of economies of distance can be seen by drawing a line between the origin and a point on the curve. The slope of this line is equal to cost per mile (analogous to output per worker in figure 1.1). As shipping distance increases, this line becomes flatter, indicating a decline in cost per mile. The reason for this decline is that the fixed terminal cost is spread over more miles as distance increases.[3]

For the current analysis, it is convenient to use a somewhat less realistic transport-cost curve that has zero terminal costs but still exhibits economies of distance. Figure 1.5 shows two such curves, with economies of distance following from their concavity (which reflects declining variable cost). The lower curve represents the cost per ton of shipping the output different distances. To understand the upper curve, suppose that the production process entails refining raw materials, with production of the refined output requiring that a portion of the input be removed and discarded. Then, to produce a ton of output, the refining factory requires more than a ton of input. The upper curve represents the cost of shipping this amount of input various distances. In other words, the curve represents the cost of shipping enough input to produce a ton of output.

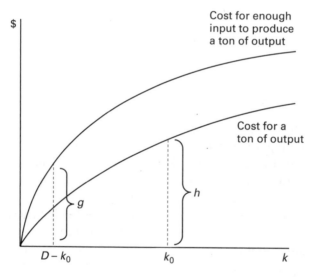

Figure 1.5
Input and output shipping.

---

3. A diagram like figure 1.4 can be used to illustrate transport mode choice between truck and train. Relative to trains, trucks have low terminal cost (they can be driven directly to a shipment pick-up point), but they have high variable cost, using more fuel and labor per ton shipped than trains. Therefore, the truck line in a diagram like figure 1.4 would start below the train line and eventually rise above it. As a result, a shipper choosing the cheapest mode would select truck for a short-distance shipment and train for a long-distance shipment.

The fact that the unrefined input and the refined output are qualitatively similar (both being, in effect, dirt) is convenient. This similarity means that the cost of shipping a ton of input or output a given distance will be the same, which ensures that the input shipping cost curve in figure 1.5 (which pertains to more than a ton) will be higher.

Things are more complicated if inputs and outputs are qualitatively different. In the baking of bread, for example, the flour input is compact but the output of finished loaves is very bulky, so that a ton of output is more costly to ship than a ton of input. Figure 1.5 would have to be modified to fit this case.

The information in figure 1.5 can be used to compute the best location for the factory. If the factory has a contract to deliver a fixed amount of output to the market, its goal is to minimize the total shipping cost per ton of delivered output. This total includes both the cost of shipping the output and the cost of shipping the input, with the latter cost pertaining to enough input to make a ton of output.

Suppose the factory is located k_0 miles from the market. Then the output must be shipped k_0 miles and the input must be shipped $D - k_0$ miles (recall that D is the distance between the mine and the market). The output shipping cost (per ton) is represented in figure 1.5 by h, and the input shipping cost (per ton of output produced) by g. The total shipping cost per ton of output at location k_0 is then $h + g$. To find the best location, this calculation procedure must be repeated for all k_0 values between 0 and D, with the location yielding the lowest total cost chosen. The required steps are cumbersome, however, and the answer is, so far, unclear.

The answer can be seen immediately, however, if figure 1.5 is redrawn as figure 1.6. This new figure has two origins, one at 0 and the other at distance D, and the input shipping curve is drawn backward, starting at the D origin. Now, total shipping cost (per ton of output) at location k_0 is equal to the height of output curve at that point plus the height of the input curve at the same point, which equals the cost of shipping the input $D - k_0$ miles. Therefore, shipping cost per ton of output is equal to the vertical sum of the two curves at any point, and the resulting curve is the upper hump-shaped one in figure 1.6. By inspection, it is easy to see the cheapest location. It is an endpoint location, with the factory located at the mine. All other locations, including the market and points between the mine and market, result in higher total shipping costs.

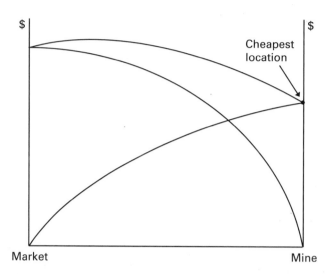

Figure 1.6
Transport-cost-minimizing location.

The mine is the best location because the production process is a "weight-losing" process. In other words, more than a ton of input is transformed into a ton of output. In this case, it doesn't make sense to ship the input at all, since some of the material will be discarded in the refining process. Only the output should be shipped.

This appealingly simple rationale partially obscures the logic of the solution. The logic has two components. First, because of economies of distance, it isn't economical to ship both the input and the output. In this case, two intermediate-distance shipments would occur, failing to exploit the lower cost per mile of longer shipments. Thus, either the output should be shipped the entire mine–market distance of D miles or the input should be shipped the entire distance. The best choice is the one that is cheaper, and, given the weight-losing nature of the production process, shipping the output all the way costs less. This argument shows that economies of distance, omitted from the partial explanation above, are crucial to the solution.[4]

---

4. If transport costs instead exhibited *diseconomies* of distance (with the curves convex), then intermediate-distance shipments would be desirable, and the best location would be an intermediate point between the mine and market. This result, which can be seen by redrawing figure 1.6 for the diseconomies case, shows that weight loss in production isn't sufficient for a mine location to be best.

Suppose the production process is, instead, weight gaining. An example would be Coca-Cola bottling, in which syrup (evidently produced under secret conditions near the company's headquarters in Atlanta) is combined with water to produce the finished product. In this weight-gaining case, the heights of the input and output curves in figure 1.5 are reversed, as are the heights in figure 1.6. The hump-shaped curve in figure 1.6 then reaches its low point at the market rather than at the mine, making the market the best location for the factory (in this case, the bottling plant). The outcome is natural since it would make little sense to ship finished Coca-Cola long distances when its main component (water) is available everywhere.[5]

In reality, the bottling of soft drinks is indeed a "market-oriented" production process, with bottling plants located in many cities across the United States. The theory says that weight-gaining production processes should all share this feature, while weight-losing processes should be oriented to the mine (or the input). This simple model, however, omits many elements of reality, including the existence of multiple markets and multiple input sites for a given firm, as well as "bulk" differences between inputs and outputs, which (as explained above) complicate the picture.[6] Nevertheless, the model shows that transport costs will affect where firms locate and thus will influence the formation of cities.

In the simple case analyzed, this influence can be delineated. The market (presumably a big city) will attract weight-gaining production processes as firms seek to minimize transport costs. Therefore, the city's existing concentration of jobs and people will attract additional jobs in weight-gaining industries via this transport-related agglomeration force. Weight-losing industries, however, will shun the market and will instead locate at the source of the raw material. Therefore, the existence of a big-city market may spawn separate employment concentrations at faraway natural-resource sites where factories built to serve the

---

5. The best factory location may sometimes lie at a "transshipment" point between the mine and the market, where the shipment must be unloaded and reloaded for some reason. Exercise 1.1 considers such a case, assuming that an unbridged river cuts the road between the mine and market, necessitating unloading, transfer to a barge, and reloading of the shipment.

6. With multiple markets and mines, it can be shown that the optimal location is usually some intermediate point, so that a market or mine location is not best.

market find it best to locate. Concentrated employment in one spot may thus cause additional remote employment concentrations to arise as a result of transport-related forces.

1.5   The Interaction of Scale Economies and Transportation Costs in the Formation of Cities

Although the desire to minimize transport costs can pull a factory toward a particular location, these costs can also play a role in the overall organization of production. In particular, transport costs can help determine whether production is centralized in one large factory or divided among a number of smaller establishments. The analysis in section 1.2 showed that a single large factory was best, but transport costs played no role in that analysis.

To illustrate the interaction between scale economies and transport costs, and to show how this interaction can affect the formation of cities, consider a simple model adapted from Krugman 1991. Suppose that the economy has five regions and a total population of N, with $N/5$ people living in each region. The regions are represented as squares in figure 1.7. Each person consumes one unit of a manufactured good, which is produced with scale economies. In this setting, scale economies are best seen via the cost function $C(Q)$, which gives the total cost of producing Q units of the manufactured good. Scale economies mean that the cost per unit of output declines as Q increases, with the factory becoming more efficient as the level of output expands. Thus, $C(Q)/Q$ falls as Q rises.

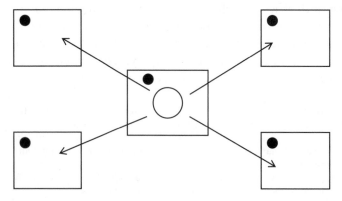

Figure 1.7
Scale economies versus transport costs.

The economy must produce N units of manufactured good to serve the population. Two different arrangements of production are possible: centralized and dispersed. Under dispersed production, a small factory, producing $N/5$ units of output, would be located in each of the five regions. These factories are represented by the small circles in figure 1.7. The cost per unit of output in each factory is $C(N/5)/(N/5) \equiv \lambda$. Under centralized production, one large factory, represented by the large circle, would be located in the central region, producing N units of output at a cost per unit equal to $C(N)/N \equiv \theta$. With scale economies, the cost per unit of output is lower in a large factory than in a small one, with $\theta < \lambda$. The total cost of production for the N units produced in the economy is θN with centralized production and λN with dispersed production, and, since $\theta < \lambda$, total cost is lower in the centralized case.

Although this conclusion led to the superiority of one large factory in the basket-weaving economy (where the output was exported), another consideration comes into play in the present setting. Since the manufactured good is consumed within the economy, adoption of centralized production means that output must be shipped from the large factory to the regions where no manufacturing plant is present. These shipments are represented in figure 1.7 by arrows. The need for shipping is avoided, however, in the dispersed case, since each region has its own factory. Let T denote the cost of shipping a unit of output from the large factory to any of the remote regions. Since four regions lack a factory, a total of $4N/5$ units of the large factory's output (which equals N units) must be shipped, at a cost of $4TN/5$. Note that $N/5$ units of output are consumed within the large factory's region and thus need not be shipped.

The overall cost of the centralized and dispersed arrangements includes both production cost and transportation cost. With transportation cost equal to zero in the dispersed case, the overall cost is just λN. In the centralized case, the overall cost is $\theta N + 4TN/5$. Therefore, the centralized (dispersed) case has a lower overall cost when λN is greater (less) than $\theta N + 4TN/5$. Rearranging, it follows that centralized (dispersed) production is preferred when $\lambda - \theta$ is greater (less) than $4T/5$. The expression $\lambda - \theta$ is the difference between cost per unit of output at the low output level of $Q = N/5$ and the higher output of $Q = N$, a positive difference given the presence of scale economies. If scale economies are strong, so that the small factory is much less efficient than the large factory, then $\lambda - \theta$ will be large, and the first inequality is likely to hold, for a fixed T. Conversely, for a fixed value of $\lambda - \theta$, the first inequality will be likely to hold when T is small. Therefore, centralized production will be favored when scale economies are strong and transports costs are low. This conclusion makes sense since strong scale economies lead to a substantial production-cost advantage for centralized production, while low transport costs mean that this advantage isn't offset by the cost of shipping the output.[7]

Although the conclusion of the analysis of basket weaving above is reaffirmed in this case, dispersed production will be preferred in an economy in which transport costs are high relative to the strength of scale economies. In this case, the second of the above inequalities will hold. This situation might describe an undeveloped economy with poor transport linkages, which would be unable to exploit potential scale economies. When economic development improves the transportation system, lowering T, production would shift to the efficient centralized arrangement.

Centralized production would presumably lead to concentrated employment for manufacturing workers, who have not been explicitly included in the analysis so far. This concentration would lead to formation of a large city in the central zone. In the dispersed case, manufacturing workers would be scattered across the regions, with no notable job concentration arising. Adding manufacturing workers would require some minor modifications to the model, but the conclusion that scale economies can interact with transportation costs in the location of production (and the hence in the formation of cities) would remain unchanged.[8]

1.6   Retail Agglomeration and the Economics of Shopping Centers

Another type of agglomeration phenomenon is retail agglomeration: the spatial concentration of retail outlets. Cities have long had shopping districts in which stores are concentrated. While such districts were the result of uncoordinated store-location decisions, they have been increasingly supplanted by shopping malls, whose owners "orchestrate" the process of retail agglomeration.

---

7. Exercise 1.2 provides a numerical example based on this model.
8. A large theoretical literature has modeled the trade-off between scale economies and transportation cost in a more elaborate and sophisticated fashion than the simple approach from above. For a survey and a synthesis of these models, see Fujita and Thisse 2002.

Two forces contribute to retail agglomeration. The first is a desire by shoppers to limit the costs of shopping trips, which include both time costs and out-of-pocket costs (such as automobile expenses, including the cost of gasoline). When a consumer has to visit multiple stores to make a variety of purchases, the cost of the shopping trip is reduced when the stores are in close proximity. Therefore, a multiple-stop shopper would prefer to carry out his or her trip at a shopping district or a mall rather than visiting a sequence of isolated stores. As a result, stores are likely to attract more customer traffic when they are spatially concentrated than when they are dispersed, and this gain can stimulate retail agglomeration.

The second force leading to concentration of stores is the benefit to consumers of comparison shopping, which can arise even when only one purchase is being made. The ability to compare similar products will generate a better purchase decision, raising the benefits from shopping. Comparison shopping, easily done in a shopping district or a mall, is costly when the stores are spatially separated. This added cost may in fact be prohibitive relative to the benefit, making comparison shopping economical only on a visit to a shopping district or a mall. Spatially concentrated stores can thus offer higher shopping benefits than isolated stores, leading to more customer traffic. This gain for stores will again stimulate retail agglomeration.

Price competition between stores selling similar products is also likely to be more intense when the stores are spatially concentrated. This competition, which leads to lower prices, is beneficial for consumers but puts downward pressure on stores' profits. The resulting loss tends to reduce the attractiveness of spatial concentration from the viewpoint of stores, offsetting some of the gains described above. The fact that owners of stores seem to prefer locations in malls and shopping districts, however, suggests that the beneficial forces dominate the loss attributable to greater price competition.

The benefits of agglomeration can be viewed as arising from inter-store externalities. For example, shoppers visiting a shoe store in a mall may also visit a clothing store, and vice versa, so that each of the store types gains from the presence of the other type. Such externalities may be weaker, however, between other types of stores. For example, visitors to clothing or shoe stores may have little reason to visit a toy store or a specialty tobacco and pipe store, and vice versa. Inter-store externalities are illustrated in figure 1.8, where the widths of the arrows represent the strength of the beneficial effects between stores.

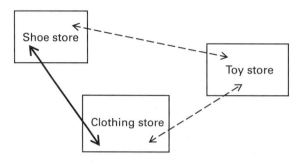

Figure 1.8
Inter-store externalities.

When retail agglomeration is orchestrated by the owner of a shopping mall, the strength and the direction of such externalities are taken into account. Since the mall's owner can charge higher rent to a store when it earns more revenue, and since revenue depends on inter-store externalities, the owner of the mall will want to choose the mix of stores and their sizes taking these externalities into account. The owner will allocate the mall's fixed square footage to stores in a way that "optimizes" the externality flows, in the proper sense. The mall's owner can reap more rental income, and thus earn more profit, by doing so.[9]

1.7 Summary

This chapter has discussed economic reasons for the existence of cities. Scale economies, which favor the creation of large business establishments, are capable of generating a moderate-size company town oriented around a single large factory. But agglomeration economies, which cause separate firms to locate near one another, are required for job concentrations substantial enough to generate a big city. Technological agglomeration economies, which raise worker productivity, can arise from knowledge spillovers among similar firms locating in close proximity. Pecuniary agglomeration economies, in contrast, reduce the cost of inputs without affecting their productivity. One pecuniary effect is the saving on transportation costs when a firm locates in a city that contains both its market and its input suppliers. But when the suppliers are remote, transport-cost considerations may pull the firm

---

9. Exercise 1.3 provides a stylized numerical example of a shopping-mall owner's optimization problem. For a formal analysis of problems of this kind, see Brueckner 1993.

toward a remote location, generating an employment concentration far from the market. Transport costs may also overturn the employment-concentrating effect of scale economies. When output must be shipped to consumers in dispersed locations, it may be better to forsake the gains from scale by putting small factories in these locations. Finally, retail agglomeration is generated by inter-store externalities, which generate gains for individual stores when they locate in close spatial proximity.

2   Analyzing Urban Spatial Structure

2.1   Introduction

Looking out the airplane window, an airline passenger landing in New York or Chicago would see the features of urban spatial structure represented in a particularly dramatic fashion. In both of those cities, the urban center has a striking concentration of tall buildings, with building heights gradually falling as distance from the center increases. The tallest buildings in both cities are office buildings and other commercial structures, but the central areas also contain many tall residential buildings. Like the heights of the office buildings, the heights of these residential structures decrease moving away from the center, dropping to three and two stories as distance increases. Single-story houses become common in the distant suburbs.

Although it is less obvious from the airplane, an equally important spatial feature of cities involves the sizes of individual dwellings (apartments and houses). The dwellings within the tall residential buildings near the city center tend to be relatively small in terms of square footage, while suburban houses are much more spacious. Thus, although building heights fall moving away from the center, dwelling sizes increase.

In walking around downtown residential neighborhoods in Chicago or New York, the traveler would notice another difference not clearly visible from the airplane. Relative to her suburban neighborhood at home, there would be many more people on the streets in these downtown neighborhoods, walking to restaurants, running errands, or heading to their workplaces. This difference is due to the high population density that prevails in central-city residential areas, which is also reflected in activities on the street. Population density falls moving away from the city center, reaching a much lower level in the suburbs.

Other important regularities of urban spatial structure aren't visible at all from an airplane or from the street. These features involve real-estate prices, and they require experience in real-estate transactions, or familiarity with urban data, to grasp. First, whereas vacant lots usually can be purchased for reasonable prices in the suburbs, vacant land near the city center (when it is available) is dramatically more expensive per acre. The same regularity applies to the price of housing floor space: the rental or purchase price per square foot of housing is much higher near the city center than in the suburbs. Consumers aren't used to thinking about prices on a per square foot basis (focusing instead on the monthly rent or selling price for a dwelling), but any real-estate agent knows that residential prices per square foot fall moving away from the city center.

Other regularities involve differences across cities rather than center-suburban differences within a single city. To appreciate these differences, suppose that our traveler is from Omaha, Nebraska. When her plane lands there on her return trip, she will notice that buildings in central Omaha, though taller than those in Omaha's suburbs, are much shorter than those in the big city she just visited. In addition, if the traveler had access to price data, she would see that a vacant lot in the center of Omaha would be cheaper than one in the center of New York.

Economists have formulated a mathematical model of cities that attempts to capture all these regularities of urban spatial structure. This chapter develops and explains the model. But it does so without relying on mathematics, instead using an accessible diagrammatic approach. As will be seen, the urban model successfully predicts the regularities described above. Since the model thus gives an accurate picture of cities, it can be used reliably for predictive purposes in a policy context. For example, the model can predict how a city's spatial structure would change if the gasoline tax were raised substantially, thereby raising the cost of driving. It can also be used to analyze how a variety of other policies would affect a city's spatial structure.

The model presented in this chapter originated in the works of William Alonso (1964), Richard Muth (1969), and Edwin Mills (1967). Systematic derivation of the model's predictions was first done by William Wheaton (1974) and later elaborated by Jan Brueckner (1987).[1]

---

1. For a comprehensive treatment of the economics of urban land use, see Fujita 1989. For a more recent book-length treatment, see Papageorgiou and Pines 1998. Glaeser 2008 also contains a chapter on this topic. For a useful overview paper, see Anas, Arnott, and Small 1998.

The presentation in this chapter is basically a nonmathematical version of Brueckner's approach.

2.2 Basic Assumptions

As is true of all economic models, the urban model is based on strategically chosen simplifications, which facilitate a simple analysis. These simplifications are chosen to capture the essential features of cities, leaving out details that may be less important. Once the model is analyzed and its predictions are derived, greater realism can be added, often with little effect on the main conclusions.

The first assumption is that all the city's jobs are in the center, in an area called the "central business district" (CBD). In reality, many job sites are outside city centers, scattered in various locations or else concentrated in remote employment subcenters. Thus, although job decentralization (the movement of jobs out of the CBD) is a hallmark of modern cities, this process is initially ignored in developing the model. It therefore applies best to cities of the early to mid twentieth century, in which jobs were more centralized than they are now. However, once the model has been analyzed, it can be realistically modified to include the formation of employment subcenters. As will be seen, many of its lessons are unaffected.

Since the goal is to analyze residential (as opposed to business) land use, the CBD is collapsed to a single point at the city center, so that it takes up no space. The model could easily be modified to allow the CBD to have a positive land area, in which case the nature of land use within the business area would become a focus in addition to residential land use outside the CBD.

The second major assumption is that the city has a dense network of radial roads. With such a network, a resident living some distance from the CBD can travel to work in a radial direction, straight into the center, as illustrated in figure 2.1. In reality, cities are criss-crossed by freeways, which are often used in combination with surface streets to access the CBD, thus leading to non-radial automobile commute paths for many residents. As will be seen below, freeways can be added to the model without changing its essential lessons.

The third major assumption is that the city contains identical households. Each household has the same preferences over consumption goods, and each earns the same income from work at the CBD. For simplicity, household size is normalized to one, so that the city consists

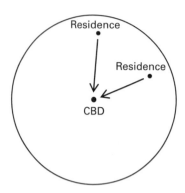

Figure 2.1
Radial commuting.

entirely of single-person households. The identical-household assumption is relaxed below by allowing the city to have two different income groups: rich and poor.

The fourth major assumption is that the city's residents consume only two goods: housing and a composite good that consists of everything other than housing. Since the model is about cities, it naturally focuses on housing. Simplicity requires that all other consumption be lumped together into a single composite commodity, which will be called "bread."

2.3   Commuting Cost

Let x denote radial distance from a consumer's residence to the CBD. The cost of commuting to work at the CBD is higher the larger is x, and this cost generally has two components. The first is a "money" (or "out-of-pocket") cost. For an automobile user, the money cost consists of the cost of gasoline and insurance as well as depreciation on the automobile. For a public-transit user, the money cost is simply the transit fare. The second component of commuting cost is time cost, which captures the "opportunity cost" of the time spent commuting— time that is mostly unavailable for other productive or enjoyable activities. Because a proper consideration of time cost makes the analysis more complicated, this component of commuting cost is ignored in developing the basic model. However, time cost is needed in analyzing a city that contains different income groups, so it will be re-introduced below.

The parameter t represents the per-mile cost of commuting. For a resident living x miles from the CBD, total commuting cost per period is then tx, or commuting cost per mile times distance. For an automobile commuter, t would be computed as follows: Suppose that operating the automobile costs $0.45 per mile, a number close to the value allowed by the Internal Revenue Service in deducting expenses for business use of an auto. Then, a one-way trip to the CBD from a residence at distance x costs $0.45x$, and a round trip costs $0.90x$. A resident working 50 weeks per year will make 250 round trips to the CBD. Multiplying the previous expression by this number yields $(250)0.90x = 225x$ as the commuting cost per year from distance x. Thus, under these assumptions t would equal 225.[2]

The fact that the same commuting-cost parameter (t) applies to all residents reflects another implicit assumption of the model: all residents use the same transport mode to get to work. Urban models with competing transport modes (and thus different possible mode choices) have been developed, but they involve additional complexity.

Let the income earned per period at the CBD by each resident be denoted by y. Then disposable income, net of commuting cost, for a resident living at distance x is equal to $y - tx$. This expression shows that disposable income decreases as x increases, a consequence of a longer and more costly commute. This fact is crucial in generating the model's predictions about urban spatial structure.

2.4   Consumer Analysis

As was mentioned earlier, city residents consume two goods: housing and "bread." Bread consumption is denoted by c, and since the price per unit is normalized to $1, c gives dollars spent on bread (all goods other than housing). Housing consumption is denoted by q, but the physical units corresponding to q must be chosen. The problem is that housing is a complicated good, with a variety of characteristics that consumers value. The characteristics of housing include square footage of floor space in the dwelling, yard size, construction quality, age, and amenities (views, for example). Although a dwelling is then best

---

2. Note that the model focuses entirely on commuting cost, ignoring the cost of trips carried out for other purposes (such as shopping). These trips might be viewed as occurring close to home at a cost that is negligible relative to the cost of commuting. Alternatively, the consumer could be assumed to shop on the way home from work at no extra cost, a behavior that appears to be common.

described by a vector of characteristics, the model requires that consumption be measured by a single number. The natural choice is square footage, the feature that consumers probably care about most. Thus, q represents the square feet of floor space in a dwelling.

With this measurement choice, the price per unit of housing is then the price per square foot of floor space, denoted by p. For simplicity, the model assumes that everyone in the city is a renter, so that p is the rental price per square foot.[3] Note that "rent," or the rental payment per period, is different from p. It equals pq, or price per square foot times housing consumption in square feet. In digesting the model, it is important to grasp this distinction between the rental price per square foot and the more common notion of rent, which is a total payment.

The consumer's budget constraint, which equates expenditures on bread and housing to disposable income net of commuting cost, is

$c + pq = y - tx.$

The budget constraint says that expenditure on bread (which equals c given bread's unitary price) plus expenditure on housing ("rent," or pq) equals disposable income. The consumer's utility function, which gives the satisfaction from consuming a particular (c, q) bundle, is given by $u(c, q)$. As usual, the consumer chooses c and q to maximize utility subject to the budget constraint. The optimal consumption bundle lies at a point of tangency between an indifference curve and the budget line, as will be shown below.

As was explained in section 2.1, one of the regularities of urban spatial structure is that the price per square foot of housing floor space declines as distance to the CBD increases. In other words, p falls as x increases. The first step in the analysis is to show that the model indeed predicts this regularity. The demonstration makes use of a simple intuitive argument, which is then reinforced by a diagrammatic analysis.

The argument relies on a fundamental condition for consumer locational equilibrium. This equilibrium condition says that *consumers must be equally well off at all locations, achieving the same utility regardless of where they live in the city.* If this condition did not hold, then consumers in a low-utility area could gain by moving into a high-utility area. This incentive to move means that a locational equilibrium has not been attained. The incentive is absent, implying that equilibrium has

---

3. The model could equally well have everyone be a homeowner, with the appropriate relabeling.

been reached, only when consumer utility—that is, the value taken by the utility function $u(c, q)$—is the same everywhere.

Utilities can be spatially uniform only if the price per unit of housing floor space falls as distance increases. Since higher commuting costs mean that disposable income falls as x increases, some offsetting benefit must be present to keep utility from falling. The offsetting benefit is a lower price per square foot of housing at greater distances. Then, even though consumers living far from the center have less money to spend (after paying high commuting costs) than those closer to the CBD, their money goes farther given a lower p, allowing them to be just as well off as people living closer in. The lower p thus compensates for the disadvantage of higher commuting costs at distant locations.

This explanation makes it clear that the lower p at distant suburban locations serves as a *compensating differential* that reconciles suburban residents to their long and costly commutes. Compensating differentials also arise in many other economic contexts. For example, dangerous or unpleasant jobs must pay higher wages than more appealing jobs with similar skill requirements. Otherwise, no one would do the undesirable work. Like the lower suburban p, the higher wage reconciles people to accepting a disadvantageous situation.[4]

While the compensating-differential perspective is the best way to think about spatial variation in p, another view that may seem easier to understand focuses on "demand." One might argue that the "demand" for suburban locations is lower than the demand for central locations given their high commuting cost. Lower demand then depresses the price of housing at locations far from the CBD, causing p to decline as x increases.

The inverse relationship between p and x can also be derived using an indifference-curve diagram, as in figure 2.2. The vertical axis represents bread consumption (c) and the horizontal axis housing consumption (q). The steep budget line pertains to a consumer living at a central-city location, close to the CBD, with $x = x_0$. The c intercept of the consumer's budget line equals disposable income, which is $y - tx_0$ for this individual. The slope of the budget line, on the other hand, equals the negative of the price per square foot of housing. Thus, the

---

4. Because the price of bread is assumed to be the same in all locations (normalized to $1 per unit), it cannot play a compensating role, as p can. Concretely, this assumption means that the prices of groceries and other non-housing goods are the same at all locations in the city. Although this requirement may not be fully realistic, it is likely to hold approximately.

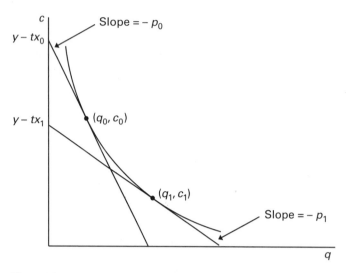

Figure 2.2
Consumer choice.

slope of the budget line for the central-city consumer equals $-p_0$, where p_0 is the price per square foot prevailing at $x = x_0$. Given this budget line, the consumer maximizes utility, reaching a tangency point between an indifference curve and the budget line. In the figure, this tangency point is (q_0, c_0). Thus, this central-city resident consumes c_0 worth of bread and q_0 square feet of housing.

Now consider a consumer living at a suburban location, with $x = x_1 > x_0$. This consumer has disposable income of $y - tx_1$, less than that of the central-city consumer. As a result, the consumer's budget line has a smaller intercept than the central-city budget line, as can be seen in the figure. The main question concerns the price per square foot of housing at this suburban location, denoted by p_1. What magnitude must this price have in order to ensure that the suburban consumer is just as well off as the central-city consumer? The answer is that p_1 must lead to a budget line that allows the suburban consumer to reach the same indifference curve as her central-city counterpart. For this outcome to be possible, the suburban budget line, with its lower intercept, must be flatter than the central-city line. When the budget line is flatter by just the right degree, the utility-maximizing point will lie on the indifference curve reached by the central-city consumer, as seen in the figure. But since the slope of the budget line equals the negative of the housing price, it follows that a flatter budget line (with a negative slope closer to zero) must have a lower price. Therefore, the suburban price p_1 must be lower than the central-city price p_0, so that $p_1 < p_0$. Figure 2.2 thus establishes that the price per square foot of housing p must fall as distance x to the CBD increases, confirming the previous intuitive argument.

Figure 2.2 contains additional important information about consumer choices. The suburban consumption bundle (q_1, c_1), which is the point of tangency between the suburban budget line and the indifference curve, can be compared with the central-city bundle (q_0, c_0). From the figure, this comparison shows that the suburban resident consumes *more square feet of housing and less bread than the central-city resident*. Therefore, suburban dwellings are larger than central-city dwellings, so that *dwelling size q rises as distance from the CBD increases*. This substitution in favor of housing and away from bread is the consumer's response to the decline in the relative price of housing as x increases.[5] Recall from above that this pattern was one of the main regularities of urban spatial structure, and the figure shows that the model predicts it.

The difference in bread consumption indicates an additional pattern: while occupying a small dwelling, the central-city resident consumes a lot of bread. Concretely, this resident has a nice car, beautiful furniture, and gourmet food in the refrigerator, and takes expensive vacations. The suburban resident's consumption, in contrast, is skewed toward housing consumption, with less emphasis on bread. Given that the city only has one income group, this prediction may be not very realistic, and it doesn't survive the generalization of the model to include multiple income groups. But the (realistic) prediction regarding dwelling-size variation with distance is robust to this generalization, as will be seen below.

So far, the model's two main predictions are that the price per square foot of housing falls, and that size of dwellings rises, as distance to the CBD increases. These outcomes can be represented symbolically as follows:

$p\downarrow$ as $x\uparrow$, $q\uparrow$ as $x\uparrow$.

With these important conclusions established, several aspects of the preceding analysis deserve more discussion. The consumer has been portrayed as choosing her dwelling size on the basis of the prevailing price per square foot at a given location. Although most consumers

---

5. Since utility is fixed, the increase in q in response to the lower housing price represents the *substitution effect* of the price change (the income effect is not present).

aren't used to thinking about the price per square foot of housing (focusing instead on total rent), the model assumes that they implicitly recognize the existence of such a price in making decisions. For example, a small apartment with a high rent would be viewed as expensive by a consumer, but the individual would be implicitly reacting to the apartment's high rental price per square foot. Indeed, commercial space is always rented in this fashion, with a landlord quoting a rent per square foot and the tenant choosing a quantity of space. But one might then argue that residential tenants aren't offered such a quantity choice (they can't, after all, adjust the square footage of an apartment), making the model's portrayal of the choice of dwelling size seem unrealistic. The response is that the consumer's quantity preferences are ultimately reflected in the existing housing stock. In other words, the size of apartments built in a particular location is exactly the one that consumers prefer, given the prevailing price per square foot.

Two additional conclusions can be drawn from consumer side of the model. The first concerns the nature of the curve relating the housing price p to distance. The curve is convex, as in figure 2.3, with the price falling at a decreasing rate as x increases. This conclusion follows from mathematical analysis, which shows that the slope of the housing-price curve is given by the following equation:

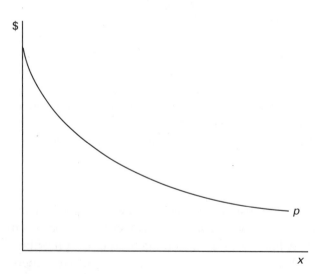

Figure 2.3
Housing-price curve.

$$\frac{\partial p}{\partial x} = -\frac{t}{q}.$$

Therefore, the slope at any location is equal to the negative of commuting cost per mile divided by the dwelling size at that location. The convexity in figure 2.3 follows because q increases with x, so that the $-t/q$ ratio becomes less negative (and the curve flatter) as distance increases. The intuitive explanation is that at a suburban location where dwellings are large a small decline in the price per square foot is sufficient to generate enough housing-cost savings to compensate for an extra mile's commute. But at a central-city location, where dwellings are small, a larger decline in the price per square foot is needed to generate the required savings.

A second conclusion concerns the spatial behavior of total rent, pq. The question is how the total rent for a small central-city dwelling compares to the total rent for a larger suburban house. The answer is that the comparison is ambiguous. Since p falls with x while q increases, the product pq could either rise or fall with x, with the pattern depending on the shape of the consumer's indifference curve in figure 2.2. The implication is that the total rent for the suburban house could be either larger or smaller than the rent for the central-city apartment, a conclusion that appears realistic.

A large body of empirical work confirms the model's prediction of a link between price per square foot of housing and job accessibility. The approach uses a "hedonic price" regression (explained further in chapter 6) that relates the value of a dwelling to its size and other characteristics, one of which is distance from the city's employment center. These regressions usually show a negative distance effect. Thus, with dwelling size held constant, value falls as distance rises, which in turn implies a decline in value (and thus rent) per square foot.[6]

2.5   Analysis of Housing Production

Now that the consumer's choice of dwelling size has been analyzed, the next step is to ask what the buildings containing those dwellings look like. To address this question, the focus shifts to the activities of housing developers, who build structures and rent the space to consumers.[7]

---

6. For an example of such a study, see Coulson 1991.
7. In reality, developers sell buildings to landlords, who then rent space to consumers, but this intervening agent is ignored.

In reality, developers produce housing floor space using a variety of inputs, including land, building materials, labor, and machinery. As in the consumer analysis, simplicity requires narrowing down the list of choice variables. Thus, the model assumes that floor space is produced with land and building materials alone, ignoring the role of labor and machinery. In one sense, this view isn't unreasonable, given that the land and materials inputs are present over the entire life of a building, while construction workers and machines (though crucial) are present only for a relatively short time at the outset.

The production function for housing floor space is written as $Q = H(N, l)$, where Q is the floor space contained in a building, N is the amount of building materials (measured in some fashion), l is the land input, and H is the production function. An engineer or an architect would point out that building materials are certainly not a homogeneous category (they include steel, wood, concrete, glass, and so on), but these distinctions are ignored for simplicity in measuring the material input. For convenience, building materials will sometimes be referred to as the "capital" input into housing production.

Several properties of the production function deserve note. The first is the diminishing marginal product of capital. This property means that, with the land input held fixed, extra doses of building materials lead to smaller and smaller increases in floor space. This property makes sense when it is recognized that increasing N while holding l fixed makes the building taller, as can be seen in figure 2.4. Diminishing returns arise because, as the building gets taller, addi-

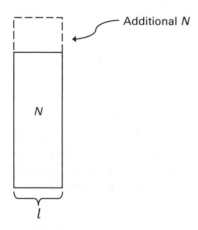

Figure 2.4
Making a building taller.

tional doses of building materials are increasingly consumed in uses that do not directly yield extra floor space. These uses include a stronger foundation, thicker beams, and more space devoted to elevators and stairways.

The second property of interest is the degree of returns to scale in housing production. In the discussion of scale economies in chapter 1, only a single input was present, and the presence of scale economies could be inferred by simply looking at the graph of the production function. Although the graph is more complicated with two inputs, economies of scale are present in housing production if doubling both the capital and land inputs leads to more than a doubling of floor space. This doubling of inputs is evident in figure 2.5, where it leads, in effect, to the construction of a second identical building adjoining the original one. The question is whether this building has more than twice the floor space of the original building. It might appear that the answer is No, with floor space instead exactly doubling. But that conclusion ignores what might be a slight gain from the fact that the exterior wall of the original building is now an interior wall, which could be thinner. Since this gain is probably small, it is safe to say that housing production exhibits approximate "constant returns to scale," with scale economies not present in any important way.

Figures 2.4 and 2.5 reflect an underlying assumption that has not been made explicit so far. The assumption is that the building completely covers the land area l, leaving no yard or open space around it. This view is logical since consumers have been portrayed as only valuing floor space, so that any land devoted to open space would be wasted. But the assumption is clearly unrealistic, at least for suburban

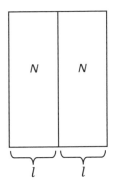

Figure 2.5
Constant returns to scale.

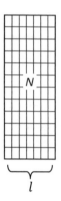

l

Figure 2.6
Division of a building into dwellings.

areas where yard space is plentiful. Strictly speaking, the model can be viewed as pertaining to a place, such as Manhattan or central Paris, where there are few yards. The model can, however, be generalized to allow yard space to be valued by consumers and provided by developers, but the resulting framework is more complex.

The housing developer will choose the capital and land inputs for his building to maximize profit, leading to a structure of a particular height. Implicitly, the developer also sets the size of the dwellings within the structure, but this decision simply responds to consumer choices. In other words, the floor space in a building is divided up into dwellings of the size that consumers want at that particular location. This division is illustrated in figure 2.6.

The revenue earned by the developer is equal to $pH(N, l)$, the price per square foot p times the square footage in the building. Input costs consist of the cost of building materials and the cost of land. To match the rental orientation of the model, both inputs are viewed as being rented rather than purchased. Thus, the developer leases land from its owner rather than purchasing it outright, an arrangement that is occasionally seen (in China, for example, all land is owned by the government and is leased to developers). Land rent per acre is thus the relevant input price, and it is denoted by r. The rental rate per unit of building materials is equal to i,[8] and this price is assumed to be independent of where the structure is built. In other words, building materials are

---

8. Note that i could instead be viewed as the annualized cost of materials that are purchased rather than rented.

delivered to any construction site, regardless of its location in the city, at a common price per unit. Combining all this information, the developer's production cost is equal to $iN + rl$.

Although i doesn't vary with location, spatial variation in land rent r is necessary to make developers willing to produce housing throughout the city. The reason is that locations far from the CBD are disadvantageous for development since the price p received by the developer per square foot of floor space is low. In contrast, locations close to the CBD are favorable since the developer can charge a high price per square foot there for his output.

In order for developers to be willing to build housing in all locations, the profit from doing so must be the same everywhere. But with close-in locations offering higher revenue per square foot than suburban locations, profits will not be uniform unless a compensating differential exists on the cost side. With the capital cost fixed, this compensating differential must come from spatial variation in land rent r. In particular, land rent must be lower in the suburbs than at central locations. With r falling as x increases, the revenue disadvantage of the suburbs is offset, and the profits from housing development remain constant over space. Because land rent must do all the work in equalizing profits, given that i is fixed, r must fall with distance much faster than p itself, declining at a greater percentage rate. Therefore, the gap between central-city values and suburban values is wider for r than for p.

As in the consumer analysis, this compensating differential can be viewed as a demand-based phenomenon. Developers will compete vigorously for land in central locations because floor space built there commands a high price. This competition bids up land rents near the CBD. Conversely, developers' lower demand for suburban land, a consequence of the low housing revenue it offers, leads to a lower land rent. Since competition for land among developers will bid up rent until profit is exhausted, the uniform profit achieved through compensating land-rent differentials is in fact a zero profit level (corresponding to "normal" economic profit).

The model thus predicts another one of the regularities of urban spatial structure: declining land rent (and thus land value) as distance to the CBD increases.[9] This pattern, in turn, generates another regularity

---

9. A number of empirical studies have confirmed the negative association between land values and distance (see, for example, McMillen 1996). However, a greater number of studies have documented the link between housing prices and distance to the CBD.

related to building heights. With the price of capital fixed and land rent rising moving toward the CBD, the land input becomes more expensive relative to the capital input as distance x declines. Producers generally shift their input mix in response to changes in relative input prices, and housing developers are no exception. In particular, as land becomes more expensive compared to capital, developers economize on the land input and use more capital in the production of floor space. But in making this substitution, the developer is building a taller structure (recall figure 2.4). Thus, as land becomes relatively more expensive moving toward the CBD, developers respond by constructing taller buildings. Conversely, as land gets cheaper moving toward the suburbs, developers use it more lavishly, constructing shorter buildings. Overall, then, building height decreases as distance to the CBD increases.

This pattern can be seen from a diagram showing cost minimization on the part of the housing developer. In figure 2.7, the capital input is on the vertical axis and the land input is on horizontal axis. The isoquant shows all the capital-land combinations capable of producing a particular amount floor space, say 150,000 square feet. Consider first the choice problem of a developer at a central-city location where $x = x_0$ and $r = r_0$. The iso-cost lines at this central location have slope $-r_0/i$, and they are relatively steep since r_0 is high. To produce 150,000

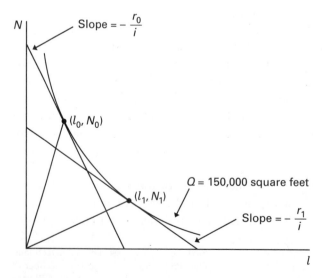

Figure 2.7
Cost minimization by housing developer.

square feet of floor space as cheaply as possible, the developer finds the input bundle on the isoquant lying on the lowest possible iso-cost line. This bundle, denoted by (l_0, N_0), lies at a point of tangency, as can be seen in the figure. In contrast, a developer building 150,000 square feet at a suburban location, where $x = x_1 > x_0$ and $r = r_1 < r_0$, faces flatter iso-cost lines. His cost-minimizing input bundle is (l_1, N_1), which has less capital and more land than the central-city bundle. Instead of building a high-rise structure like the one at x_0, this developer builds a garden-apartment complex.

Building heights in the two developments are reflected in the amount of capital per acre of land, given by the ratios N_0/l_0 and N_1/l_1. These ratios are equal to the slopes of the rays shown in the figure that connect the input bundles to the origin. With the central-city ray steeper, it follows that the building at x_0 is taller than the building at x_1. Thus, building height falls moving away from the CBD.[10]

The two main predictions from the producer analysis are that land rent per acre and building height both fall as distance to the CBD increases. Symbolically,

$r \downarrow$ as $x \uparrow$, building height $\downarrow$ as $x \uparrow$.

2.6   Population Density

A final intracity regularity is the decline of population density with distance to the CBD, which the model also generates. Population density, denoted by D, is equal to people per acre. But since dwellings contain a single person, D is just dwellings per acre. Figure 2.8 illustrates the difference between dwellings per acre in the central city and the suburbs. The central-city location has a tall building (with high capital per acre) that is divided into small dwellings, while the suburban location has a short building divided into large dwellings. From the figure, dwellings per acre is clearly higher at the central-city location than in the suburbs. In other words, since suburban buildings have less floor space per acre of land and contain larger dwellings than central-city buildings, the suburbs have fewer dwellings per acre than the central city. Thus, D falls moving away from the CBD. Symbolically,

$D \downarrow$ as $x \uparrow$.

---

10. This prediction is confirmed by McMillen 2006 and by other studies.

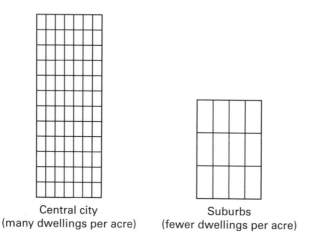

Central city
(many dwellings per acre)

Suburbs
(fewer dwellings per acre)

Figure 2.8
Population density.

Most empirical testing of the urban model has focused on testing this prediction about the spatial behavior of population density. Dozens of empirical studies have investigated the relationship between density and distance to the CBD for individual cities all over the world.[11] These studies rely on the fact that cities are divided into small spatial zones for census purposes, with the population of the zones tabulated. Once the land area of each zone has been estimated, the zone's population density can be computed by dividing the population by its area. In addition, the distance from the zone to the CBD can be measured. The result is a point scatter in density-distance space like that shown in figure 2.9. The empirical researcher then runs a regression, which generates a curve passing through the point scatter, as shown in the figure.[12] The estimated density curves for the world's cities are almost always downward sloping, confirming the prediction of the model.

The entire set of intra-city predictions is summarized in figure 2.10, which shows the logical linkages involved in the predictions. The solid boxes in the figure contain the two fundamental equilibrium conditions in the model: spatially uniform consumer utility and spatially uniform

---

11. See McDonald 1989 for a survey.
12. A common assumption is that density follows a negative exponential relationship, with $D = \alpha e^{-\beta x}$. Taking natural logs, this relationship reduces to $\log D = \theta - \beta x$, showing a linear relationship between $\log D$ and x. With density measured in logs, the regression curve in figure 2.9 is then replaced by a straight line.

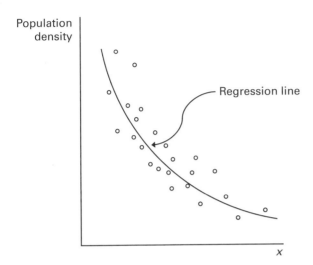

Figure 2.9
Population-density regression.

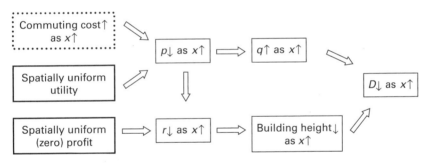

Figure 2.10
Logical structure of the model.

(zero) developer profit. The dashed box in the figure contains the crucial real-world fact that drives the entire model: the increase in commuting cost as distance increases. The logical arrows show how this real-world fact and the two equilibrium conditions combine to generate the various predictions. The increase in commuting cost with distance and the requirement of uniform utility imply that p falls with x, which in turn implies that q rises with x. The zero-profit requirement and the decline in p with x imply that r falls with x. The decline in r then implies that building height falls with x. Finally, the rise in q and decline in building height as x increases imply that D falls with x.

2.7   Intercity Predictions

As was explained earlier, the model also generates intercity predictions
that match observed regularities. For example, the model predicts that
large cities will have taller buildings than small cities. To generate these
predictions, it is necessary to analyze what might be called the "supply-
demand" equilibrium of the city. Basically, the equilibrium requirement
is that the city fits its population, or that the "supply" of housing equals
the "demand" for it.

    The size of the land area occupied by a city determines how much
housing the city contains. The city's land area is, in turn, the result of
competition between housing developers and farmers for use of the
land. Suppose that farmers are willing to pay a rent of r_A per acre of
land. This agricultural rent will be high when the land is very productive or when the crops grown on it command a high price. Although
r_A might vary with location, being higher near the delivery points for
agricultural output (where transport cost is low), this rent will instead
be viewed as constant over space, thus being independent of x. Figure
2.11 shows the graph of r_A, which is a horizontal line, along with the
downward-sloping urban land-rent curve. Like the housing-price
curve in figure 2.3, the land-rent curve is convex, with r decreasing at
a decreasing rate as x increases.

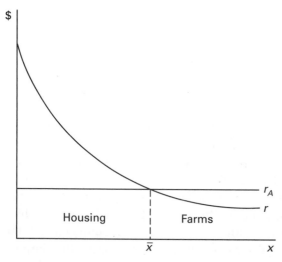

Figure 2.11
Determination of city's edge.

A landowner will rent his land to the bidder who offers most for it.[13] Figure 2.11 shows that the housing developer is the highest bidder at locations inside the intersection point of the r curve and the r_A line, while the farmer is the highest bidder at locations outside this intersection. Therefore, housing is built inside the intersection, while the land outside the intersection is in agricultural use. The intersection point, which is $\bar{x}$ miles from the CBD, thus represents the edge of the city. For the city to be in supply-demand equilibrium, its fixed population (denoted by L) must exactly fit in the housing available inside $\bar{x}$.

The city's supply-demand equilibrium depends on the four key parameters of the model: population (L), agricultural rent (r_A), commuting cost (t), and income (y).[14] By changing a particular parameter and deducing the resulting changes in urban spatial structure, the intercity predictions can be derived.[15]

2.7.1 The effects of population and agricultural land rent

Consider first the effect of population size. The city is assumed to start in equilibrium, exactly fitting its population L. Then the population size is hypothetically increased—a change that disrupts the equilibrium, since the larger population doesn't fit in the existing city. The analysis then deduces the changes in urban spatial structure that must occur in order to restore equilibrium, allowing the city to fit the now-larger population.

This thought experiment shows how the spatial structure of a particular city would respond to an increase in population. Since the city gets rebuilt in response to the population increase (as will be explained below), the predicted changes must be viewed as occurring over a very long time period. But the results of the thought experiment can be interpreted in a different, more useful way. In particular, the differences between the pre-change and post-change cities can be used to predict the differences between two separate cities, one small and one large, *at a given point in time*. In other words, the long-run changes in spatial structure that would occur in a single city as its population expands should also be reflected in the differences between *two coexisting cities* with different population sizes.

---

13. Landowners are assumed to be "absentee" (that is, living outside the city). Otherwise, rental income would be earned by city residents, which would complicate the model.
14. The cost i of housing capital is another parameter, but its effect isn't of interest here.
15. Exercise 2.1 involves an analysis of this type for a simplified version of the model.

Suppose a particular city, which starts in equilibrium, experiences a one-time increase in its population L. The sequence of impacts unfolds as follows:

1. Although the city's housing stock fit the original population, the stock is now too small, leading to *excess demand* for housing (a housing shortage).

2. This excess demand leads to an increase in the price per square foot of housing p at all locations in the city.

3. With housing now more expensive, consumers choose smaller dwelling sizes. Thus, q falls at all locations, an adjustment that occurs in the long run as the city is rebuilt.

4. By raising housing revenue per square foot, the higher price p boosts the profits of housing developers. With development now more profitable, developers compete more vigorously for land, driving up land rent r at all locations.

5. In response to the higher cost of land, developers economize on its use, constructing taller buildings at all locations. This change occurs in the long run as the city is rebuilt.

6. With buildings taller and dwellings smaller at each location, the number of dwellings per acre of land rises, leading to higher population density D at all locations.

7. With r rising at all locations, the urban land-rent curve shifts up to r_1, as shown in figure 2.12 (where r_0 is the original rent curve). As a result, the distance $\bar{x}$ to the edge of the city increases from to $\bar{x}_0$ to $\bar{x}_1$.

8. Since population density increases everywhere, and since the city's land area is now larger, it fits a larger population. Thus, the excess demand for housing is eliminated, restoring the supply-demand equilibrium.

Since these adjustments can be used to predict differences between cities with small and large populations at a given point in time, the following conclusions emerge. The larger city occupies more land than the smaller city. At a given distance from the center, the larger city has taller buildings, smaller dwellings, a higher housing price per square foot, higher land rent, and higher population density than the small city. These predictions match many of the observed differences between large and small cities in the real world.[16]

---

16. Empirical tests of the predicted effects of L, y, r_A, and t on city land areas have been carried out. They are discussed in chapter 4.

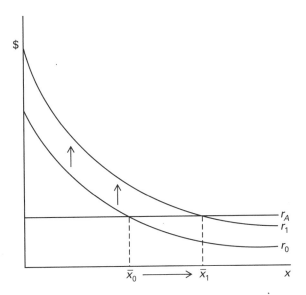

Figure 2.12
Effect of a higher *L*.

Now consider the effect of an increase in agricultural rent r_A on the city's spatial structure, with population held fixed. This thought experiment can be used to predict the differences between two coexisting cities, one in a region with a high r_A and one in a region with a low r_A. The first region might be the state of Illinois, which has highly productive farmland; the second might be the state of Arizona, where much of the land is desert and thus has little or no value in agriculture.

An increase in agricultural rent from r_{A0} to r_{A1} raises the height of the r_A line in figure 2.13. With the urban land-rent curve held fixed at r_0, the $\bar{x}$ value at the intersection point decreases from $\bar{x}_0$ to $\bar{x}'$. Taken literally, this change means that the existing housing between $\bar{x}_0$ and $\bar{x}'$ is bulldozed and the land is returned to agricultural use. But after this shrinkage in the housing stock, the city no longer fits its population, which leads to excess demand for housing. This situation is exactly the one encountered under step 1 of the population-driven adjustment process above. As a result, the subsequent steps 2–8 unfold in exactly the same fashion as before. Note that the upward shift in the land-rent curve in step 7 leads some of the land initially bulldozed to be returned to urban use, as can be seen in figure 2.13. But the final value of $\bar{x}$, again denoted by $\bar{x}_1$, must be smaller than the initial value $\bar{x}_0$. The reason is

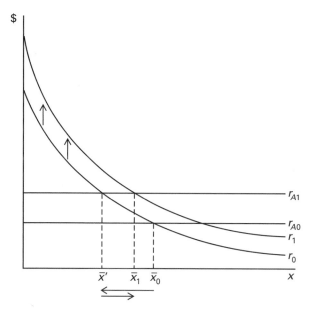

Figure 2.13
Effect of a higher r_A.

that the city is now denser (recall step 6), which means that its fixed population fits in a smaller land area.

Given these conclusions, a city in a high-r_A state (say, Peoria, Illinois) differs from a city with approximately the same population located in a low-r_A state (say, Tucson, Arizona), in the following ways: The high-r_A city is spatially smaller, and at a given distance from the CBD, it has taller buildings, smaller dwellings, a higher housing price per square foot, higher land rent, and higher population density than the low-r_A city. In view of the spread-out, low density nature of desert cities, these predictions seem realistic.

2.7.2   The effects of commuting cost and income

Now consider the effect of an increase in the commuting-cost parameter t. Such an increase could be due to a higher price of gasoline, or to an increase in the gasoline tax. When t increases, the existing spatial pattern of housing prices doesn't adequately compensate for long suburban commutes. As a result, suburban commuters will want to move toward the center to reduce their commuting costs. This movement bids up housing prices near the CBD, and reduces them at suburban locations. As a result, the housing-price curve rotates in a clockwise direction. The profit of housing developers then rises near the center and falls in the suburbs, leading to stronger competition for central land and weaker competition for suburban land. Land rents then rise near the center and fall in the suburbs, causing a clockwise rotation in the land-rent curve that mimics the rotation of the housing-price curve. This rotation (seen in figure 2.14) leads to a decline in $\bar{x}$ from $\bar{x}_0$ to $\bar{x}_1$. Thus, with the higher commuting cost causing residents to move inward, the land area of the city shrinks.

In response to the land-rent rotation in the figure, building heights rise near the center and fall in the city's shrunken suburbs. Dwelling sizes fall near the center, so that central population density rises given the increase in building height. However, mathematical analysis shows that the change in q is ambiguous in the suburbs, which makes the change in density ambiguous there as well.

As before, these changes can be used to predict the differences between two coexisting cities, one of which has a high t and the other a low t (but whose populations have the same size). Since gasoline taxes are much higher in Europe than in the United States, the first city could be European and the second American. The analysis predicts that the European city is more compact, with a smaller land area than its American counterpart. In the center, it has taller buildings, smaller dwellings, a higher housing price per square foot, a higher land rent,

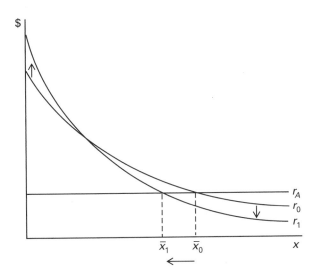

Figure 2.14
Effect of a higher t.

and higher population density than the American city. If gasoline taxes were to rise substantially in the United States, then American cities would eventually assume the more compact form of their European counterparts.

Finally, consider the effect of an increase in consumer income y. Mathematical analysis shows that these effects are exactly the opposite of the effects of a higher t. The housing-price curve rotates in a counterclockwise direction, causing the same kind of rotation in the land-rent curve, seen in figure 2.14. As a result, $\bar{x}$ rises from $\bar{x}_0$ to $\bar{x}_1$, so that the city expands spatially. Building heights decrease near the center and increase in the (expanded) suburbs. Dwelling sizes increase, and population density decreases, near the center, although changes are ambiguous in the suburbs.

These changes arise from a consumer's changing locational incentives when income increases. With a higher income, consumers will want larger dwellings and will thus have an incentive to move outward, attracted by the lower price per square foot of housing at greater distances. This desire for outward movement will push p up in the suburbs and reduce it in the center, leading to counterclockwise rotation of the housing-price and land-rent curves. The resulting spatial expansion of the city makes sense since higher incomes will raise the aggregate demand for housing and thus the aggregate derived demand for land.

Making intercity comparisons, the analysis predicts that a high-income city will be larger spatially than a low-income city. Near the center, it will have shorter buildings, larger dwellings, a lower housing price per square foot, lower land rent, and lower population density than the low-income city.

These intercity predictions have been tested empirically, with a focus on the $\bar{x}$ predictions. As will be explained in more detail in chapter 4, the empirical studies carry out regression analysis relating a city's land area to its population, income, commuting cost, and the agricultural rent on the surrounding land, with results that support the theory.

2.7.3 Migration between cities
The preceding analysis ignores the possibility of migration between cities, in effect looking at a given city in isolation. To analyze intercity migration, the first step is to note that when L, r_A, y, or t increases, the welfare of urban residents (as measured by their common utility level) is affected. When L increases, for example, the resulting increase in the housing price p raises the city's cost of living, which makes the

residents worse off. Conversely, an increase in y makes the urban residents better off.[17]

Given these effects, variation in L and y across cities can lead to welfare differences, with residents reaching high utility levels in some cities and low utilities in other cities. But if consumers are able to migrate between cities, such utility differences are unsustainable. Just as in the case of the intracity equilibrium, in which consumer utility was the same at all locations, an *intercity migration equilibrium* must make consumers equally well off regardless of *which city they live in*. If this requirement were not met, people would move from low-utility cities to high-utility cities until welfare was equalized.

When migration is possible, a high-income city, where consumers would otherwise be better off, must have a larger population than a low-income city. The larger population cancels the welfare gain from the higher income, leading to the same utilities in both cities. Intercity migration is the source of the larger population: residents migrate from the low-income city to the high-income one, and migration stops when the city's population has grown enough to cancel the advantage of its higher income. Therefore, once intercity migration is allowed, the model predicts a *positive correlation between city population and income*, a relationship that has been confirmed empirically.[18]

Intercity migration requires reconsideration of the intercity predictions made in section 2.6. Those predictions pertain to a "closed city," where migration is impossible and the population is set exogenously. When migration is allowed, the "open city" model is appropriate instead. Section 2.6 analyzed the effect of a higher income on the city's spatial structure with L held fixed, but a different exercise is needed for an open city. In this case, the higher y is automatically accompanied by a larger L (a consequence of migration). The resulting effect on the city's spatial structure is then the combination of two separate effects: the effect of a higher y, *with L held fixed*, plus the additional effect of a higher L. Since each change separately leads to an increase in $\bar{x}$, the

---

17. Although the p curve rotates rather than shifts up when y increases (making the impact on the cost of living ambiguous), mathematical analysis nevertheless shows that a higher income raises consumer welfare, as intuition would predict. Conversely, an increase in commuting cost t makes the city's residents worse off, as does an increase in r_A.

18. Since an increase in either commuting cost or agricultural rent makes a city's residents worse off, a population decrease would be required to restore the original utility level. Therefore, intercity migration equilibrium requires cities with high t values or high r_A values to have small populations.

combined change also raises $\bar{x}$, so that the city's land area increases. Therefore, with intercity migration, high-income cities are spatially larger than low-income cities, just as in the closed-city model. The other spatial-structure effects of the simultaneous increase in y and L can be derived mathematically.[19]

2.8 Summary

This chapter has analyzed urban spatial structure using a diagrammatic version of the standard urban model. The model generates realistic intracity predictions, which show that the price per square foot of housing, land rent, building heights, and population density fall moving away from the CBD, while dwelling size increases. The model also generates intercity predictions, which show that more populous cities are spatially larger, denser, and more expensive than small cities. The model predicts realistic differences between desert cities and cities located on productive agricultural land, as well as differences between cities with expensive vs. cheap commuting and high vs. low incomes. The model is a useful and powerful tool for understanding urban spatial structure.

---

19. The net effect of these simultaneous changes is an upward shift in the housing-price curve, which leads to a decrease in dwelling size q at all locations. The higher p curve generates an upward shift in the land-rent curve, leading to an increase in building heights at all locations. Population density rises at all locations. The open-city effects of a higher t (and the accompanying decrease in L; see note 18) are the reverse of the effects of a higher y, just as in the closed-city case. In contrast, in an open city, a higher r_A (and the accompanying decrease in L) has no effect on p, q, r, building height, or D. The only effect is a shrinkage of the city's land area. See Brueckner 1987 for details.

3   Modifications of the Urban Model

3.1   Introduction

The urban model presented in chapter 2 imposed a number of simplifications so that simple conclusions could be derived. The purpose of this chapter is to introduce modifications to the model and appraise their separate effects. The first modification adds a second income group to the city, which then contains both "rich" and "poor" households. The second modification adds a freeway to the city's transportation system, so that all commutes are no longer radial. The third modification introduces job sites (either widely dispersed employment locations or distinct subcenters) outside the central business district. The fourth modification explicitly recognizes the durability of housing capital, allowing the city to contain both old and new buildings. The fifth modification puts the model in the context of a developing country, where rural–urban migration occurs.

3.2   A City with Two Income Groups

Suppose that, instead of having a common income, some households in the city are rich, earning income y_R, and some are poor, earning income $y_P < y_R$. In addition, suppose that money cost continues to be the only commuting cost, which is then the same for both groups and equal to t (time cost will be introduced below).

An important question regarding the spatial structure of the two-group city concerns the relative locations of the rich and poor residential areas. In reality, high-income households tend to locate in the suburbs of U.S. cities, and poor households tend to live near the center. What, then, does the model predict about the relative locations of the two income groups?

With rich and poor households, there will be two housing-price curves, one denoted by p_R and one by p_P. When paying housing prices per square foot along the p_R curve, members of the rich group will be locationally indifferent, reaching the same utility in all locations. Similarly, when paying housing prices along the p_P curve, members of the poor group will be locationally indifferent, reaching the same utility in all locations. But to actually reside at a particular location, members of a given income group must be *the highest bidder* for housing at that location, outbidding the other group. For example, if the rich and poor price curves have the form shown in figure 3.1, then the poor group is the highest bidder for housing inside the intersection point $\hat{x}$ of the p_P and p_R curves, whereas the rich group is the highest bidder outside $\hat{x}$. Thus, in the situation shown in the figure, the poor live in the central part of the city and the rich in the suburbs.[1]

The urban model's remarkable prediction is that this location pattern is the *only one possible* under the maintained assumptions (which include a common t). To see why, recall that the housing-price curve's slope is equal to $-t/q$. With q differing between the groups, the p_R curve then has a slope of $-t/q_R$, where q_R denotes housing square footage for the rich, and the p_P curve has a slope of $-t/q_P$, where q_P denotes housing

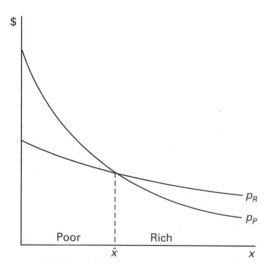

Figure 3.1
Locations of rich and poor.

---

1. The price per square foot of housing as a function of distance thus follows the upper curve at each location, with the lower curve not relevant since the corresponding group is outbid.

square footage for the poor. One would expect q_R to be larger than q_P, but this relationship is guaranteed to hold only at a location where both groups face the same price per square foot of housing, in which case the rich group's higher income implies greater housing consumption. But a common p is exactly what the two groups face at distance $\hat{x}$, where the p_R and p_P curves intersect. Therefore, at this location, q_R is larger than q_P, and the slope $-t/q_R$ of the p_R curve is less negative than the slope $-t/q_P$ of the p_P curve. Thus, *at a point where the curves intersect, the p_R curve must be flatter than the p_P curve, so that price-curve diagram must look like figure 3.1.* The location pattern in the figure, with the poor in the center and the rich in the suburbs, is then a prediction of the model.

The intuitive explanation for this prediction borrows from chapter 2's analysis of the effect of y on urban spatial structure. That discussion argued that the increase in desired dwelling size following from an increase in income gives a household an incentive to move farther from the CBD, to locations where the price per square foot is lower. Because the rich are then drawn to low-p areas of the city, they are able to outbid poor households for suburban locations. Poor households, in contrast, can tolerate a high per-square-foot housing price better than the rich because their dwellings are small. Therefore, the poor are able to outbid the rich for housing in the center, where p is high.

The predicted central location of the poor, however, depends crucially on the absence of time cost as a component of commuting cost. Including time cost in the model in a proper way would involve adding a third good—leisure time—to the utility function. A longer commute would then reduce the amount of time available for work and leisure, and the consumer would end up valuing this loss at w per hour, where w is the wage. However, the presence of leisure time in the model prevents the derivation of many of the simple conclusions of chapter 2.

A simpler, though ad hoc, approach to generating time costs is more workable. The approach assumes that leisure time is fixed, with commuting time (unrealistically) reducing available work hours in one-to-one fashion. Then, if an extra mile of commuting distance reduces work time by some fraction δ of an hour, that mile reduces income by δw dollars. Adding this loss onto the money cost t of commuting then yields a new commuting cost per mile, equal to $m = \delta w + t$. But since the rich have higher wages than the poor ($w_R > w_P$), two different commuting costs emerge, equal to $m_R = \delta w_R + t$ and $m_P = \delta w_P + t$, with the rich one higher ($m_R > m_P$). With this modification, the slopes of the housing-price curves are modified, with t replaced by m_R or m_P in the slope expression. In other words, the slope of the p_R curve is equal to $-m_R/q_R$, and the slope of the p_P curve is $-m_P/q_P$. But with $m_R >$ m_P and $q_R > q_P$, the relationship between the slopes is unclear: the p_R curve could either be flatter or steeper than the p_P curve at their intersection point. Thus, figure 3.1 could still apply, or the figure could be reversed. In the latter case, the p_R curve would be steeper than p_P curve, and the rich would live in the center and the poor would live in the suburbs. Therefore, when time costs are present, *the model doesn't offer a clear prediction about the relative locations of the rich and the poor*.[2]

The source of this ambiguity is the presence of two conflicting forces. The desire to rent their large dwellings at a low price per square foot pulls the rich toward the suburbs, while a desire to limit their high time cost of commuting pulls the rich toward the center. Depending on the relative strengths of these forces, either location for the rich group is possible.[3]

Although many American cities (including New York and Chicago) have high-income enclaves near the CBD, the overall correlation between income and distance from the center is positive in the United States. The contrast between this strong pattern and the model's ambiguous predictions is striking, and this disparity has prompted researchers to seek other explanations for the observed pattern that do not rely on a strict interpretation of the urban model. Glaeser, Kahn, and Rappaport (2008), for example, use a transport mode-choice explanation. They argue that the poor, being unable to afford automobiles, must rely on public transit, and that central cities are the only parts of urban areas that are dense enough to support convenient public transit (for example, subways with closely spaced stations). The implication is that poor households must live in central cities in order to have mobility, thus yielding the location pattern observed in the United States.[4]

---

2. Empirical researchers have used data to try to measure the slopes of the price curves and thus dispel the model's ambiguity. However, they disagree on the conclusions to be drawn from the data. See Wheaton 1977 and Glaeser, Kahn, and Rappaport 2008.

3. Formally, the housing force dominates the time-cost force if the income elasticity of housing demand is greater than the income elasticity of commuting cost per mile.

4. LeRoy and Sonstelie (1983) offer a more nuanced analysis of the effect of mode choices on location. They assume that time costs are dominant in location choices when the rich and poor both rely on the same transport mode, in which case the rich live in the center. But when a new, fast, and expensive transport mode is introduced (say, the streetcar in the nineteenth century), the rich choose it while the poor continue to use the original mode (walking). But the mode's speed reduces the time cost of commuting for the rich, allowing them to move to the suburbs, with the poor occupying the central city. This model thus predicts that location patterns may change with the adoption of new transport modes.

Brueckner and Rosenthal (2009), in contrast, show that a different picture of locational incentives emerges when the age of dwellings is taken into account. According to their argument, high-income households prefer newer housing, whereas the poor tolerate older housing. Since a city's newest dwellings are usually found in the suburbs, far from the CBD, these suburban locations end up attracting the rich, whereas the poor occupy older dwellings near the center. But Brueckner and Rosenthal point out that when the central city's old buildings wear out and are replaced, the center's new housing may then attract the rich, leading to "gentrification" and a reversal of the typical location pattern.

The challenge faced by the urban model in explaining locational patterns by income becomes even harder when it is realized that the American pattern is not always repeated in other countries. For example, the pattern is reversed in Paris, where the central city is rich and the suburbs are poor. Other European cities, and some cities in Latin America, also have a pattern opposite to that of the United States. In attempt to explain the resulting puzzle, Brueckner, Thisse, and Zenou (1999) focus on urban amenities such as historical monuments, fine architecture, and natural amenities, such as an ocean front or a river front. They argue that if such amenities are present in the central city, and if the rich value living near them more than do the poor, then a force arises that may reverse the American locational pattern. Paris is a prime example of a city with an amenity-rich center, and this theory may explain why rich households occupy the central city rather than living in the suburbs.

The discussion in Brueckner, Thisse, and Zenou 1999 makes clear another implicit omission in the development of the urban model in chapter 2. In particular, locations in the basic model are distinguished only by differences in commuting cost. In effect, amenities are absent, so that aside from commuting-cost differences, no location is better or worse than any other. This implicit assumption may be unrealistic for some cities, in which case the model's predictions about housing price patterns and other spatial features may not be fully accurate.

More generally, the foregoing discussion shows that the urban model is less successful at explaining the locations of different income groups within the city than at predicting regularities in spatial structure such as the decline in building heights moving away from the CBD. Developing a better understanding of these group location patterns remains a task for ongoing research.

3.3   Commuting by Freeway

The model so far portrays the city as having a dense network of radial roads. Suppose instead that a single freeway passes through the city in an east–west direction, allowing access to the CBD (see figure 3.2). Suppose also that the freeway can be accessed from city streets at any point, with an onramp available on every block. Since freeway traffic moves faster than traffic on city streets, commuters living near the freeway will use city streets to access it, driving the rest of the way to work on the freeway. But some commuters will find it better to use city streets for their entire trip. Figure 3.2 shows that a commuter living at location A will travel diagonally to the freeway and then to the CBD, whereas a commuter living at location B will travel straight in to the CBD on city streets without using the freeway.[5] The freeway's "catchment area" (which consists of locations where use of the freeway is preferable, such as A) consists of the two triangular-shaped areas inside the dashed lines in the figure.

Since freeway trips are fast, the distance traveled is no longer a proper measure of commuting cost, assuming that time cost matters along with money cost. As a result, a freeway-using commuter who lives relatively far from the CBD in either the easterly or the westerly direction will have the same commuting cost as a commuter who lives closer to the CBD but in the northerly or the southerly direction and commutes on slow city streets. In other words, locations A and B could have the same commuting cost even though A is farther from the CBD.

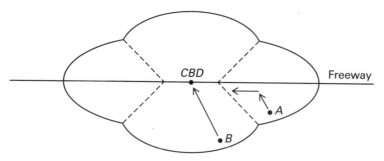

Figure 3.2
City with freeway.

5. Note in figure 3.2 that the commuter living at A drives in a non-radial direction to access the freeway, which means that the street pattern allows such a path as well as allowing radial trips.

The price p per square foot of housing would then be the same at A and B, which in turn implies that land rent r would be the same in both locations despite A's greater distance from the center. This conclusion implies that, within the freeway catchment area, *land rent falls more slowly as distance to the CBD increases than it does outside the catchment area*. As a result, land rent takes longer to fall to the agricultural rent level inside the catchment area, which in turn means that edge of the city is farther from the CBD inside the catchment area than outside it. Thus, the city is elongated within the freeway catchment area, although its radius is not affected outside that area. This pattern can be seen in figure 3.2.

Aside from this change in the shape of the city, all the intracity predictions of the model are unaffected. The housing price p, land rent r, building heights, and population density D all decrease moving away from the CBD, although their rates of decline are less within the freeway catchment area. Dwelling size again increases with distance, subject to the same qualification.

3.4 Adding Employment Outside the CBD

As was mentioned earlier, not all employment in real-world cities is concentrated in the CBD. Although employment may be high in the center, additional jobs may be widely dispersed throughout the city or concentrated in secondary employment centers. How do these different employment patterns affect the predictions of the model?

3.4.1 Dispersed employment

Consider first the dispersed-employment case, in which the CBD remains the only job center but other businesses are scattered throughout the city without any significant spatial concentration. Consider a CBD worker living at distance x^* who makes a radial trip from his residence that passes by one of these business establishments, which is located at distance x^{**} from the center. That employer could lure this worker away from CBD employment by offering an income equal to $y - tx^{**}$. This income would give the worker a disposable income equal to $y - tx^{**} - t(x^* - x^{**})$, where the last term is commuting cost from the residence distance x^* to the noncentral location x^{**} of the new workplace. Since this disposable income expression reduces to $y - tx^*$ (note that tx^{**} cancels), which equals the worker's disposable income with CBD commuting, the worker loses nothing from the switch and is thus happy to make it. Note that the worker saves tx^{**} in commuting cost by stopping at the noncentral job site rather than going all the way to the CBD, and the employer cuts his income relative to the CBD income y by exactly this amount, making the worker indifferent between the two work sites.

This argument shows that if dispersed employers located outside the CBD pay incomes of $I(x) = y - tx$, where x is the distance of the establishment from the center, then they can skim off previous CBD commuters without affecting their disposable incomes. Since the spatial decline of disposable income thus remains the same as in the case when all jobs are at the CBD, all of the model's predictions are unaffected. Thus, a city where some jobs are at the CBD and the rest are dispersed across other locations is indistinguishable from one where all the jobs are centralized. The incomes paid at these dispersed worksites fall with their distance to the CBD, a pattern known as a "wage gradient." Various empirical studies have established the existence of wage gradients in real cities.[6]

3.4.2   Employment subcenters

Now suppose that, instead of being dispersed, the city's non-CBD employment is concentrated in a secondary business district (SBD). Extending the logic of the basic model, the existence of such a center would, in effect, generate a second city joined to the original city. Figure 3.3 shows an aerial view of the resulting "polycentric" city, and figure 3.4 shows the pattern of housing prices along a line between the CBD and the SBD.

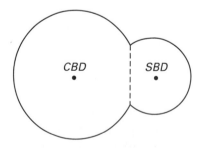

Figure 3.3
Subcenter.

---

6. See, for example, Eberts 1981.

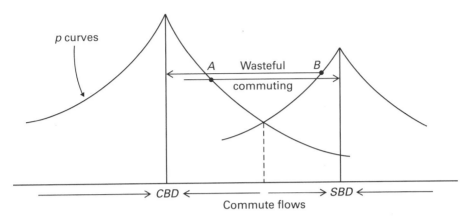

Figure 3.4
Wasteful commuting.

The figures show that residents living near the CBD commute to that center, while residents living closer to the SBD commute to it. At the boundary between the commute areas, shown as a dashed line in figure 3.3, disposable incomes net of commuting costs are equal. As can be seen in the figure, the border may be farther from the CBD than from the SBD, an outcome that arises if the CBD pays a higher income than the SBD. Figure 3.4 shows that the housing price p declines moving away from each center, with the respective price curves intersecting at the commute boundary. Given the illustrated price behavior, the additional predictions of the model would apply around each employment center. In particular, moving away from either center, land rent will decline along with p, as will building heights and population density. As the commute boundary is crossed, the pattern will reverse itself, with these four variables then rising as the other center is approached. Dwelling sizes will exhibit corresponding behavior.

This portrayal thus views a city with two employment centers as the effective union of two "monocentric" cities. The predictions of the resulting model appear to be fairly realistic, with access to a nearby center in a polycentric city generating housing-price premia.[7] However, the portrayal misses an important and puzzling feature of existing polycentric cities: "wasteful commuting." Under this pattern,

---

7. A number of empirical studies attempt to identify and count subcenters in large U.S. cities. See, for example, Giuliano and Small 1991. Fujita and Ogawa (1982) develop a complex model that explains the formation and location of subcenters.

a resident living at location B in figure 3.4 would commute to the CBD rather than to the closer SBD, while a resident living at location A would commute to the SBD rather than to the closer CBD. This arrangement is wasteful because if the two commuters were to switch residences they would continue to pay the same housing price p, but each would have a shorter commute.

Hamilton (1982) showed that the volume of wasteful commuting is large in U.S. cities, a finding that remains puzzling even after much subsequent research on the topic. There are several possible explanations for this pattern, although none has been firmly established as the cause. First, residents may have idiosyncratic preferences for particular neighborhoods as a result of local amenities or the close proximity of relatives. For example, the resident at A may have once worked in the CBD (which accounts for her choice of this location), and she may have to come to enjoy A's amenities. Therefore, she refuses to leave her adopted neighborhood after taking a new job at the SBD, thus engaging in a wasteful commute.[8] A second explanation focuses on multiple-worker households. If the head of a household appears to engage in a wasteful commute, the reason may be a desire to be close to the spouse's employment site. If employment for such secondary workers isn't tabulated, the data might give the impression that residential choices are irrational and wasteful when a good unobserved reason exists. A third possible reason for wasteful commuting is employment uncertainty. For example, the resident at A may be uncertain about whether she can keep her SBD job, and if laid off, she would expect to search for work in the CBD. Maintaining a residence close to the CBD may then make sense.[9]

3.4.3 Employment decentralization and spatial mismatch

When jobs move to the suburbs, the result may be worse employment outcomes for some urban residents. Members of poor households living near the CBD, who may belong to a racial minority, are now far from the new jobs. Public transit service to the suburbs may be inadequate, making it hard to access the jobs from central-city residences. In addition, racial discrimination may be present in suburban housing markets, making it hard for the poor households to move near the jobs. The result is what is known as "spatial mismatch": an insurmountable

---

8. For a model illustrating this possibility, see Ng 2008.
9. For a model illustrating this idea, see Crane 1996.

mismatch between residential and job locations for poor households. Substantial evidence has accumulated showing that spatial mismatch leads to a higher level of unemployment, and to longer unemployment durations, for minority members.[10]

3.4.4   Commuting in the information age

The information age and the rise of the Internet have begun to change commuting patterns, with many workers "telecommuting" from home instead of physically commuting to job sites, at least for part of the work week. Since with telecommuting, fewer commute trips are made per period, the effect of this change is to decrease the commuting-cost parameter t. Thus, as the results of subsection 2.7.2 suggest, the rise of telecommuting should causes cities to spread out and become less dense in their centers.[11]

3.5   Durable Housing Capital

The urban model as presented in chapter 2 doesn't recognize age differences between buildings. In effect, the model assumes that housing capital is "perfectly malleable," so that buildings can be easily replaced as conditions change. Recall, in particular, the analysis of the supply-demand equilibrium, in which the city was rebuilt in response to changes in population or income. But a look at any real city shows that this malleability assumption is inaccurate. In many locations, a brand-new building stands next to a very old one, an outcome that would never exist with malleable capital. With malleability, the old structure wouldn't have been left standing while the adjacent location was redeveloped.

When new and old buildings are in close proximity, the result may be a pattern of building heights that violates the predictions of the model. For example, the new building may be a tall high-rise structure, while the old building, having been constructed decades earlier, may be relatively short. But the model predicts that building heights should decline smoothly as distance to the CBD increases, so that buildings that are adjacent to one another should be nearly identical. The question then is this: How do the predictions of the model change when it

---

10. For a survey of the evidence, see Ihlanfeldt and Sjoquist 1998. For a survey of models of spatial mismatch, see Gobillon, Selod, and Zenou 2007.
11. For further analysis, see Rhee 2008.

is modified to allow housing capital to be durable, leading to the coexistence of old and new buildings?

A large literature (summarized in Brueckner 2000a) is devoted to analyzing urban models with durable housing capital. An important lesson of this complex literature can be developed using a simple example. In the example, the city grows outward over time by a fixed distance each year, adding "rings" as a tree does. Each ring is referred to as a "block," and years are denoted by T. The city comes into being at year 0, thus adding its first block at $T = 0$. New buildings are constructed in a block when it is added to the city, and they are held in the housing stock for a fixed amount of time before being replaced. For simplicity, the life span of a building is set at 3 years, although a more realistic number might be 75 or 100 years. Therefore, a building constructed at $T = 0$ is replaced at $T = 3$, one constructed at $T = 1$ is replaced at $T = 4$, and so on.

Table 3.1 gives the age pattern of buildings at three dates ($T = 2, 3$, and 8), and the upper panel of figure 3.5 illustrates the age pattern for $T = 8$. From table 3.1, observe that at $T = 2$, first-generation buildings occupy blocks 0, 1, and 2. The buildings in block 2 are brand new, those in block 1 are 1 year old, and those in block 0 are 2 years old. Then, at $T = 3$, the buildings in block 0 reach the end of their life span and are replaced with new second-generation structures, while new structures are also built in block 3, which is newly added to the city. This growth pattern continues, and by $T = 8$, the interaction of spatial growth and redevelopment has generated the "sawtooth" pattern of building ages shown in the top panel of figure 3.5.

Table 3.1
Building-age contours.

$T = 2$		$T = 3$		$T = 8$	
Block	Age	Block	Age	Block	Age
0	2	0	0	0	2
1	1	1	2	1	1
2	0	2	1	2	0
		3	0	3	2
				4	1
				5	0
				6	2
				7	1
				8	0

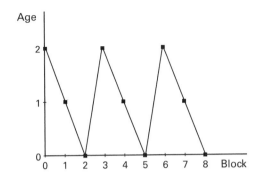

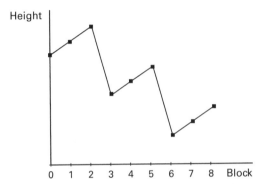

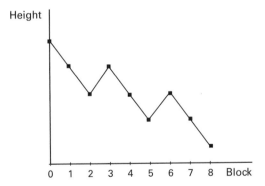

Figure 3.5
Patterns of building age and building height.

Now consider the spatial pattern of building heights at $T = 8$. This pattern depends on the effects of both location and construction date on the height of buildings. For buildings constructed *at a given date*, those farther from the CBD will be shorter, following the basic model. For buildings constructed *at a given location*, suppose that those constructed later (belonging to a subsequent generation) are taller. Thus, the partial effect of distance on building height is negative, whereas the partial effect of the construction date is positive.

Given these facts, consider the pattern of building heights at $T = 8$, focusing initially on blocks 0, 1, and 2. Buildings in block 1 were built later than those in block 0, and this difference tends to make them taller. However, block 1 is farther from the CBD, and this difference tends to make its buildings shorter than those in block 0. Although the net effect is ambiguous, suppose that the age effect dominates the distance effect, so that buildings in block 1 are taller than those in block 0, as shown in the middle panel of figure 3.5. Since buildings in block 2 were built later than those in block 1, the same principles apply, and buildings there are taller than those in block 1.

In contrast, in moving from block 2 to block 3, the age and distance effects work in the same direction. The reason is that buildings in block 3 were built *earlier* than those in block 2 (they are 2 years old instead of brand-new), and this difference tends to make them shorter. Since the distance effect reinforces this tendency, building heights decline sharply moving from block 2 to block 3. These patterns are repeated in blocks 3–8, generating a cyclical pattern of building heights.

Other cyclical patterns are possible. For example, if the age effect is weak, the distance effect will dominate within the block ranges 0–2, 3–5, and 6–8, leading to downward-sloping height contours over these ranges. As before, heights will drop sharply between the ranges. Yet another pattern emerges if the age effect is reversed, with a later construction date making the buildings in a given location *shorter* rather than taller. The distance and age effects then work in the same direction in block ranges 0–2, 3–5, and 6–8, implying that building heights decline over these ranges, as can be seen in the bottom panel of figure 3.5. The discontinuous increase in age across blocks 2 and 3 now implies a jump in building heights, which is repeated across blocks 5 and 6.[12]

These examples show that the interaction between the city's spatial growth and the redevelopment of its buildings generates irregular height patterns that contrast sharply with the smoothly declining

---

12. Exercise 3.1 generates a numerical example based on this discussion.

contours of a city with malleable housing capital. Over blocks 2–3 and 5–6, figure 3.5's middle panel shows exactly the kind of height disparity noted above, with tall new buildings adjacent to old short ones.

Despite these differences, the height pattern in figure 3.5 is consistent with the pattern from the basic model on a more fundamental level. In particular, the *trend of building heights over distance is downward*, just like in the basic model. To see the reason, recall that for buildings constructed at the same date, less central structures are shorter. For example, height falls with distance in figure 3.5 over blocks 0, 3, and 6, where buildings are all 2 years old, and in blocks 2, 5, and 8, where they are all new. Since the age pattern repeats itself over distance, the result is an overall downward trend in building heights. Therefore, while capital durability leads to irregular local building-height contours, the global height pattern looks very much like that of the model with malleable capital.

3.6   Cities in Developing Countries

The analysis in chapter 2 briefly considered a city that was open to migration from other cities. However, it is interesting to consider a different type of open city: one that experiences in-migration from rural areas rather than from other cities. This kind of migration plays an important role in developing countries, where the growth of manufacturing and service production in cities attracts large numbers of workers from the countryside. This process of rural–urban migration has been largely completed in developed Western economies, leaving relatively small rural populations, but it is still unfolding in a major way in developing countries.

The migration process often generates very large cities, and serious urban problems, in developing countries. By adapting the urban model from chapter 2, the equilibrium city size determined via rural–urban migration can be analyzed.

Suppose that rural residents earn an income y_A, which is lower than the urban income y. Since the rural residents live next to the fields where they work, no commuting cost is incurred. Therefore, the rural resident's disposable income is just equal to y_A.

When will a rural resident want to move to the city? He will wish to do so if earning the urban income y and paying for commuting and urban housing makes him better off than living in the countryside. But in order to decide whether migration will raise his standard of living, the rural resident need only compare his situation with that of the urban resident living at the city's edge. The reason is that all urban residents are equally well off (recall the fundamental urban equilibrium condition), so that a comparison with any one of them is sufficient to judge relative standards of living.

Comparison with the edge resident is especially easy because that resident and the rural resident pay the same price for housing.[13] Therefore, standards of living can be compared by simply *comparing disposable incomes*. For the edge resident, disposable income is just $y - t\bar{x}$, urban income minus commuting cost from the city's edge. If this disposable income is greater than y_A, then the rural resident gains by moving to the city, and he will do so (migration costs are assumed to be zero). Since the incentive to move will be absent once $y - t\bar{x}$ becomes equal to y_A, the equality of these two values is the condition for rural–urban migration equilibrium. In other words, no further incentive to move to the city exists, and migration equilibrium is achieved, when $y - t\bar{x} = y_A$.

To use this condition to determine the equilibrium city population L, recall from the supply-demand analysis that $\bar{x}$ and L are positively related, with an increase in population leading to an increase in $\bar{x}$. As a result, the city's edge distance can be written as an increasing function of L, with $\bar{x} = \bar{x}(L)$. Substituting this function, the equilibrium condition $y - t\bar{x} = y_A$ can be rewritten as

$$y - t\bar{x}(L) = y_A.$$

This new condition determines the equilibrium value of the city's population under the rural–urban migration process. When L is of just the right size, $y - t\bar{x}(L)$ and y_A will be equal, and there will be no incentive for rural–urban migration.

The above condition can be used to determine the effect of the relevant variables on the equilibrium city size. For example, suppose y_A is low, perhaps as a result of poor agricultural productivity in the countryside. Then, to reach migration equilibrium, $y - t\bar{x}(L)$ must also have a small magnitude. But this requirement means that $\bar{x}(L)$ must be large and hence that L itself must be large. Therefore, in a country with a low rural income, rural–urban migration will not stop until the city has reached a large population size. This large population means a long commute (and thus a low disposable income) for the edge resident,

---

13. To see why, note that the land used in rural housing production has rent r_A, which is the same as the rent paid by urban housing developers at the city's edge. Since the price of housing capital i is the same everywhere, both input prices are then the same. As a result, rural and city-edge housing will rent for the same price per square foot.

pushing the urban standard of living down to the low rural level. Thus, the model predicts that *developing countries with low rural incomes should contain especially large cities.*[14]

It is also possible to analyze the effect of the city's income y and its commuting cost per mile t on the equilibrium L. Doing so is less straightforward than before, because $\bar{x}$ itself depends on y and t. But the required analysis shows that *cities with high incomes or low commuting costs will attract a large number of rural migrants*, growing to a large equilibrium population L.

These latter conclusions can be verified in a simpler model in which population density is constrained to be constant across locations. This outcome would occur if only one dwelling size were available and if buildings were the same height everywhere. With individual land consumption fixed at some constant $1/\mu$, the land area of the city is equal to μL (acres per person times population). Thus, the radius $\bar{x}$ of the city satisfies $\pi\bar{x}^2 = \mu L$, so that $\bar{x} = (\mu L/\pi)^{1/2}$. Then the migration-equilibrium condition can be written $y - t(\mu L/\pi)^{1/2} = y_A$. It is easy to see from this equation, that if y increases or t falls, then L must also increase to maintain the equality. Thus, a higher urban income or a lower commuting cost leads to a more populous city.

The model can also be used to consider another issue that is important in the phenomenon of rural–urban migration: high unemployment in cities in developing countries. The persistence of migration flows in the face of such unemployment looked puzzling to many researchers until Harris and Todaro (1969) developed their model. That now-famous model pointed out that expected income (in a probabilistic sense) is what should matter to migrants. As a result, migrants will move to the city even with a relatively small chance of landing a job as long as that job pays a lot better than rural employment.

The Harris-Todaro dimension can easily be added to the model. Suppose that the number of jobs in the city is fixed at J, with each job paying a high income level y. Then the chance of getting such a job is equal to J/L, the number of jobs divided by the city's population. If a migrant earns zero income if she doesn't land a job, expected income is then yJ/L. Replacing y in the previous migration equilibrium condition by expected income, the condition becomes

---

14. The largest cities in a number of developing countries (for example, Mexico City) are extremely large relative to the country's population, a pattern that is usually not seen in developed countries. The above model isn't really adequate to explain this pattern, but various empirical studies have attempted to find its source.

$yJ/L - t(\mu L/\pi)^{1/2} = y_A.$

The urban standard of living now falls with L for two reasons. First, as before, a bigger L means a longer commute for the edge resident, reducing disposable income. Second, a bigger L reduces expected income by adding to the pool of people competing for the fixed number of high-paying urban jobs. The previous conclusions hold for this Harris-Todaro version of the model: the equilibrium city population L rises when y increases or when t or y_A falls. But a new linkage also emerges. If the number of jobs J in the city rises, then L must also rise to restore equality in the equilibrium condition. The increase in J raises expected income, increasing the urban standard of living, and this change encourages more people to migrate to the city. Thus, cities with more jobs grow to a larger population size, a natural conclusion.[15]

The foregoing analysis shows how the basic urban model can be used to help understand the forces that drive urbanization in developing countries.[16]

3.7   Summary

This chapter has explored modifications of the urban model. In a city with two income groups, the model predicts that the poor live in the center and the rich live in the suburbs. But when a time-cost component is added to commuting cost, the model no longer yields a clear prediction as to where the rich and the poor live. Adding a freeway to the radial road network changes the city's shape without altering the main qualitative conclusions of the model. Adding dispersed employment has no effect on the model, while adding a secondary employment center effectively creates a second city joined to the original one. When housing capital is durable instead of malleable, spatial building-height patterns become irregular, but the trend is still downward moving away from the central business district, as in the basic model. The model can also be used to analyze rural–urban migration and the determination of city sizes in developing countries.

---

15. For a numerical example based on this analysis, see exercise 3.2 below. For more general analysis of a model that adds a Harris-Todaro component to the basic framework, see Brueckner and Kim 2001.

16. For a more ambitious computable general equilibrium approach to modeling cities in developing countries, see Kelley and Williamson 1984.

4   Urban Sprawl and Land-Use Controls

4.1   Introduction

Strong sentiment against "urban sprawl" has emerged in the United States in recent years. Critics of sprawl argue that urban expansion consumes too much agricultural land, leading to a loss of amenity benefits from open space as well as a loss of scarce farmland. They also argue that the long commutes resulting from urban expansion create excessive traffic congestion and air pollution. In addition, they allege that growth at the urban fringe depresses the incentive for redevelopment of land closer to city centers, leading to decay of downtown areas. Some critics also claim that, by spreading people out, low-density suburban development reduces social interaction, weakening the bonds that underpin a healthy society. Finally, critics draw a link between sprawl and obesity, arguing that life in the automobile-dependent suburbs deprives people of the benefits of exercise from walking.

Using data from satellite imagery from the period 1976–1992, Burchfield et al. (2006) document the spatial growth of U.S. cities. Although their data show that only 1.9 percent of the U.S. land area was built up by 1992, the percentage was much lower (1.3) in 1976, only 16 years earlier. Thus, the developed land area grew at the very high rate of 2.5 percent per year over that period, with the share of developed land rising by almost half. Other sources show that the rate of spatial growth in many U.S. cities far exceeded their rates of population growth.

In response to concerns about sprawl, state and local governments have adopted policies designed to restrict the spatial expansion of cities. At least twelve states have enacted growth-management programs, the best-known being New Jersey's 1998 commitment to spend

$1 billion of sales tax revenue to purchase half of the state's remaining vacant land. In addition, cities all over the country have imposed a variety of anti-sprawl policies, including growth boundaries and charges levied on development. The November 1998 election saw 240 anti-sprawl initiatives appearing on ballots nationwide, and many additional measures were put before the voters in the 2000 election and in subsequent contests.

Do the criticisms of urban sprawl have merit? Do cities take up too much space? Should policy measures designed to restrict the spatial growth of cities be adopted? This chapter addresses these questions, making use of the urban model developed in chapters 2 and 3.[1] Since land-use controls offer one means of attacking sprawl, the chapter then turns to an analysis of these policies. The discussion first considers urban growth boundaries, a primary tool for limiting sprawl, and it then turns to other land-use controls, such as building-height restrictions and zoning, that aren't related to sprawl.

4.2 Empirical Evidence on the Spatial Sizes of Cities

The phenomenon lamented by the critics of sprawl, the spatial expansion of cities, is captured theoretically by the urban model developed in chapters 2 and 3. The model showed how $\bar{x}$, the distant to the edge of the city, responds to changes in four variables: $\bar{x}$ rises when the city's population L or income level y increases, and $\bar{x}$ falls when commuting cost per mile t or agricultural rent r_A increases. The first step in appraising the criticism of urban sprawl is to determine, using data, whether these variables really affect $\bar{x}$ (and thus the city's spatial area, $\pi\bar{x}^2$) in the manner predicted by the model.

Brueckner and Fansler (1983) and McGrath (2005) present regression analyses relating urban land areas to measures of L, t, y, and r_A. Measurement of these variables is straightforward except for the commuting-cost variable t. Whereas Brueckner and Fansler use two different proxies for commuting cost,[2] McGrath instead uses the transportation component of the consumer price index to measure a city's t. Brueckner and Fansler rely on data for a single year (1970) for 40 small and

---

1. Much of the discussion in the first half of the chapter draws on Brueckner 2000b. See Glaeser and Kahn 2004 and Nechyba and Walsh 2004 for surveys of the issues involved in urban sprawl. For a non-economist's perspective on sprawl, see Bruegmann 2005.
2. The proxy variables are the city's share of commuters using public transit (with a high value indicating a high t) and the share using autos (with a high value indicating a low t).

Table 4.1
Elasticities of urban area land with respect to various variables.

	Brueckner and Fansler (1983)	McGrath (2005)
Population (L)	1.10	0.76
Commuting cost (t)	0	−0.28
Income (y)	1.50	0.33
Agricultural rent (r_A)	−0.23	−0.10

medium-size cities, but McGrath uses data for 153 cities at ten-year intervals over the period 1950–1990.

Table 4.1 gives the elasticity estimates from the regressions in these two studies. Recall that an elasticity equals the percentage increase in the dependent variable from a 1 percent increase in an independent variable. Thus, Brueckner and Fansler's results show that a 1 percent increase in population leads to a 1.1 percent increase in the city's land area, whereas McGrath's results show a smaller increase of 0.76 percent. Brueckner and Fansler's results show a strong income impact (a 1.5 percent land-area increase from a 1 percent increase in y); McGrath's show a smaller effect. Both studies show a negative impact of agricultural rent, with Brueckner and Fansler's measured effect again stronger. Brueckner and Fansler find no commuting-cost effect, presumably because their t proxies are crude, but McGrath, using a better measure, finds the predicted negative impact of commuting cost on land area.

Although the numerical magnitudes of the estimated elasticities differ between the two studies, these empirical findings show that the predictions of the urban model are confirmed by real-world data. Therefore, the model can be used reliably to understand the spatial expansion of cities, allowing an appraisal of criticisms of urban sprawl.

Given table 4.1's evidence on the link between land areas and the variables L, y, and t, it is easy to see why American cities have experienced strong spatial growth over past decades. First, city populations have increased, reflecting the overall growth of the U.S. population. Second, household incomes have grown substantially over the decades since 1950. Third, over this period, governments at all levels have made substantial investments in transportation infrastructure, mainly in the form of freeways, which have reduced the cost of road travel within cities as well as between them. Since an increase in L or y, or a decline in t, each separately leads to an increase a city's land area, the combined historical changes in these variables likely account for much of the observed spatial growth of cities.[3] Thus, urban spatial expansion appears to be caused mainly by "fundamental forces": rising populations and incomes and falling commuting costs.[4]

With this understanding, it may be hard to find fault in the process of urban spatial expansion, even if its consequences (paving over the landscape) may seem undesirable. After all, an expanding population needs space in which to live, and higher incomes naturally cause households to consume more land as they buy bigger dwellings. Also, freeway investments meant to ease commuting naturally encourage longer commutes and thus cause cities to spread out. Moreover, table 4.1 shows that the operation of these fundamental forces is restrained by agricultural land rents. Cities don't spread out as much when r_A is high, indicating that productive farmland is more resistant to urban expansion than unproductive land (perhaps easing concerns about farmland loss).

But despite the apparently benign operation of the fundamental forces, criticism of urban spatial expansion may be justified if these forces are distorted by "market failures." A market failure arises when the decentralized activities of economic actors fail to achieve the right outcome from society's point of view. The classic example of market failure is industrial pollution, where a dirty factory fails to consider the damage caused by the pollution it creates and thus pollutes too much (this problem is analyzed in detail in chapter 9). The question, then, is whether market failures are present in the economic process that determines the spatial sizes of cities, making them too big from society's point of view.

---

3. Additional evidence on the effect of lower commuting costs is provided by Baum-Snow (2007). He shows that, over the period 1950–1990, metro areas with a larger number of radial highways connecting the center to outlying areas experienced a larger decrease in central-city populations, and thus more suburbanization, than less well-connected metro areas. Thus, investment in freeways spurred suburbanization.
4. Another force leading to the spatial expansion of cities may emerge from the public sector. Instead of residing in a city that contains both rich and poor households, with public services shared between the two groups, high-income households may have an incentive to form their own homogeneous communities at the edge of the city, reinforcing the tendency toward spatial expansion already spurred by the above fundamental forces (see Nechyba and Walsh 2004). Public-sector issues are discussed in detail in chapter 8.

4.3   Market Failures and Urban Sprawl

4.3.1   The market failure related to open-space amenities

Urban economists have identified several market failures that may be relevant to urban sprawl. The first involves the amenity benefits generated by open space, which are lost when this space is consumed by urban development. Suppose, in particular, that each acre of agricultural land yields b dollars of open-space benefits to society, over and above the benefits resulting from the crops it produces. The problem is that these open-space benefits aren't taken into account when the land is converted from agricultural to urban use. Whereas the landowner will rent his land to housing developers when the urban land rent r they pay exceeds the rent r_A paid by the farmer, society would make a different calculation in the presence of open-space amenities. In particular, society (represented by a "social planner") would want the landowner to take the lost open-space benefit of b into account when deciding whether to switch an acre of land to urban use. The planner would want the land switched only if the urban rent could compensate for both the lost agriculture-rent income *and* the lost open-space benefits. Thus, the planner would want the land in urban use only if $r \geq r_A + b$. From the planner's point of view, the boundary of the city should be set at an x value where $r = r_A + b$, not an x value where $r = r_A$.

In effect, the socially optimal city is the city that would emerge if the agricultural rent were $r_A + b$, not r_A. This "effective" agricultural rent includes the open-space benefit generated by the land in addition to the benefit from its agricultural use, as measured by r_A. The resulting city is shown in figure 4.1, which is similar to figure 2.13. The higher "effective" agricultural rent leads to all the effects discussed earlier, including an upward shift in the urban land-rent curve and a decrease in $\bar{x}$. This latter effect provides the crucial conclusion: *In the presence of an open-space amenity, the socially optimal city is spatially smaller than the city generated by the free-market equilibrium.* Therefore, the free-market city takes up too much space, exactly as the critics of urban sprawl allege.

What policy intervention could society carry out in order to fix this market failure? One possibility would be to use the price system, in the form of a tax on developed land. Suppose that the landowner has to pay a tax of b to the government on each acre of developed land that he rents to a housing developer. Then, the landowner's net income

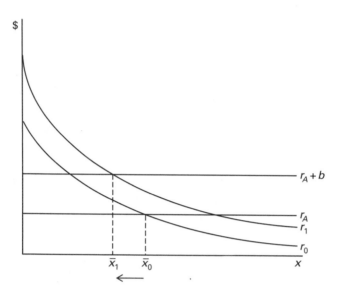

Figure 4.1
Open space externality.

from developed land is $r - b$, the urban land rent minus the tax. The landowner will switch the land from agricultural to urban use only when $r - b \geq r_A$, and this relationship will hold with equality at the edge of the city, implying $r = r_A + b$. But since this is the condition that determines the boundary $\bar{x}$ of the socially optimal city (recall figure 4.1), the urban equilibrium with a development tax is socially optimal.

Since imposition of the development tax is equivalent to an increase in the effective agricultural rent, the resulting city has smaller dwellings and is more expensive to live in than the city with no tax (recall figure 4.1). These changes would ordinarily make the city's residents worse off, as was seen at the end of chapter 2. But once the gain from having additional open space is counted, the population would end up better off, an outcome that was the goal of the government intervention.

Even though this discussion is sound in principle, one might wonder whether open-space amenities are important in a practical sense, especially as they are portrayed in this model. Although some people may care in the abstract about the open space surrounding cities and suffer an amenity loss when it is developed, other people may place little or no value on open space that is far from their residences. Such consumers may care instead about open space in the form of neighborhood parks, which can be enjoyed after a walk or a short drive from a residence. As long as land is devoted to such parks, as is done in most cities, such individuals may have little interest in the preservation of open space on the urban fringe.

Since preserving such open space seems to be a major goal of sprawl critics and of existing policies toward sprawl, this uncertainty about social benefits is problematic. One can imagine a situation in which the individuals in charge of implementing sprawl policies value open space at the urban fringe but the average person doesn't. Then, imposing an anti-sprawl policy such as a development tax may seem right to the policy makers but may make the average person worse off by reducing dwelling sizes and raising the urban cost of living (with no attendant amenity benefits). In this sense, misguided anti-sprawl policies can be harmful, undermining an important element of the American standard of living (consumption of ample amounts of housing floor space) with no accompanying gain.

4.3.2 The market failure related to traffic congestion

A second market failure relevant to urban sprawl is related to traffic congestion, and its source is the "congestion externality." This externality arises because the presence of a single extra car on a congested road slows down all the other cars slightly, raising the time costs of commuting for their drivers. Even though each driver's loss is small, summing these cost increases across all the affected drivers leads to a total impact that is non-negligible. The problem is that, since these congestion costs are felt by other drivers, no individual driver has an incentive to take them into account in making decisions. The upshot is that the private cost of commuting, which includes an individual's own time and money costs, is less than the social cost. This latter cost includes the private-cost elements *plus the externality damage done to other drivers in the form of higher time costs resulting from the presence of the extra car.* To correct for the presence of this externality (and the resulting market failure), commuters should be charged a congestion toll equal to the dollar value of the congestion costs they impose on other drivers. When this toll is charged, the commuting choices of consumers will be better from society's point of view than in the absence of tolls.

Chapter 5 will present a full analysis of congestion tolls and their consequences in a non-spatial model. For present purposes, the goal is to understand how the imposition of congestion tolls, which corrects the congestion externality and eliminates the resulting market failure, affects urban spatial structure. The answer is that the imposition of tolls, by raising the cost of commuting, leads to a spatial shrinkage of the city (a decline in $\bar{x}$). In response to the higher cost of accessing the central business district, urban residents choose to make shorter trips on average, moving closer to the center. Since congestion tolls, by correcting the market failure, lead to a socially optimal outcome, it follows that *the city's spatial size in the free-market equilibrium, without tolls, is too large*. Thus, the free-market city again takes up too much space, exactly as the critics of sprawl allege.

The decline in $\bar{x}$ with congestion tolls is similar to the impact of an increase in t in the urban model from chapter 2. However, it is important to note that the earlier model doesn't actually incorporate traffic congestion. If congestion were present, commuting cost per mile t wouldn't be a fixed constant but would instead increase along with the population L of the city. The reason is that traffic volumes would rise with L, clogging the city's streets. In addition, the presence of congestion would mean that the cost of commuting a mile near the city center, where streets are highly congested, would be higher than the cost in the less congested suburbs, so that t would depend on distance x.

Urban models with congestion have been analyzed extensively, however, and the qualitative effect of imposing congestion tolls in these models is very similar to the effect of raising t in a model without congestion. Tolls would be levied (perhaps electronically) for each mile of travel, and the toll per mile would increase as the CBD was approached, reflecting greater central congestion. In response, population would shift toward the center, the land-rent curve would rotate (as in figure 2.14), and $\bar{x}$ would fall.

Unlike in the case of open-space amenities, there can be little disagreement about the importance of the congestion-related market failure and its effect on urban land areas. After careful study, congestion tolls on the order of $0.17 per mile have been proposed by transportation economists.[5] Mathematical analysis of urban models with traffic congestion shows that, when appropriate tolls are charged, $\bar{x}$ decreases by approximately 10 percent, and population densities rise dramatically near the city center.[6]

---

5. See Small and Verhoef 2007.
6. See Wheaton 1998 and Brueckner 2007.

Although economists have long lobbied for the use of congestion tolls, their adoption has been relatively recent. Tolls were first used extensively in Singapore, and they were more recently adopted in London, where a substantial charge is levied on traffic entering the central city.[7] Stockholm recently adopted a similar scheme, charging peak-hour tolls on the bridges used to access the center. The urban model predicts that these cities will become more compact, at least in the long run, than they would have been in the absence of tolls, and that their residents will be better off.[8]

4.3.3 Other distortions affecting urban land areas

A number of other distortions, which may not be best described as market failures, can also affect the urban land areas. These distortions arise from the actions of governments, which means that they could be called government failures rather than market failures.

The first such distortion is related to the financing of urban infrastructure, such as streets, sewers, parks, and schools. To understand this distortion, note first that the provision of some types of infrastructure may be subject to decreasing returns to scale. For example, extending sewer lines farther and farther from the city center as suburbs expand may entail increasing costs, with the lines and related pumping equipment more expensive to build far from the center than closer in, given the greater distance from sewage-treatment plants. Historically, these higher costs were shared among all the city's residents, with suburban households not penalized for being more costly to serve. In particular, infrastructure costs were paid through property taxes, and the city's property tax rate was raised slightly when taxes on new suburban houses were insufficient to pay the high infrastructure costs associated with those houses. With the higher tax rate, the existing residents helped pay for the cost of servicing the new suburban houses. As a consequence of this cost sharing, the new suburban residents did not have to pay the true "marginal cost" of providing infrastructure to their houses. As a consequence, the cost of occupying a suburban house (inclusive of taxes) would look artificially cheap to new residents, encouraging growth of the suburbs. If the tax system instead made the new residents face the true infrastructure costs associated with their houses, suburban growth

---

7. For a discussion of the London toll, see Leape 2006.
8. In addition to creating congestion, commuting also involves another market failure through its contribution to air pollution. This market failure could be addressed by adding a pollution component to an existing congestion toll.

would seem less attractive, and less suburban development would occur. Thus, tax arrangements can lead to the "underpricing" of urban infrastructure, which encourages excessive urban expansion.

In fact, taxation practices in many localities have changed in recent years in a way that eliminates or reduces this underpricing distortion. The change involves adoption of "impact fees," which require housing developers to pay directly for the cost of the infrastructure required by their developments. Developers might pay a road impact fee or a school impact fee, with the revenue used to cover the cost of roads and schools that the government must build. Since these costs are passed on to home buyers, they show up in a higher selling price for the house rather than in property tax payments. But the ultimate effect is the same: new suburban residents are charged for the marginal cost of serving them. The use of impact fees, although not universal, tends to eliminate the infrastructure-underpricing distortion, thus restraining the excessive spatial growth of cities.

Three other government financial practices also affect urban land areas. The first effect operates through the federal income tax system, which creates a "tax subsidy" to homeownership. As will be discussed in more detail in chapter 6, this tax subsidy reduces the cost of home-ownership for high-income households, encouraging large dwelling sizes. Big houses in turn use lots of land, which causes cities to take up more space than they would in the absence of a tax subsidy to home-ownership. The second financial practice is the subsidization of auto-mobile transportation. This subsidy arises because gasoline taxes aren't high enough to cover the full cost of building and maintaining roads. As a result, driving is artificially cheap (with t too low), and urban residents do too much of it. The result is excessively long commute trips and cities that are more spread out than they would be in the absence of a subsidy, as was illustrated in figure 2.14. Public transit is also subsidized, but these subsidies can be partly justified on grounds of economic efficiency (which would require transit users to pay only the low marginal cost of serving them). A third government financial practice works in the opposite direction, tending to restrict urban land areas. This practice involves government policies toward agriculture, which bolster farmers' incomes through crop price supports and other programs. By making farming more profitable than it would otherwise be, these policies allow farmers to pay higher land rents than would be possible in their absence. Since a higher r_A leads to a smaller urban land area from the analysis in chapter 2 (recall figure 2.13), it follows that cities are more compact than they would be in the absence of favorable agricultural policies.

4.3.4 Sprawl and blight

As was mentioned above, critics of sprawl allege that excessive urban spatial expansion depresses the incentive for redevelopment of downtown areas, leading to decay and blight. Since the basic urban model doesn't recognize the deterioration of buildings as they age, it cannot address this claim. However, using an extended version of the model in which the extent of building maintenance is a decision variable of housing developers, Brueckner and Helsley (2011) confirm the connection between sprawl and blight. They show that the market failures leading to sprawl also generate under-maintenance of buildings in the central city. When sprawl remedies such as a development tax or congestion tolls are imposed, the city becomes more compact and its central-city buildings are revitalized, confirming the allegations of the sprawl critics.

Others have argued that higher-income households move to the suburbs to *escape* urban blight. From this perspective, *blight causes sprawl* rather than vice versa. Each of these views probably contains elements of truth.[9]

4.3.5 Scattered development and sprawl

So far, sprawl has been viewed as a problem of too much land being devoted to housing, leading to a city that is too spread out. But many commentators equate sprawl with the phenomenon of *scattered* development, which leaves many areas of undeveloped land within the outer boundaries of the city. Although scattered development may not make the amount of land devoted to housing too large, critics argue that it wastes resources by failing to generate compact cities.

Scattered development poses a puzzle since it appears to raise commuting costs relative to compact development, an outcome that consumers would seem not to favor. However, explicitly dynamic models of cities, which put the model of chapter 2 into an intertemporal context, show that housing developers may wish to leave some interior land vacant as a city grows. Such land is reserved for later development at high densities once future residents arrive, an outcome that can be socially optimal. Despite this conclusion, criticisms of scattered

---

9. See Bradford and Kelejian 1973.

development may still have merit, insofar as such patterns may involve market failures.[10]

4.4 Behavioral Impacts of Urban Sprawl

Critics of sprawl allege that low-density suburban living puts distance between people and makes them less likely to form friendships and to engage in social activities. With their high population densities, central cities instead put people in close proximity, thus (it is argued) stimulating interaction. Brueckner and Largey (2008) show that these claims are exactly backward. They provide empirical evidence that social interaction is higher, not lower, in less dense areas. They use a variety of interaction measures from a national survey that indicate whether people talk to their neighbors, belong to social clubs, and so on. For most measures, interaction falls as density rises, indicating that there is more interaction in the low-density suburbs than in central cities. Thus, urban sprawl appears to promote, rather retard, social interaction.

On the obesity question, the expectation is that automobile-reliant suburban living promotes a sedentary lifestyle, contributing to obesity. Central-city residents, in contrast, may walk more, and the resulting exercise is expected to help maintain a proper weight. The expected association between suburbanization and obesity is confirmed by a number of studies, but Eid et al. (2008) argue that self-selection may drive the findings, with people who would be obese anyway tending to choose suburban locations (perhaps because walking can be avoided). They control for self-selection by focusing on individuals who moved between central cities and suburbs, measuring their weight change. The results show no impact of such a move, indicating that suburban living has no causal effect on obesity.

Thus, these two studies suggest that both of the alleged behavioral impacts of urban sprawl are absent in the data.

4.5 Using Land-Use Controls to Attack Urban Sprawl

4.5.1 Urban growth boundaries and sprawl
The discussion in section 4.3 showed that two price-based instruments can be used to address urban sprawl. The first of these instruments

---

10. In their empirical work on the determinants of sprawl, Burchfield et al. (2006) equate sprawl with scattered development.

was a development tax, designed to correct the market failure associated with open-space amenities. The second was a congestion toll, designed to correct the market failure associated with the congestion externality.

An alternative anti-sprawl instrument is quantity-based rather than price-based, and it is known as an urban growth boundary (UGB). A UGB attacks a symptom of sprawl (excessive spatial expansion), rather than its root cause, by restricting the quantity of land that may be converted to urban use. In terms of the model, a UGB imposes an upper limit on $\bar{x}$, the distance to the edge of the city, prohibiting development beyond this limit.

If properly set, a UGB has exactly the same effect as a development tax. In figure 4.1, the socially optimal size of the city is $\bar{x}_1$, and it results from imposing a development tax of b per acre. But the same outcome could be generated by dropping the tax and instead imposing a UGB that prevents development outside $\bar{x}_1$. The resulting boundary of the city is obviously the same as under the tax, and exactly the same upward shift in the urban land-rent curve occurs (leading to identical urban spatial structures under the two instruments).

UGBs are in place in a number of U.S. cities, the most famous example being in Portland, Oregon. Since UGBs are easy to implement, they tend to be preferred over development taxes and other price-based instruments. But the use of a UGB involves the same pitfall as a development tax used to preserve open space: potentially excessive restriction of urban land areas. In other words, zealous policy makers, believing that their city will tend to expand far too much, could impose a draconian UGB that greatly restricts its land area. But if the average consumer sees no benefit from the preservation of open space, the increase in density and living costs generated by the UGB represents a pure loss, with no offsetting benefit. Therefore, UGBs should be imposed with great caution, recognizing the large downside from unwarranted restriction of urban land areas.

Is a UGB a good instrument for attacking the sprawl that results from the congestion-related market failure? The answer might seem to be affirmative, since this market failure again leads to excessive spatial expansion, a symptom that the UGB treats. But the UGB is in fact a poor substitute for a congestion toll, as was shown by Brueckner (2007). The problem is that the UGB treats one symptom without leading to other needed adjustments in spatial structure. In particular, the UGB tends to increase density throughout the city rather than causing a substantial shift of population toward the center. This shift is socially desirable given the congestion phenomenon, and a congestion toll achieves it whereas a UGB doesn't, even though it can shrink the city's land area. Thus, although the UGB is equivalent to a price-based remedy in the case of the open-space market failure, this equivalence doesn't carry over to the congestion case.

4.5.2 Another motive for imposing a UGB

Although UGBs can be used to address market failures, other less noble motives may lead to their adoption. These motives are explored in a large body of research on "urban growth controls," which suggests that landowners have an incentive to restrict the supply of housing in a city.[11] A supply restriction drives up the price of land, conferring capital gains on those who own it, while hurting renters, who pay a higher price for their housing. This view suggests that UGBs might be imposed even in the absence of a concern about sprawl, reflecting the power of property owners to engineer policies for self-enrichment.

To analyze this motive, recall that landowners in the urban model are assumed to live outside the city. They live, say, in Florida, getting their land-rent checks in the mail. This assumption is obviously unrealistic, but it allows a simple analysis. A more complicated model in which the landowners live in the city can be constructed, and it has the basically same message regarding the motive for imposing a UGB.

To understand the landowners' incentives, consider figure 4.2. If landowners act as a group, total land rent is what they care about. This figure illustrates the change in total land rent that occurs when $\bar{x}$ is restricted by a UGB that prevents development beyond $\bar{x}_1$. With the land-rent curve shifting upward from r_0 to r_1, the change in total rent is easy to see in the figure. The UGB forces the land between $\bar{x}_1$ and $\bar{x}_0$ back into agricultural use, so it earns r_A instead of the higher urban rent level given by the r_0 curve. The rent loss on this portion of land is thus given by the area V in the figure. On the other hand, the land between the CBD and $\bar{x}_1$ earns a higher rent, and the total rent gain is given by the area S.[12] Since S > V, total land rent rises when a UGB at $\bar{x}_1$ is imposed. Landowners thus gain from imposing the UGB, and they

---

11. For an overview of this literature, see Brueckner 1999.
12. For these areas to correctly represent land rent changes, the city must be linear, consisting of a long narrow rectangle instead of a circle, with the CBD at the midpoint of the rectangle. The areas S and V must be adjusted in the circular case, but the overall message is not affected.

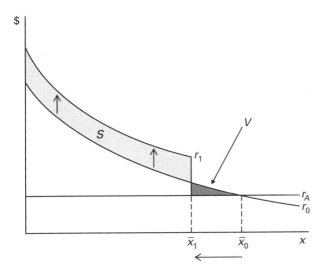

Figure 4.2
UGB enriches landowners.

might be able to gain even more by making it even tighter. In other words, if $\bar{x}$ is reduced further to $\bar{x}_2$ (not shown in the figure), then the r curve shifts up further, rent falls to r_A between $\bar{x}_2$ and $\bar{x}_1$, and new areas analogous to V and S are generated. As long as the new S is larger than the new V, this further restriction is in the landowners' interest. When land rent stops rising (when the relevant S and V areas are equal), no further tightening of the UGB is desirable. At this point, total land rent has been maximized.[13]

Since open-space amenities are absent, the UGB makes the city's residents worse off, as was discussed earlier. As a result, the UGB isn't in society's interest, even though it enriches landowners.[14] But if land-owners have sufficient political power, imposition of a UGB may happen anyway.

In a more realistic model, the city would contain both renters and homeowners, who may own the city's rental property along with their owner-occupied houses. The same motives would drive homeowners in such model. By imposing a UGB, they could increase the value of their houses, although renters would be hurt through higher rents.

---

13. Exercise 4.1 offers a numerical example based on this analysis.
14. It can be shown that the losses to urban residents more than offset the gains to landowners.

Does this self-enrichment motive help to explain the widespread attempts to limit development in cities across the United States, or can such attempts be traced to more benign motives (such as attacking sprawl)? Although the answer isn't clear, an intermediate explanation that includes quality-of-life considerations may also be appealing. Politically powerful homeowners, disliking the congestion and other negative effects of city expansion, could limit growth through a UGB. This limitation serves to improve their quality of life, while at the same time generating a bonus in the form of housing capital gains.[15]

4.6 Other Types of Land-Use Controls

4.6.1 Building-height and density restrictions

A number of cities around the world have imposed building-height restrictions. In the United States, the most prominent example is Washington, where no building in the District of Columbia portion of the metro area can be taller than the U.S. Capitol. Another example is Paris, where tall buildings are generally prohibited in the central city, although a few high-rises exist as a result of past exceptions to the rule. A less well-known case involves the Indian cities of Mumbai and Bangalore, which have developed under tight height restrictions. Whereas the Washington and Paris height limits are in place for aesthetic reasons, those in India appear to be motivated by concerns that high population densities might overwhelm aging urban infrastructure.

Technically, height restrictions specify a limit on a building's floor area ratio (FAR). This ratio is equal to the square footage of floor space in the building divided by the lot area. If a building covers its entire lot, the floor space on each floor would equal the lot area, and an FAR limit of 8 would then restrict the building's height to 8 stories. If the building covers half of its lot, the same FAR limit would restrict its height to 16 stories.

When height restrictions are imposed, they constrain land use in the central part of the city, where buildings would otherwise be taller than the limit. The urban model shows that the overall effect of a height limit follows the pattern shown in figure 4.3, which plots FAR as a function of distance. Building heights are at the FAR limit in the central part of the city, thus being shorter than they would be in the absence of a limit. But heights *increase* in the outer part of the city, as shown in the figure.

---

15. For a formal analysis of these motives, see Brueckner and Lai 1996.

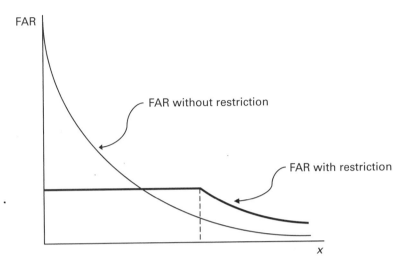

Figure 4.3
Effect of building-height restrictions.

In addition, the city expands spatially, with $\bar{x}$ growing. This latter effect is natural since the height limit reduces the land's ability to accommodate residents, so that the city must expand to fit its population. But the effect is also striking in the sense that the height restriction *leads to urban sprawl*.

Mathematical analysis of the urban model shows that the price p per square foot of housing increases at all locations, which leads consumers to reduce their dwelling sizes. In locations where the height restriction isn't binding, the higher p leads to an increase in land rent r, which leads to taller buildings and a higher FAR at those locations, as figure 4.3 shows.[16] The irony of this outcome is that an attempt to limit building heights in one part of the city causes them to increase in other areas.

With housing more expensive and dwellings smaller, the height restriction makes the urban residents worse off. Thus, for the restriction to be desirable from society's point of view, an offsetting gain must be present. In Washington and Paris, this gain is the aesthetic one that comes from preserving the historic character of the central cities. Whether the gain is large enough to offset consumer losses is, however, hard to judge.

---

16. See Bertaud and Brueckner 2005.

A building-height restriction is just one of a broader class of density restrictions. For example, many high-income suburban communities impose minimum-lot-size restrictions, which require lots for single-family houses to be no smaller than, say, half an acre. These restrictions end up limiting the number of people per acre, thus constraining densities. Such restrictions (discussed further in chapter 8) have the same effect on $\bar{x}$ as a building-height restriction, causing the city to spread out and creating sprawl. Thus, density restrictions can be added to the previous list of government policies that encourage spatial expansion of cities.

4.6.2 Zoning

The most pervasive land-use controls in U.S. cities are zoning laws. These laws specify the allowable type of land use in a given area, the broad categories being commercial, industrial, high-density residential, and low-density residential (meaning detached houses). Typical zoning laws include subcategories under these general headings, which may involve FAR requirements.[17]

Zoning laws are designed to separate land uses, with the goal of limiting the impact of negative externalities. Factories, which generate noise and perhaps pollution, are prohibited from locating amid residences or in shopping areas, and gas stations are prevented from locating in residential neighborhoods. Apartment buildings, which generate traffic and other nuisances, aren't allowed to be built amid detached single-family houses.

The rationale for zoning laws is shown in figure 4.4. For simplicity, this diagram depicts a rectangular city located on an island (say, Manhattan). Everyone in the city works from home, so no commuting occurs (there is no CBD). As a result, the price per square foot of housing would be the same at all locations in the absence of any negative externalities. However, two fully automated factories want to locate in the city. Although they employ no workers and take up no space (being represented by single points), the factories are noisy and dirty. These negative externalities affect housing prices around the factory locations. In order to be compensated for the presence of a factory, consumers require a substantial discount in the housing price p. Thus, p is lower within several blocks of each factory, as is shown in the upper panel of figure 4.4.

---

17. For an extensive overview of the economics of zoning laws, see Fischel 1985.

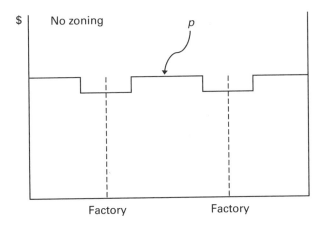

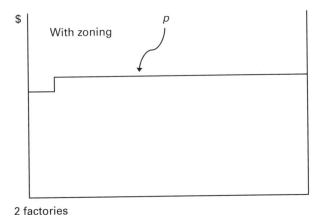

Figure 4.4
Effects of zoning.

Although consumers living near a factory are compensated for the undesirable location, the presence of a factory hurts landowners. With p lower near a factory, land rent r will be lower as well, reducing the landowners' income. With the two factories locating separately amid the city's residential area, as in the top panel of the figure, these land-rent losses will extend over many blocks.

A zoning law will instead require the two factories to locate in a place that minimizes the externality effect and thus the rent losses. That location is at one end of the island, as seen in the lower panel of figure 4.4. With the factories located next to one another at the city's edge, the area experiencing the negative externality is reduced by 75 percent, with landowners' lost income reduced by the same proportion. Thus, the city should institute a zoning law that creates an industrial zone at the edge of the city, with only residences allowed outside that zone. This example is, of course, highly stylized, but the principle it illustrates applies generally in more realistic settings.

Might different land uses separate naturally, so that zoning laws will not be necessary? For example, might the two factories in the above example prefer to locate at the city's edge in any case (perhaps so as to be close to an interstate highway), so that no government intervention is necessary? This view has motivated different approaches to zoning, with some cities imposing no zoning laws at all. The most famous example is Houston, which is not zoned.

Land-use patterns in Houston don't look much different from those in other zoned cities, which suggests that zoning may not be essential. However, Houston—a relatively young city that grew rapidly—experienced more large-scale development than older American cities, which grew in a more piecemeal fashion. Since a large housing subdivision controlled by a single developer is designed to minimize negative externalities, commercial zones are located so as to limit the negative effects of traffic. As a result, the need for zoning laws is lower in Houston than in a city where development is less coordinated and where externalities may not be taken into account. Thus, the success of non-zoning in Houston doesn't necessarily mean that zoning could have been forgone elsewhere.

4.6.3 Empirical evidence on the effects of land-use controls

There is a large empirical literature exploring the effect of land-use controls on housing prices. With the model showing that UGBs, building-height restrictions, other density restrictions, and impact fees all raise the price p per unit of housing, the expected effect is in a positive direction. A common recent approach (see, for example, Ihlanfeldt 2007) is to measure the intensity of land-use restrictions using data from a survey of local governments. The survey indicates how many types of restrictions each government has in place (whether it has a UGB, levies impact fees, and so on), and the intensity measure is a simple count of the number of restrictions. This count measure is then used as an explanatory variable in a regression in which the dependent variable is a house price measure. The regression includes a variety of other control variables. The results from this type of study typically show the expected effect: house prices in a locality rise with an increase in the number of land restrictions in place.

Taking a different approach to exploring the effects of regulation, Glaeser, Gyourko, and Saks (2005) measured the gap between the price per square foot of housing and construction cost per square foot in different communities. Noting that the two values should be equal in a competitive market, they argue that a large gap indicates the presence of government regulations that inhibit housing supply.

4.7 Summary

Rising populations and incomes and falling commuting costs have led to substantial spatial expansion of cities. Although these forces are benign, they may be distorted by market failures, causing cities to expand more than they should. Such market failures arise from open-space amenities, which aren't taken into account in development decisions, and from traffic congestion, which involves an externality. The resulting overexpansion of cities can be addressed by price-based remedies: a development tax in the presence of open-space amenities, congestion tolls in the presence of traffic congestion. An urban growth boundary, a quantity-based remedy, can also be used to correct some market failures. Regardless of the instrument used, policy makers should recognize that excessively tight limits on urban spatial expansion may reduce social welfare.

In addition to UGBs, other land-use controls include building-height restrictions and alternative types of density limits, which contribute to urban sprawl while serving other goals. Zoning laws are also applied in most cities, with the goal of minimizing negative externalities by separating land uses.

5   Freeway Congestion

5.1   Introduction

Road congestion is a universal problem. Commuters and other drivers spend many hours each year stuck in slow-moving traffic on streets and freeways in cities around the world. The problem is severe in many U.S. cities and often worse in other countries, especially in less developed regions. The millions of hours of personal time that are lost as a result of congestion represent a large social cost.

As was noted in chapter 4, road congestion involves an externality: each car slows down all the other cars on a congested roadway by a small amount, generating higher time costs for their drivers. These costs add up to a non-negligible total even though they are individually small, making the congestion externality quantitatively important. To correct the externality, each car must pay a congestion toll equal to the external costs it generates. Chapter 4 showed that when congestion tolls are levied in the city portrayed by the urban model, the higher cost of commuting leads the residents to shorten their commutes by moving toward the central business district, which makes the city more compact.

This chapter analyzes the congestion externality and the imposition of congestion tolls in more detail. Rather than using a model with flexible residence locations, in which the length of commute trips can change as people move closer to the CBD, the length of these trips is fixed in the analysis. Commute trips are assumed to occur between a suburb and the central city on a freeway of fixed length, which is subject to congestion. Commuters respond to congestion tolls on the freeway not by changing the length of their commutes but by choosing a different way of getting to work (commuter rail, for example) or by choosing to travel at a different, uncongested time of day. In reality, commuters would probably adjust to congestion tolls along these dimensions while also moving their residences. But a model with a fixed commute is easy to analyze, and its lessons extend to more realistic settings. The rest of the chapter derives these lessons.

5.2 Congestion Costs

Figure 5.1 illustrates the spatial setting. A freeway connects a suburb to the central city, which contains the urban area's jobs. During the morning rush hour, a cluster of commuters travels down the freeway to work. The extent of rush-hour congestion on the freeway depends on how many commuters are present. The easiest way to think of this connection is to imagine that the speed of the traffic cluster as it moves down the freeway depends on how big the cluster is. The larger is the cluster, the slower it moves.[1] This heuristic view corresponds to a more precise formal representation involving a continuous flow on the freeway.[2]

Let T denote the number of cars on the freeway, or the size of the traffic cluster. The relationship between the traffic speed s (the rate at which the cluster moves down the freeway) and T is illustrated in figure 5.2. Speed is unaffected by the traffic volume as long as T is low. Because the freeway isn't congested, adding a car to the traffic cluster has no effect on s, and traffic continues to move at the speed limit. But

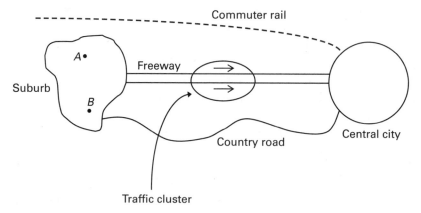

Figure 5.1
Map of metro area.

---

1. There will be a symmetric return rush hour in the evening, which need not be explicitly considered.
2. See Small and Verhoef 2007.

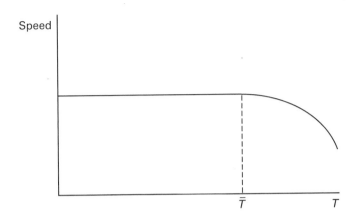

Figure 5.2
Speed falls with T.

when T rises above the freeway's design capacity, denoted by $\bar{T}$, the traffic slows down and s falls. Speed drops sharply as T increases beyond $\bar{T}$.

To derive the connection between commuting cost and T, suppose that the money cost of the entire commute trip equals m. To derive the time cost, let D denote the length of the freeway in miles. Then the time duration of the trip is D/s hours, which equals the distance in miles divided by speed in miles per hour. If commuting time is valued at the hourly wage w, then time cost equals wD/s. The total cost of the commute trip is then $g = m + wD/s$.

Given the behavior of s in figure 5.2, the relationship between commuting cost g and T is as shown in figure 5.3. When the freeway is uncongested, an increase in T has no effect on commuting cost. But over the congested range, a higher T leads to a reduction in the traffic speed s, which increases the trip's duration and thus its time cost (wD/s in the g formula rises when s falls). Therefore, the commuting-cost curve in figure 5.3 is the mirror image of the speed curve in figure 5.2, with cost rising where speed is falling. Let commuting cost be written as a function of T, so that $g = g(T)$.

When the freeway is congested, the $g(T)$ function is upward sloping, and adding one more car (increasing T) raises each driver's commuting cost. This effect leads to a congestion externality. To see the externality, consider how an increase in T affects the aggregate commuting cost incurred by all drivers on the freeway. This aggregate cost equals $Tg(T)$, the number of cars times cost per car. When one more car is added to

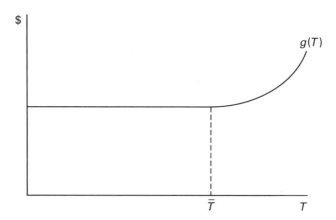

Figure 5.3
Cost of using freeway.

the freeway, the effect on aggregate cost is found by taking the derivative of this expression with respect to T. Using the product rule, this derivative is equal to

$$\frac{d}{dT}(\text{aggregate commuting cost}) = g(T) + Tg'(T).$$

This formula shows that, when one more car is added to a congested freeway, aggregate costs rise for two reasons. First, the added car itself incurs a cost, equal to $g(T)$. Second, the added car imposes costs on all the existing cars on the freeway. The increase in cost for each of these cars is captured by the derivative $g'(T)$. Since T cars are present, the costs for all of them together rise by T times this amount, or $Tg'(T)$. This expression is the *externality damage resulting from an added car*, and it quantifies the congestion externality.

Since the above formula gives the increase in aggregate cost $Tg(T)$ when a car is added, it represents the *marginal cost* of an added car, denoted by MC. Corresponding to MC is an average cost, denoted by AC. Average cost equals aggregate cost divided by the number of cars, or $Tg(T)/T$, which is simply $g(T)$. Therefore, AC = $g(T)$, which is just the individual cost per car, while MC = $g(T) + Tg'(T)$. Note that MC = AC + $Tg'(T)$. In other words,

MC = AC + externality damage resulting from an added car.

MC and AC both depend on the traffic volume T, as is shown in figure 5.4 (where the AC curve is the same as the curve in figure 5.3).

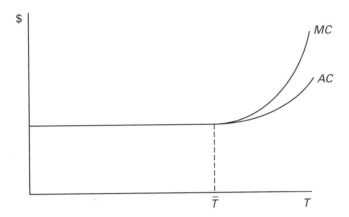

Figure 5.4
AC and MC curves.

If the freeway is uncongested, then the externality damage from an added car is zero, and the MC and AC curves coincide (see the preceding formula). But when the freeway is congested, the MC curve lies above than the AC curve. Moreover, *the vertical distance between the curves equals the externality damage resulting from an added car.*

Chapter 4 made a distinction between the private and social cost of commuting, and this distinction can be clearly seen in the present setup. The private cost of commuting is simply the cost that an individual car incurs in using the freeway. This cost is just AC. The social cost of commuting is the increase in the aggregate commuting cost when one more car is added to the freeway, or MC. This social cost is the cost borne by the added car itself, represented by AC (or private cost), plus the increase in costs for the other cars, which equals the externality damage. Therefore, social cost = private cost + externality damage = MC.

5.3 The Demand for Freeway Use

To derive the demand for use of the freeway, consider again figure 5.1, which depicts a commuter rail line that connects the suburb to the central city and a winding country road that also passes between the suburb and the city. These other options represent *alternate routes* that can be used, rather than the freeway, to access the central city. As can be seen in the figure, the best alternate route may differ across commuters. For the commuter living at location A in the suburb, the best alternate route would probably be the commuter rail line. For the commuter living at B, the best alternate route might be the winding country road (especially if that commuter owns a sports car). For each commuter, the preferred alternate route is best in the sense that it has the lowest cost among alternatives to the freeway. Let this (lowest) alternate cost be denoted by g_a, and suppose for simplicity that each consumer has a different value of g_a. These differences could arise from differences in the routes taken (rail vs. country road) or from different valuations of a particular best alternative across commuters.[3] In contrast, the cost of using the freeway is the same for all commuters, and it is given by $g(T)$, or AC.

This information can be used to derive an individual's demand curve for use of the freeway. Like any demand curve, this curve gives the quantity chosen as a function of cost. For a single day's freeway use, the quantity can either be 0 or 1: the commuter either uses the freeway or doesn't use it, and in the latter case, the alternate route is used. Figure 5.5 shows how this quantity decision depends on the cost of the freeway. This cost is represented on the vertical axis, and the number of freeway trips, 0 or 1, is represented on the horizontal axis and denoted by R. The diagram pertains to commuter 1, whose alterna-

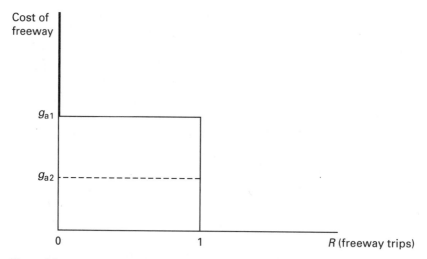

Figure 5.5
Individual demands.

---

3. For example, the country road may be the best alternative for a number of commuters, but those with sports cars (whose enjoyment of driving reduces their cost of getting to work) might find it less costly.

tive cost is g_{a1}. When the freeway cost is above g_{a1}, the alternative is cheaper and the freeway isn't used, so $R = 0$. When the freeway cost is below g_{a1}, then the freeway is used and $R = 1$. Therefore, the demand curve is a "step function," shown by the solid lines in the figure. Above g_{a1}, the curve lies on the vertical axis; below g_{a1}, the curve is a vertical line at $R = 1$. The two vertical segments are then connected by a horizontal segment.

The demand curve for commuter 2, whose alternate cost is $g_{a2} < g_{a1}$, is derived similarly. Above g_{a2}, the curve lies on the vertical axis, and below g_{a2}, it is a vertical line at $R = 1$. The curve has the same form as commuter 1's demand curve, except that its horizontal segment is lower, as shown by dashed line in figure 5.5 (whose height is g_{a2}).

To decide how many commuters use the freeway, the aggregate demand curve must be derived, and this step is easily carried out using the individual curves. Suppose for the moment that the suburb contains only two commuters, 1 and 2, so that the aggregate demand curve is based on them alone. Figure 5.6 shows that curve, which is the horizontal sum of the individual curves. When the freeway's cost is above g_{a1}, it is more expensive than the alternate routes for both commuters, and no one uses it, so that $R = 0$. When the freeway cost is between g_{a1}

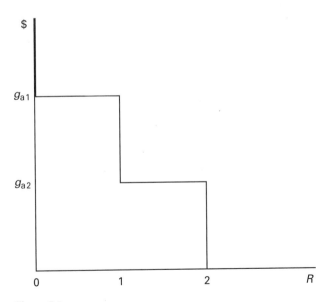

Figure 5.6
Aggregate demand.

and g_{a2}, consumer 1 uses it, but commuter 2 still finds his alternative cheaper. Thus, $R = 1$. However, when the freeway cost is below g_{a2}, it is cheaper than the alternative for both commuters, so both commuters use the freeway, and $R = 2$. Therefore, the aggregate demand curve is a step function with two steps, one at g_{a1} and one at g_{a2}.

Now suppose that the suburb contains a large number of commuters (equal to n), each with a different alternative cost. Then the aggregate demand curve will be a step function like figure 5.6, but with a large number of steps. Each of these steps will look very small on a redrawn version of figure 5.6, which would be rescaled to reflect the possibility of thousands of trips. With the steps tiny in size, the aggregate demand curve D can then be approximated by a smooth curve, as shown in figure 5.7. Note that since total freeway trips is the same as T (the number of cars on the freeway), trips R can be replaced by T on the horizontal axis.

The identities of the individual commuters will be important in the ensuing analysis. Therefore, as in the two-commuter example, let the suburban commuters be numbered according to their alternate cost. Commuter 1 has the highest alternate cost, commuter 2 has the next highest cost, commuter j has the jth highest cost, and commuter n has the nth highest cost (the lowest). With this numbering scheme, an important feature of the aggregate demand curve can be stated: *The*

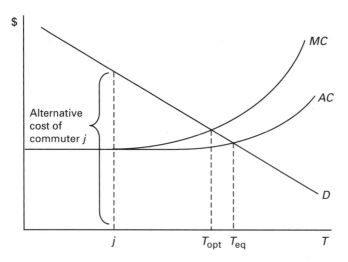

Figure 5.7
Aggregate demand with a large number of commuters.

height up to the demand curve at T = j is equal to the alternate cost of com-muter j for j = 1, 2, . . . , n. This feature is illustrated in figure 5.7. To verify this property of the demand curve, reconsider figure 5.6. In that figure, the height of the two-person aggregate demand curve at $R = 1$ equals g_{a1} (commuter 1's alternate cost), and the height of the curve at $R = 2$ equals g_{a2}, as claimed.

5.4 Traffic Allocations: Equilibrium and Social Optimum

In addition to showing the smooth demand curve, figure 5.7 also shows the AC and MC curves and their intersections with the D curve. These intersections are crucial because they show the equilibrium traffic volume on the freeway as well as the socially optimal traffic volume. The equilibrium is represented by the intersection of D and AC, and it has a traffic volume of T_{eq}. The social optimum is represented by the intersection of D and MC, and it has a traffic volume of T_{opt}. Since $T_{eq} > T_{opt}$, too many cars use the freeway in equilibrium. The following discussion explains why these intersections represent the equilibrium and social optimum and why the freeway is overused.

5.4.1 The equilibrium
Since consumers, in deciding how to get to their workplaces, will compare the private cost of using the freeway to their alternate cost, it makes sense that the intersection of demand and AC represents the equilibrium. Although this intersection tells how many cars use the freeway in equilibrium (T_{eq}), the description of the equilibrium involves more than just a simple traffic count. The *identities* of the freeway users, as well as the identities of the commuters using their alternate routes, must be specified. In equilibrium, commuters 1 through T_{eq} use the freeway, while commuters $T_{eq} + 1$ through n use their alternate routes. This division makes sense since commuters high on the list have high alternate costs (which make the freeway attractive) while those low on the list have low alternate costs (which make alternate routes attractive).

To prove that this division of commuters represents an equilibrium, a definition of this concept is needed. In the urban model of chapter 2, the crucial feature of equilibrium was that no consumer had an incentive to change location. The same notion applies in the congestion model. An equilibrium allocation of traffic has the property that *no commuter has an incentive to switch routes.* In other words, no

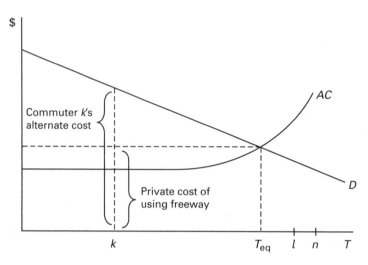

Figure 5.8
Equilibrium allocation of traffic.

freeway commuter would be better off switching to his alternate route, and no alternate-route user would be better off switching to the freeway.

To verify that the above traffic allocation is an equilibrium, it must be verified that no commuter has an incentive to switch routes. This step can be carried out by using figure 5.8. First, observe that the cost of using the freeway under the given traffic allocation is the height up to the AC curve at $T = T_{eq}$. For reference, a dashed line at this height is shown in the figure. Now consider commuter k, who is assumed to be a freeway user. Would this individual want to switch to his alternate route? The answer is No, because the figure shows that commuter k's alternate cost, which equals the height up to the demand curve at $T = k$, is greater than the cost of using the freeway, which equals the height up to the dashed line. The same argument applies for any consumer who, like commuter k, has a number smaller than T_{eq} and is thus a freeway user.

Now consider commuter l, who is assumed to use his alternate route. Would this person want to switch to the freeway? The answer is No, because the figure shows that commuter l's alternate cost, which equals the height up to the demand curve at $T = l$, is less than the cost of using the freeway, which equals the height up to the dashed line. The same argument applies to any commuter who, like commuter l, has a number larger than T_{eq} and is thus an alternate-route user. ·

Commuter T_{eq} remains to be considered, but this commuter is indifferent between the freeway and his alternate route. The height up to the demand curve at $T = T_{eq}$, his alternate cost, equals the height up to the dashed line. Therefore, commuter T_{eq} also has no incentive to switch routes.

5.4.2 The social optimum

The socially optimal traffic allocation *minimizes the total cost of commuting*, including the costs of both freeway users and alternate-route users. Equivalently, the socially optimal allocation is one in which *total commuting cost cannot be reduced by switching any commuter between routes*. In figure 5.7, the social optimum is represented by the intersection between the demand curve and MC curve, which leads to a traffic volume T_{opt} that is smaller than the equilibrium volume T_{eq}.

As with the equilibrium, the social optimum involves a particular assignment of commuters to routes. Under the optimal allocation, commuters 1 through T_{opt} use the freeway, while commuters $T_{opt} + 1$ through n use their alternate routes. As in the equilibrium allocation, the commuters with the highest alternate costs use the freeway, while those with the lowest alternate costs use their alternative routes. But a social planner would ask an intermediate group of commuters, $T_{opt} + 1$ through T_{eq}, to switch from the freeway to their alternate routes in order to achieve the socially optimal allocation.

To verify that this traffic allocation is indeed socially optimal, minimizing total commuting cost, consider figure 5.9, which is similar to figure 5.8. Recall that the MC curve represents the *increase in aggregate commuting cost on the freeway when one more car is added*. The height up to the MC curve at $T = T_{opt}$ thus gives the increase in freeway cost from adding a car when T_{opt} cars are already using the freeway. Note that this height also gives the *reduction* in total freeway costs if a car is *removed*. For reference, a dashed line is drawn in figure 5.9 at this MC height.

As before, consider switching commuter k (a freeway user under the optimal allocation) to his alternate route or switching commuter l (an alternate-route user) to the freeway. But instead of asking whether these individuals have a *private incentive* to switch, consider the *effect of the switch on total commuting cost*. If commuter l were switched from his alternate route to the freeway, aggregate cost on the freeway would go up by an amount equal to the height of the dashed line. But the commuter's alternate cost (equal to the demand height at $T = l$) would

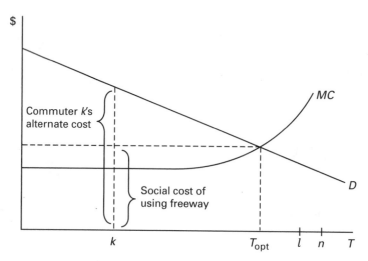

Figure 5.9
Socially optimal allocation of traffic.

no longer be incurred. Since the first height is larger than the second height, the switch would increase the total cost of commuting, which would make it undesirable.

Now suppose commuter k were switched from the freeway to his alternate route. Aggregate cost on the freeway would go down by an amount equal to the height of the dashed line in figure 5.9. But the commuter's alternate cost (equal to the demand height at $T = k$) would now be incurred. Since the second height is larger than the first height, the switch would again raise total commuting cost, making it undesirable. Since the same arguments apply to other commuters like l and k, it follows that, starting at the assumed traffic allocation, total commuting cost cannot be reduced by switching any consumer between routes. Therefore, the allocation is socially optimal.[4]

5.4.3 Another approach to finding the social optimum

A different diagrammatic approach is also helpful in illustrating the determination of the social optimum. This approach assumes that the consumers with the highest alternate costs will be assigned to the freeway, and then asks where the cutoff T value (the value that divides users of the freeway from users of the alternate routes) lies. The

---

4. Exercise 5.1 provides a simple numerical example illustrating the equilibrium and socially optimal traffic allocations.

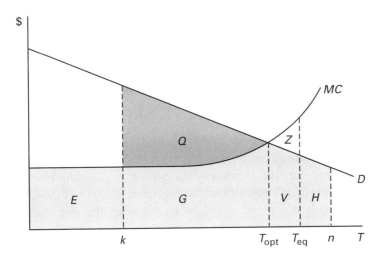

Figure 5.10
Total commuting cost at optimum.

approach makes use of the fact that the aggregate freeway cost equals the area under the MC curve up to the cutoff T value, which reflects the usual property of MC curves.

Suppose that the cutoff T value is equal to k, as shown in figure 5.10, so that commuters 1 through k are on the freeway. Then the aggregate freeway cost is the area E (the area under MC up to k), while the aggregate cost on alternative routes is the area $Q + G + V + H$ (the area under the demand curve between k and n). This latter area is generated by summing the heights up to the demand curve (which equal alternate costs) for all commuters over the range $k + 1$ through n, who use their alternative routes. Summing E and this latter area then yields total commuting cost when the cutoff T value equals k. The resulting area is represented by the shaded region in figure 5.10.

The optimal cutoff value is the one that minimizes this area. It is easily seen that the right value is T_{opt}, represented in figure 5.10 by the intersection of D and MC. To see why, observe that, in moving from the k cutoff to T_{opt}, aggregate freeway costs rise by the area G, while aggregate alternate costs fall by the area $Q + G$. The net effect is a reduction in total commuting cost equal to Q. Total commuting cost at T_{opt} is then equal to the area $E + G + V + H$.

Although increasing the cutoff value from k up to T_{opt} was desirable, a further increase is not. For example, in moving the cutoff up from T_{opt} to T_{eq}, freeway costs rise by $Z + V$, while alternate costs fall by V, for a net cost increase of Z. Therefore, total commuting cost at the optimum is smaller than at the equilibrium by an amount equal to the area Z.

Since the intersection of D and MC occurs on the rising part of the MC curve, the freeway remains congested at the social optimum, and this conclusion may seem counterintuitive. One might think that society's goal should be to entirely eliminate congestion, forcing freeway traffic down to the level $\bar{T}$. The analysis shows that, given the position of the demand curve D in the various figures, this conclusion is incorrect. Commuters' alternatives are costly, and society will want to weigh these costs against the cost of freeway congestion in deciding on the best allocation of traffic. Thus, although congestion is too high in equilibrium given each commuter's failure to consider the externality damage he generates, reducing it to zero through a large diversion of traffic to alternate routes isn't in society's interest.

5.5 Congestion Tolls

5.5.1 The toll schedule
The equilibrium has too many freeway commuters, and the reason is that no commuter has an incentive to consider the social cost of using the freeway. Commuters focus instead on the smaller private cost, which doesn't include the externality damage. The congested freeway thus appears artificially cheap to commuters, with the result that some commuters use it when society would prefer that they took an alternate route instead. Naturally, the commuters who should be diverted are those with the lowest alternate costs among the equilibrium group of freeway users (consumers $T_{opt} + 1$ through T_{eq}), for whom a switch would be least objectionable. The remaining freeway users have alternate costs high enough that society is happy to keep them on the freeway.

Stated differently, the problem is that consumers look at private costs (the AC curve) in making decisions, while a social planner would look at social costs (the MC curve) in deciding on the traffic allocation. In order to get commuters to do the right thing, society should ensure that their decisions mimic those of the planner, which can be done by forcing commuters to consider the MC curve in their choices.

This outcome can be achieved by charging congestion tolls, which will raise the private cost of using the freeway until it coincides with the MC curve. To generate this coincidence, the toll must equal the

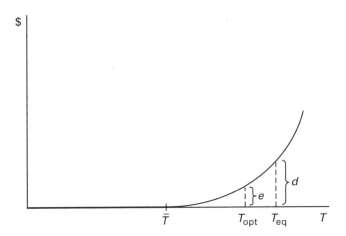

Figure 5.11
Toll schedule.

vertical difference between the MC and AC curves, so that the new
private-cost curve (given by the AC curve plus the toll) is the same as
the MC curve. But since the vertical distance between the MC and AC
curves is just the externality damage, the toll charges each commuter
for this damage.

More specifically, the social planner will compute a "toll schedule,"
which gives the toll per car as a function of the traffic volume T. This
schedule is shown in figure 5.11, and its height equals the vertical distance between the MC and AC curves at each T. The schedule shows
that the toll is zero when the traffic volume is below $\bar{T}$ and externality
damage is absent, but that the toll is positive when T is above $\bar{T}$.

Concretely, a toll schedule would be implemented by installing electronic devices along the freeway that would measure traffic. The
devices would then compute the proper toll at the prevailing traffic
level, and they would announce the dollar amount of the toll in an
electronic display visible to commuters (who would pay electronically).
On the system's first day of operation, before commuters know what
to expect, the previous equilibrium number of cars (T_{eq}) would enter
the freeway, and the toll would be equal to the height d in figure 5.11.
With a toll this high, many commuters would regret their decision to
use the freeway, so the traffic volume would be lower the next day, as
would the toll (with its magnitude again given by the schedule). Eventually, traffic would settle at the level T_{opt}, where the AC curve augmented by the toll schedule (the MC curve) cuts the demand curve.

The actual toll charged would be equal to the height e in figure 5.10.[5] As for the actual dollar magnitude of e, recall from chapter 4 that the proper magnitude of congestion tolls is on the order of \$0.17 per mile. Using this number, e would then equal \$0.17 times the length of the freeway.

A key feature of the toll system is that all freeway users pay the same toll, regardless of their alternate costs. In other words, all commuters under the toll system would pay an amount equal to e. The reason is that, regardless of their identities, freeway users impose the same external cost on their fellow travelers and must be charged symmetrically for that cost.

5.5.2 Time-of-day considerations

The discussion so far has focused on rush-hour commuting without considering other times of day, when the freeway is less crowded. For example, at night, when fewer people need to travel, the demand curve D for freeway use would be lower. In this case, D might intersect the AC and MC curves on their flat portion, where congestion is absent. No externality damage is then present, and no toll is charged (the electronic display would show a toll of zero). Therefore, an idealized congestion-toll system would generate tolls that vary by time of day. Tolls would be high during rush hours and zero at off-peak times. In practice, however, the government may wish to collect additional toll revenue, so that tolls would be positive even during off-peak hours. But to appropriately restrict rush-hour traffic, a large toll differential between the hours of peak use and the off-peak hours is needed.

Another observation concerns the model's alternate-route option. Other types of alternatives besides the commuter-rail and country-road alternatives in figure 5.1 can be envisioned. Some alternatives might involve use of the freeway itself. For example, the freeway could have an uncongested lane dedicated to express bus service. Bus riders would incur no congestion cost, but they would incur an inconvenience cost

---

5. Rather than using a toll schedule, a different approach would be to impose a toll equal to e that would be paid regardless of the volume of traffic on the freeway. Under this approach, the new private-cost curve for use of the freeway is given by the AC curve shifted up in parallel fashion by the amount e. The intersection of the demand curve with this shifted curve occurs at $T = T_{opt}$, so that the resulting traffic volume is socially optimal. This alternate approach matches the usual one under Pigouvian taxation, whereas the toll-schedule approach is different but more transparent.

associated with reliance on public transit. The alternate cost would then be the sum of this cost, the bus fare, and the uncongested time cost. Similarly, the freeway might have a car-pool lane where congestion is absent and no toll is levied. Like the express bus, the car-pool alternative is inconvenient because of the need to coordinate with other commuters, and this inconvenience cost would comprise part of the alternate cost.

A better reinterpretation of the alternate route may be in a time-of-day context. To see this point, note that some freeway users may not be commuters but instead may be morning shoppers headed for the central city. Although these rush-hour shoppers would have some reason for preferring to shop early, they could also reschedule their shopping trips to a less congested period with modest cost. Thus, their "alternate route" could be a freeway trip at *a different time of day*. The alternate cost for the shoppers would be cost of an uncongested, off-peak freeway trip plus the loss attributable to having to shop at a less preferred time. Congestion tolls would tend to divert the rush-hour shoppers, leading them to shop later in the day. Something similar might happen for those rush-hour commuters with flexible work schedules, who might delay arriving at and leaving their workplaces in order to avoid rush-hour tolls.

5.5.3   Real-world congestion tolls

Since 2000, congestion-toll systems have been adopted in two major cities: London and Stockholm. They join Singapore, where a toll system has been in place for decades. In each case, tolls are levied for entry into the congested central city. Stockholm uses a purely electronic payment system, and London uses a more complex approach where video cameras record license plate numbers to verify electronic payment of the toll.

Adoption of toll systems must confront an issue that has been overlooked in the analysis so far: political support for tolls. In order for such support to be realized, the toll revenue, which constitutes a tax on commuters, must be returned in some fashion. Otherwise, commuters who pay the toll will end up worse off and will not support its imposition. To see this point, note that the private cost of using the freeway equals the height of the AC curve at $T = T_{eq}$ without the toll, but equals the height of the MC curve at $T = T_{opt}$ when the toll is present (see figure 5.7). As a result, commuters 1 through T_{opt}, who continue to use the freeway when the toll is imposed, incur a higher cost and are worse off, and they would vote against imposition of the toll system. But if the toll revenue is returned to commuters, say by reducing income or gasoline taxes for everyone (including commuters who don't use the freeway), a majority of the commuters may support imposition of the toll system, making it politically feasible. Such support is necessary for congestion tolls to be implemented.

5.5.4 Alternate price-based mechanisms

Because congestion tolls aren't especially easy to implement, it is natural to wonder if other price-based options might be available. Raising the gasoline tax would increase the cost of road use. But since all road users would pay the higher tax whether they travel at congested or uncongested times, the tax increase wouldn't have the desired effect of reducing traffic just during peak, congested hours. A more effective alternative would focus on parking charges. After their morning rush-hour trip, many workers enjoy free parking provided by their employers. If workers instead had to pay for their parking at market rates (which are usually high in big cities), with employers raising their wages accordingly, the effect would be similar to levying rush-hour congestion tolls. Rather than pay the new parking fees, workers might pocket the money from higher wages and take public transit to work. This simple idea, promoted by Shoup (2005), could reduce peak-hour congestion.

5.5.5 Subsidies rather than tolls?

Although the congestion externality is remedied by tolls, could subsidies for use of a roadway ever be desirable, at least in principle? It is possible to generate an example, albeit a fanciful one, in which this outcome would ensue. In particular, suppose that commuters *benefit* from the presence of more cars on the freeway at very low traffic volumes. Such a benefit could arise for emergency-related reasons: additional cars on the freeway would improve the chances that a commuter could get help in the event of a breakdown, a flat tire, or some other problem. When such a benefit exists, the AC curve would fall over its initial range as T increases. Since the benefits of higher traffic presumably would vanish once a modest volume was reached, the AC curve would flatten out before eventually rising as congestion sets in. However, it is convenient to ignore the flat range, drawing the curve as U-shaped, as in figure 5.12.

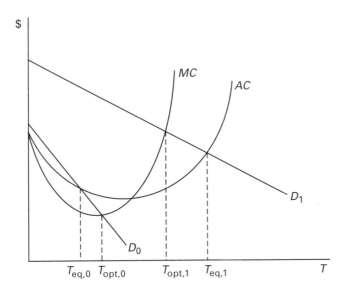

Figure 5.12
U-shaped costs.

When the AC curve is U-shaped, the MC curve shows the familiar pattern seen in figure 5.12, being itself U-shaped and cutting the AC curve at its minimum. The MC curve then lies below the AC curve at low traffic volumes, indicating that the social cost of using the freeway is *less than the private cost* over this range. The reason is that the presence of an extra car confers benefits on other commuters, these benefits being *subtracted from private cost* to generate social cost.

Figure 5.12 shows two possible positions for the demand curve: D_0 and D_1. When D_1 is the relevant curve, the freeway is congested in equilibrium, and the preceding discussion applies. The socially optimal traffic volume, denoted by $T_{opt,1}$, is smaller than the equilibrium volume, denoted by $T_{eq,1}$. But when the lower demand curve D_0 is relevant, the MC intersection lies *to the right* of the AC intersection, so that the socially optimal traffic volume, $T_{opt,0}$, *exceeds* the equilibrium volume, $T_{eq,0}$. The reason is that, in deciding between the freeway and alternate routes, commuters fail to consider the benefits they generate through their presence on the freeway. As a result, some commuters choose their alternate routes when society would be better served if they were on the freeway.

In order to generate the social optimum when demand is low, use of the freeway must be subsidized. On the same principle used in the computation of tolls, the subsidy per car is equal to the external benefit the car generates. At a given T, the subsidy thus equals the vertical distance between the AC and MC curves. With the subsidy reducing the commuter's cost, the MC curve gives the new private cost of using the freeway, and the equilibrium then coincides with the social optimum.

Note that the toll schedule in figure 5.11 now becomes a "subsidy/ toll" schedule. Rather than lying on the horizontal axis at low T values, the schedule now lies below it, indicating a negative toll (a subsidy). But the schedule lies above the axis, as in figure 5.11, when T is large and a toll is required.

This unrealistic example is intended to illustrate some useful principles. Although subsidization of freeway use wouldn't be expected in practice, the logic behind such a possibility is illuminating.[6]

5.6 Choice of Freeway Capacity

The AC and MC curves in the preceding figures are conditional on the capacity of the freeway, which is determined by its width or its number of lanes. The capacity determines the traffic volume $\bar{T}$ at which congestion sets in and the AC and MC curves start to slope upward. A higher capacity causes the curves to slide over to the right, with no change in the height of their horizontal portions, as can be seen in figure 5.13. That height remains fixed because, under uncongested conditions, wid-

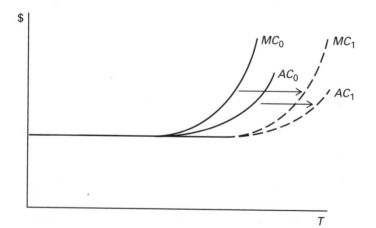

Figure 5.13
An increase in freeway capacity.

6. Exercise 5.2 consists of a numerical example using a similar setup. The example concerns a hot tub, which, like freeways and other facilities, can be subject to congestion.

ening the freeway will have no effect on the traffic speed and thus no effect on commuting cost (s remains at the speed limit).

Since enlarging the freeway can forestall the onset of congestion, how wide should the freeway be? If capacity were increased enough so that the demand intersection were to fall on the flat part of the shifted AC and MC curves, then congestion would be absent in equilibrium. Should the freeway be this wide? Or would a smaller freeway, which experiences some congestion, be better?

The answer is that the *optimal-size freeway should be congested*. This conclusion may seem counterintuitive, but the logic is simple, as follows. Expanding a freeway is expensive, so there must be some benefit from doing so. This benefit is a reduction in total commuting cost. When the freeway is at an optimal size, the cost of a slight expansion should equal the benefit from the expansion. But for there to be such a benefit, the freeway must be congested (otherwise making it bigger would have no effect). Therefore, since it is optimal to stop expanding the freeway when there is still a benefit from doing so, the resulting freeway is congested.[7]

This argument can be illustrated using figure 5.14. The marginal cost curve is given by MC_0 before a slight freeway widening and by MC_1

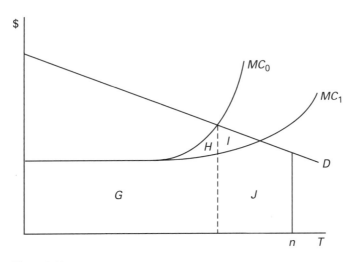

Figure 5.14
Benefits from freeway widening.

---

7. Recognizing that a brand-new freeway, built in anticipation of future traffic growth, may not be congested at the outset, this principle can be modified. In particular, an optimal-size freeway should be congested *at some point during its life*.

afterward. Recalling figure 5.10, total commuting cost before the freeway widening is given by the area G + H + I + J, while total commuting cost after the widening is the area G + J. Therefore, the reduction in commuting cost resulting from the expansion is the area H + I. If this area exceeds the cost of the freeway widening, then the expansion is desirable. However, if the widening cost happens to exactly equal H + I, then the benefit from the expansion (lower commuting cost) equals the cost of carrying it out. In this situation, society is indifferent between widening and not widening the freeway. Its size is therefore optimal.

The important point is that for an area like H + I to be present, the demand curve must cut the MC curve on its upward sloping range, indicating the presence of congestion. If the freeway is so wide that D cuts MC on its flat portion, then the H + I area is gone and the freeway has been made too wide.

Because the MC curve is used to determine the traffic volume in figure 5.14, congestion tolls are implicitly being levied. The use of the revenue from these tolls has not been discussed so far, but a natural use would be to pay for the cost of freeway construction (specifically, the interest on the bonds used to finance the construction). But would the toll revenue be enough to cover that cost, or would there be a shortfall? The answer is given by the famous *self-financing theorem*, which says that, under reasonable conditions, *the toll revenue exactly pays for the cost of the freeway.*[8] Two conditions must hold. First, freeway costs must exhibit constant returns to scale, so that doubling the freeway's width doubles its cost. Second, doubling the width of the freeway and doubling the traffic volume must leave traffic speed (and thus congestion) unchanged. Under these conditions, both of which are plausible, tolls exactly cover the freeway's cost, so that no additional tax revenue is needed.

5.7 Application to Airport Congestion

Like freeways, airports around the world exhibit their own type of congestion. When the number of planes attempting to land or take off exceeds the number that the airport can handle per unit time, queues develop, either on the ground or in the air. The result is flight delays, which impose time costs on passengers and resource costs on the air-

---

8. See Small and Verhoef 2007.

lines. These resource costs include the cost of longer crew hours and extra fuel (for planes queuing in the air) and reduced aircraft utilization (planes stuck in traffic can't make as many flights per day).

As in the freeway case, aircraft using a congested airport impose external costs by slowing down other planes. Therefore, each plane should be charged a congestion toll that captures these external costs. In response, some airlines might shift flights from a congested airport to an uncongested facility in the same city (analogous to an alternate route in the freeway case). But most of the adjustment would be on the time-of-day dimension. In other words, airlines would shift some flights to off-peak hours in response to the imposition of congestion tolls.

For example, a flight from Hawaii scheduled to land in Chicago at 5 p.m., a peak hour, might be rescheduled to land at 8 p.m. instead. Although the passengers (vacation travelers) could easily tolerate the switch, a flight arriving at 5 p.m. from New York (and full of business travelers) wouldn't be rescheduled. These passengers would want to get home to their families at a reasonable hour after a day's work in New York, and the airline, recognizing this desire, wouldn't reschedule the flight.

Although the analogy between airport and freeway congestion is close, there is one important difference. Freeway users are "atomistic," each being small, but airlines are "non-atomistic." Rather than operating a single flight, airlines tend to operate simultaneous flights to different destinations from a single airport. These flights can congest one another, and airlines have an incentive to take this self-imposed congestion into account. Recognizing that scheduling an extra peak-hour flight will slow down its other peak-hour flights, an airline may be reluctant to add the extra flight. Airlines, then, "internalize" self-imposed congestion, taking it into account in their scheduling decisions. Since self-imposed congestion is recognized, the toll system need not charge airlines for it. The toll system need only charge an airline *for the congestion imposed on other carriers, not for the congestion imposed on itself.*[9]

As in the freeway case, airport congestion tolls would vary by time of day, being high during peak hours and zero during off-peak hours, when congestion is absent. Although such tolls could easily replace the current system of aircraft landing fees, which are time-invariant and

---

9. For further discussion and references, see Brueckner 2002.

depend on aircraft weight, congestion tolls aren't currently levied at any of the world's airports, despite some past experimentation. Since tolls would require only a change in the billing system currently used to collect landing fees, they could be imposed with little resource cost (in contrast to the larger investment required for freeways). The resulting gains to passengers and airlines could be substantial.

5.8 Summary

Freeway congestion involves an externality, with commuters not considering the congestion they impose on their fellow freeway users. As a result, freeways are overused, and congestion tolls must be levied to reduce traffic to a socially optimal level. Tolls would be absent during off-peak periods, but their presence during peak periods would cause some travelers to use alternate routes or to travel at a different time of day. Congestion can be reduced by an expansion of freeway capacity, but expansions that eliminate congestion entirely aren't socially desirable. The principles underlying freeway congestion tolls can also be applied to airports, with some modification.

6 Housing Demand and Tenure Choice

6.1 Introduction

Housing is probably the most important commodity that consumers purchase. It provides essential shelter and an environment for many activities, most significantly the activity of raising a family. Owner-occupied housing is also an investment, usually providing capital gains for homeowners in the long run. While housing consumption played a central role in the urban model developed in earlier chapters, many important aspects of the housing commodity were omitted. Housing consumption was equated with the consumption of floor space, leaving out many other housing attributes. Also, because everyone in the city was assumed to be a renter, the issue of housing "tenure choice" (that is, the choice between owning and renting) was ignored. The possibility that consumers earn housing capital gains was thus suppressed, and other elements such as mortgage costs that affect the cost of housing were ignored.

To provide a fuller picture of housing, this chapter introduces the previously omitted elements. The chapter starts with a discussion of the traditional demand function for housing and how it is estimated empirically. The discussion then turns to the alternate approach in which housing is treated as a bundle of attributes. Under this approach, researchers are interested in the demands for individual attributes, which are identified by first estimating a "hedonic price function," a relationship that connects a house's selling price to the levels of its attributes. Returning to the traditional approach, the next task is to derive the "user cost" of housing. The user cost incorporates previously omitted elements (mortgage costs, capital gains, depreciation, and taxes) to derive an accurate formula for the "effective" price per unit of housing. The formula shows how taxes and the mortgage interest rate affect this price, and how optimistic capital-gains expectations can cause "housing bubbles."

Renter-occupied housing and owner-occupied housing have different user-cost formulas. These formulas can be used to analyze the rent/own decision, which involves choosing the cheaper mode of tenure. The resulting tenure-choice model offers predictions about the factors that determine an economy's homeownership rate. Other factors that affect tenure choice but are not included in the model are also discussed.

6.2 Housing Demand: The Traditional and Hedonic Approaches

6.2.1 The traditional approach

The traditional approach to housing demand assumes that housing consumption can be measured unidimensionally—in other words, by a single number. In the urban model, the unidimensional measure was the amount of floor space in a dwelling. Empirical researchers, however, have been able to estimate the demand function for housing without having to specify exactly how consumption is measured.

To see how, let the demand for housing be given by the demand function

$$q = \alpha p^\beta y^\theta,$$

where q is housing consumption measured in some fashion, p is the price per unit of housing, and y is income. The parameters β and θ, which are negative and positive respectively, give the price and income elasticities of demand. A goal of housing researchers is to estimate the magnitudes of these elasticities. This estimation is made possible by multiplying both sides of the above equation by p, which yields

$$pq = \alpha p^{\beta+1} y^\theta.$$

If the demand equation applies to a renter, the expression pq on the left of this equation is total "rent." If the equation applies to an owner-occupier, then p is the purchase price, as opposed the rental price, per unit of housing, and pq is the value of the house. Let pq (housing "expenditure") be denoted by E, representing either rent or value. Then the previous equation is written as

$$E = \alpha p^{\beta+1} y^\theta.$$

After taking natural logarithms, it can be rewritten as

$$\log E = \gamma + (\beta + 1) \log p + \theta \log y,$$

where $\gamma = \log\alpha$. This new equation gives housing expenditure as a function of the price p and income y, but its beauty is that the equation *doesn't require physical measurement of housing consumption*. The income and price elasticities can be estimated by regression analysis using data on rents or house values, and measures of price and income, without having to decide how to measure housing consumption q.

A measure of p, the price per unit of housing, is still needed, but empirical researchers often use a city-level housing price index to represent this variable. Then, individual data, drawn from households in a variety of cities, is typically used to measure E and y. The usual focus is on homeowners rather than renters, so that E measures house values rather than rents. The elasticity estimates from such empirical studies typically show that the elasticities satisfy $-1 < \beta < 0$ and $0 < \theta < 1$. Thus, housing demand is price inelastic, indicating low price responsiveness. In addition, with $\theta < 1$, housing consumption rises less than proportionally with income. As a result, housing expenditure comprises a smaller and smaller share of income as y rises. For a summary of evidence on the magnitudes of price and income elasticities, see Mayo 1981.

6.2.2 The hedonic approach

In contrast to the traditional approach to housing demand, the "hedonic" approach recognizes that a dwelling is a bundle of attributes such as floor space and lot size, making it hard to measure housing consumption using a single variable. Thus, instead of being written as $u(c, q)$, the consumer's utility function is written as $u(c, a_1, a_2, \ldots, a_m)$, where a_i is the level of the ith housing attribute, of which there are m in total (recall that c is "bread" consumption). With preferences expressed in this way, consumers have "demands" for individual attributes rather than a demand for a generalized housing commodity.

To isolate these demands empirically, the first step is to estimate a "hedonic price function." Such a function relates the selling price of a house to the levels of its various attributes. A hedonic function can be estimated using the kind of data available to real-estate agents and home buyers, which includes a host of property characteristics. However, the actual selling price of the house is used rather than the seller's asking price.

Grether and Mieszkowski (1974) estimated one of the first hedonic housing price regressions, using data on house sales in New Haven, Connecticut, during the period 1962–1969. Here is the equation they estimated:

House value = 36 + 5.2 × square footage + 0.89 × lot size + 800 × number of bathrooms + 580 × family room + 830 × fireplace + 790 × one-car garage + 1,270 × two-car garage – 5.2 × average room size – 0.07 × age × square footage + additional attribute effects.

The hedonic coefficients are known as the "implicit prices" of the attributes, and the results show the magnitudes of these prices. The house values in the sample are very low by today's standards (averaging $22,000), so the implicit prices are themselves modest. For example, another 100 feet of floor space raises a house's value by $520, and the same increment to lot size raises the house's value by $89. A second bathroom is worth $800, a family room $580, and a fireplace $830. Relative to a house without a garage, a one-car garage adds $790 to value while a two-car garage adds $1,270. With square footage held constant, larger rooms reduce a house's value. Older houses are also worth less. Note that age is interacted with square footage, so that the dollar age discount rises with the size of the house. Mieszkowski and Grether's hedonic regression includes many additional variables capturing the house's condition, its exterior materials, and some of its interior characteristics.

The demand for housing attributes can be recovered in a second step once the hedonic price function has been estimated.[1] The approach is basically to regress the implicit price on the level of the corresponding attribute and on the characteristics of the household buying the house (income, family size, and so on).[2] The estimated coefficient on the attribute variable gives the slope of attribute demand function, thus revealing the price responsiveness of the consumer's attribute choice.

---

1. The two-step hedonic method was pioneered in a famous paper by Sherwin Rosen (1974).

2. Because Mieszkowski and Grether's regression is linear, the implicit attribute prices are constants. The dependent variable in the second-step procedure is thus constant, which would rule out a proper second-step regression. (The authors did not attempt to carry out such a regression, being interested only in the hedonic function itself.) More flexible specifications of the hedonic equation (semi-log, for example) generate non-constant implicit prices, thus allowing the second step to be carried out. For an example of a study that includes both steps, see Quigley 1982.

6.3   The User Costs of Housing

6.3.1   Preliminaries

To provide a fuller picture of cost of homeownership, and to analyze the choice between owning and renting, it is necessary to return to the traditional view of housing, in which consumption is measured in a unidimensional fashion and a price per unit can be identified. When housing is rented, the price per unit is simply the rental price, denoted by p in the context of the urban model. But when a consumer owns the housing she occupies, characterization of the cost per unit is more complicated. As an owner, the consumer will make a mortgage payment, pay property taxes, incur depreciation on the dwelling, and earn housing capital gains. Additional costs of ownership include maintenance costs and insurance.

To capture these costs, let V denote the value of the house. In addition, let i denote the mortgage interest rate, h denote the property tax rate, d denote the depreciation rate, and g denote the rate of capital gains (the annual percentage change in house values). Suppose that the consumer buys the house using a 100 percent mortgage, with no down payment (the analysis is unchanged if a down payment is allowed). In addition, suppose for simplicity that the mortgage is of the "interest-only" kind. Then the consumer's annual interest cost is equal to iV (that is, the interest rate times the amount of the mortgage loan, which equals the house's full value). Along with this cost, the property tax payment is hV (the tax rate times the house's value).[3]

Depreciation captures the annual decline in the value of the house as it wears out. Houses are thought to depreciate by 1–2 percent per year, a decline that is captured by d. Therefore, the annual loss due to depreciation is dV. Finally, general appreciation in house values (due, say, to rising overall demand in the economy) leads to housing capital gains, with g measuring the percentage gain in value. The consumer then realizes a benefit equal to gV each year, which tends to offset the previous costs. It is possible, of course, that g could be negative, in which case gV represents an actual cost. With all the previous elements gathered, the annual costs incurred by the homeowner are given by $(i + h + d - g)V$. For simplicity, the costs of maintenance

---

3. If the consumer makes a down payment of D, the mortgage interest payment is $i(V - D)$. But by putting D into the house purchase, the consumer forgoes investment income of iD (if the investment return equals the mortgage interest rate). When this loss is added to the interest payment, the sum equals iV, just as if no down payment were made.

and insurance are omitted from this formula, but they could easily be added.

Let q again denote the amount of housing consumption, which in the urban model was measured by square feet of floor space. In addition, let v denote the purchase price per unit of housing, as distinct from the rental price p. Then the house's value V is equal to vq, with the owner-occupier's cost given by $(i + h + d - g)vq$. Given this formula, the housing cost *per unit of consumption* is then $(i + h + d - g)v$. When deciding whether to be an owner-occupier or a renter, a consumer might compare this cost-per-unit expression to the cost per unit as a renter, given by p. But two adjustments must be made before this comparison can be carried out. First, the fact that some of the owner's costs are tax deductible must be taken into account. Second, the rental price p will depend on the value v per unit of housing, in a manner that again depends on taxes, and this dependence must also be considered in comparing the costs of owning and renting.

6.3.2   The tax treatment of housing

The tax treatment of owner-occupiers affects their housing costs, and the tax treatment of the landlords who supply rental housing affects the rents they charge, as reflected in p, the rental price per unit. Table 6.1 summarizes the treatment of the various housing-cost elements for both owner-occupiers and landlords under the U.S. income tax code, indicating whether the costs are tax deductible. Mortgage interest, property taxes, and depreciation are all tax deductible for landlords. Mortgage interest and property taxes are deductible for owner-occupiers, but depreciation isn't.[4]

The benefits accruing to landlords are the rental income they earn from their properties and the capital gains they enjoy. Both of these benefits are taxable, as can be seen in table 6.2. Capital gains are among the benefits accruing to owner-occupiers, as was discussed above. But another benefit consists of the rental payments they avoid by owning rather renting their dwellings. This benefit is measured by *imputed rent*, which equals the amount the consumer would have to pay in rent if she occupied her dwelling as a renter rather than an owner. This benefit isn't taxable, and capital gains are also not taxable for most individuals (to be taxed, they must exceed a high threshold).

---

4. In order to claim the deductions, an owner-occupier must itemize deductions in computing her tax liability rather than taking the standard deduction. In addition, there is an upper limit on the amount of mortgage interest that can be deducted.

Table 6.1
Tax treatment of housing costs.

Cost element	Tax deductible for owner-occupier?	Tax deductible for landlord?
Mortgage interest	Yes	Yes
Property taxes	Yes	Yes
Depreciation	No	Yes

Table 6.2
Tax treatment of housing benefits.

Benefit	Taxable for owner-occupier?	Taxable for landlord?
Rental income or imputed rent	No	Yes
Capital gains	No for most taxpayers	Yes

Tables 6.1 and 6.2 show that the tax treatment of owner-occupiers and landlords is asymmetric. In contrast to the treatment of landlords, neither of the housing benefits is taxed for owner-occupiers, and one of the housing costs (depreciation) isn't tax deductible. These differences in the treatment of owner-occupiers are favorable, on balance. In other words, the gain to owner-occupiers from not having to pay taxes on housing benefits exceeds the loss from being unable to deduct depreciation. As a result, relative to the treatment of landlords, the tax code involves a tax subsidy to homeownership.

This tax subsidy would be eliminated if an owner-occupier were treated as a landlord renting to herself. The owner-occupier would then be viewed as paying herself rent (even though no money changes hands), and this implicit income would be taxed. She would be allowed to deduct depreciation as a business expense and would have to pay a tax on capital gains. Since the resulting change in the owner-occupier's tax liability would come mostly from taxation of imputed rent, the failure to tax this benefit is the main source of the tax subsidy to homeownership.[5]

---

5. A popular view is that eliminating the mortgage interest deduction is the right approach to reducing the tax subsidy. Although this change would raise the costs of homeownership, it would *increase*, not decrease, the asymmetry in the tax treatment of owner-occupiers and landlords. It should be noted that, even though taxation of imputed rent involves some challenges (particularly estimating the rent that an owner-occupied house would command), some countries, notably Germany, require it.

6.3.3 The user cost of owner-occupied housing

The tax deductibility of mortgage interest and property taxes requires an adjustment in the previous formula for the owner-occupier's housing cost. To make the adjustment, let τ denote the owner-occupier's income-tax rate.[6] Deductibility means that, for every dollar of mortgage interest the owner-occupier pays, she can reduce her taxes by τ dollars via the deduction. Therefore, a dollar of mortgage interest costs the owner-occupier only $1 - τ$ dollars, and the same is true of property taxes. Modifying the previous formula, the annual cost of housing is then equal to

$$[(1 - \tau)(i + h) + d - g]V,$$

where the cost $(i + h)V$ of interest and property taxes is replaced by the after-tax cost, $(1 - \tau)(i + h)V$.

As before, let V be replaced in this formula by vq, where v is the purchase price per unit of housing. The owner-occupier's cost per unit of housing, adjusted for taxes, is then given by

$$[(1 - \tau)(i + h) + d - g]v = \text{user cost of owner-occupied housing.}$$

To capture housing demand by owner-occupiers in a realistic way, this "user-cost" expression would replace the price per unit p in the demand formula in subsection 6.2.1. The quantity demanded, q, will then depend on all the elements in the user-cost formula. If the purchase price per unit of housing v rises, q will fall, and the same thing will happen if the mortgage interest rate i or the property tax rate h were to rise. The effect of i establishes the important point that the cost of a mortgage contributes to the cost of owner-occupied housing.

In addition, higher depreciation would raise the user cost, causing the quantity demanded to fall, whereas an increase in the capital gains rate g would have the opposite effect. By producing a financial payoff from homeownership, higher capital gains reduce its cost, thus giving consumers an incentive to consume more housing.

---

6. For simplicity, the analysis makes an unrealistic assumption about taxes. In particular, it assumes that a consumer is subject to a *proportional* income tax, paying a fixed proportion τ of taxable income to the government. In addition, as will be discussed later, τ is assumed to be higher for higher-income individuals. This feature is meant to mimic the actual income tax system, whose progressivity means that the marginal tax rate rises as income increases. A fully realistic depiction of taxes would complicate the analysis without changing its basic message.

6.3.4 Inflation and housing bubbles

Although the capital-gains effect provides the key to understanding housing bubbles, first consider the effect of a less dramatic phenomenon: inflation that affects the prices of all goods. Suppose that the rate of overall inflation rises by 1 percentage point (say, from 4 percent to 5 percent). Then g goes up by 0.01, and, in addition, the mortgage interest rate rises by 0.01. This second effect occurs because the nominal interest rate generally equals an underlying real interest rate plus the rate of inflation.

How do these combined changes and i and g affect the user cost of owner-occupied housing? With Δ denoting change, the change in the user cost is

$$[(1 - \tau)\Delta i - \Delta g]v = [(1 - \tau)(0.01) - 0.01]v = -0.01\tau v < 0.$$

Therefore, general inflation reduces the user cost, encouraging owner-occupiers to demand more housing. This reduction in user cost means that the tax code's effect on housing costs is non-neutral with respect to inflation.

A housing bubble arises when widespread expectations of high housing capital gains are self-fulfilling, so that the expectations are confirmed. From the user-cost formula, it is easy to see how a bubble works. Suppose that consumers start to expect high housing capital gains, so that g increases, but that they don't expect generalized inflation, so that i is unchanged. Then, as was noted above, the user cost falls. But a lower user cost raises the demand for housing, so that consumers increase their desired consumption. This higher demand, in turn, drives housing prices up, confirming and even heightening consumers' capital-gains expectations. With even greater price appreciation expected, demand via the user cost increases further, fueling the bubble. This kind of process led to the large run-up in U.S. housing prices over the period 2000–2006. The collapse of capital-gains expectations, caused in part by the growing unaffordability of houses over this period, led to a severe drop in prices and the end of the bubble.

Many observers argued that low mortgage interest rates also helped to start the housing bubble, and this effect can be seen in the user-cost formula. As was noted above, a low i pushes up the demand for housing, leading to price escalation and the anticipation of further capital gains.

6.3.5 The user cost of rental housing

To compute the user cost of rental housing, consider a landlord who purchases a dwelling at a per-unit price of v and rents it out at a per-unit price of p. Suppose that, like the consumer, the landlord buys the property with a 100 percent mortgage, while paying property taxes and incurring depreciation. Since all these costs are tax deductible, the landlord's after-tax cost per unit of housing purchased is

$$(1 - \lambda)(i + h + d)v,$$

where λ is the landlord's income-tax rate. In addition, the landlord earns capital gains at rate g, but he is able to keep only $(1 - \lambda)gv$ of these gains, since they are taxed. Finally, the landlord earns rental income of p per unit of housing, but this income is taxed, leaving $(1 - \lambda)p$ in after-tax income. The landlord's profit per unit of housing, which equals after-tax income minus after-tax costs, is then

$$(1 - \lambda)p - [(1 - \lambda)(i + h + d)v - (1 - \lambda)gv] = (1 - \lambda)[p - (i + h + d - g)v].$$

As was explained in chapter 2, competition in the housing market drives profit down to zero, and this outcome pertains to landlords as well as housing developers. Therefore, the above profit expression must be zero, which means that the rental price p must bear a particular relationship to the purchase price v. In particular, it must be true that

$$p = (i + h + d - g)v = \text{user cost of rental housing.}$$

Thus, the price p is equal to a user-cost expression that is similar to the user cost of owner-occupied housing but doesn't contain any income-tax term.[7]

6.4 Tenure Choice

6.4.1 Tenure choice in the basic model

In deciding whether to rent or to own, the consumer will choose the cheaper tenure mode. In other words, the consumer will compare the user costs under owning and renting, and then choose the mode with

---

7. If the costs of maintenance and insurance were added to the model, they would be treated like depreciation, being tax deductible for the landlord but not for the owner-occupier. It is useful to note that, in the maintenance category, the tax code allows deductions for repairs, but not for improvements to the property (defined as changes that prolong its life). Since the depreciation deduction allows landlords to treat the wearing out of the property as a cost, allowing them to also deduct improvements that reverse the wearing out process would involve double counting.

the lower user cost (and thus the lower cost per unit of housing). Using the above user-cost formulas, the result of this comparison is immediate. Since the owner-occupier's cost is the same as the renter's user cost except for the appearance of the $1 - \tau$ term, which multiplies i and h, it follows that the owner's user cost is smaller. This relationship holds regardless of the magnitude of the income-tax rate τ, as long as the rate is positive (ensuring that $1 - \tau < 1$). Therefore, a consumer will always choose to be an owner-occupier, no matter what her tax rate is.

Since about one-third of households in the United States are renters, with the rest homeowners, this prediction of universal homeownership isn't accurate. But the model so far omits an important element of the tax code by failing to realistically incorporate an important element in the treatment of depreciation. The next subsection shows what happens when that element is included.

6.4.2 Tenure choice with a realistic depreciation deduction

The depreciation term d in the formulas above is meant to represent *economic depreciation*, which captures the actual wearing out of buildings over time. The U.S. tax code, however, allows landlords to deduct *accelerated depreciation*, under which buildings are treated as wearing out faster than they really do.[8] Accordingly, let the depreciation rate allowed for tax purposes be $d + e$, where e is the rate of *excess depreciation* over and above d, the rate of economic depreciation.

Incorporating accelerated depreciation, the profit expression for the landlord is written as

$$(1 - \lambda)p - [(1 - \lambda)(i + h + d)v - \lambda ev - (1 - \lambda)gv]$$
$$= (1 - \lambda)[p - (i + h + d - g)v] + \lambda ev.$$

Note that accelerated depreciation creates an additional taxing saving of λev, equal to landlord's tax rate λ times the dollar amount of excess depreciation per unit of housing (ev). The second profit expression shows that the net result is the addition of λev to the previous profit formula. As before, the landlord's profit must equal 0, and this requirement can be used to determine p. Setting the last profit expression above equal to 0 and solving for p yields

$$p = (i + h + d - g)v - \lambda ev/(1 - \lambda) = \text{new user cost of rental housing.}$$

---

8. The tax code assumes that buildings wear out (that is, are fully depreciated) after 27.5 years of use. Actual economic depreciation, in contrast, would lead to a life span of 75–100 years.

Therefore, the new user-cost expression is the same as the previous one, except that the term $\lambda ev/(1 - \lambda)$, which captures the effect of excess depreciation, is subtracted off.[9]

This new renter user-cost formula generates a more complicated and realistic answer to the tenure-choice question than did the old formula. Now, even though the owner-occupier's user cost is smaller than the $(i + h + d - g)v$ expression in the above formula, the presence of the subtracted term reduces the magnitude of the renter's user cost, making it unclear which user-cost expression is smaller.

To compare the user costs, recall that the owner-occupier's user cost depends on the income-tax rate τ, and that this tax rate will differ across households. Reflecting the progressivity of the actual income tax code, the tax rate τ will be high for high-income households and low for low-income households.[10] Since the user cost falls as τ increases, a graph with τ on the horizontal axis will show user cost as a linear, downward-sloping curve, as in figure 6.1.[11] In contrast, since the renter's user cost doesn't depend on the household's income-tax rate, its

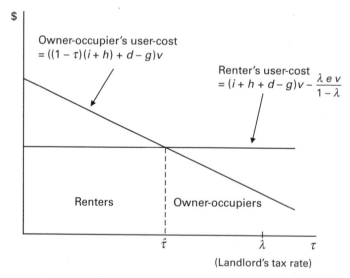

Figure 6.1
Housing tenure choice.

9. This user-cost derivation follows Sonstelie and Narwold 1994.
10. Recall from note 6 that the proportional tax assumed in the model is unrealistic, in that the income tax is actually progressive.
11. Linearity can be seen from the above user-cost formula, which indicates that the slope is $-(i + h)v$.

graph is just a horizontal line in the diagram. The crucial feature of figure 6.1 is that the owner's user cost starts out above the renter's user cost when τ is small and falls below it once τ becomes large. This property can be verified using the formulas.[12] Thus, the major conclusion from the diagram is that renting is cheaper than owning for households with low τ's and that owning is cheaper than renting for households with high τ's. Recalling that τ rises with income, it follows that low-income households will be renters and that high-income households will be owner-occupiers.

Figure 6.1 could apply to a world with a continuum of income-tax rates, in which case the cutoff tax rate that divides renters and owners would equal $\hat{\tau}$. Real-world tax codes have a only a handful of rates, but in this case the figure's implications are unchanged. Consumers in a tax bracket whose rate lies below $\hat{\tau}$ will be renters, whereas consumers in a bracket whose rate lies above $\hat{\tau}$ will be owner-occupiers. Another thing to note from the figure is that the landlord, who is likely to be a rich individual, will have a high tax rate. As a result, the landlord's tax rate λ (which helps determine the level of the renter's user cost) lies far to the right on the horizontal axis, as seen in the figure.

The division of high-income and low-income households between owning and renting has a simple intuitive explanation. The question for a household is whether to take advantage of the tax deductibility of mortgage interest and property taxes as an owner-occupier or to take advantage of the deductibility of excess depreciation (whose benefits are passed on by the landlord) as a renter. Because the owner-occupier's deductions aren't worth much to a household with a low income-tax rate, such households (which have low incomes) prefer to take advantage of the landlord's tax benefits by being renters. However, the high tax rate of high-income households makes the deductions of mortgage interest and property taxes worth more to them. These households thus prefer to be owner-occupiers rather than taking advantage of the landlord's tax benefit as renters.

This model of tenure choice can generate a number of additional predictions. Consider, for example, the effect of an increase in the landlord's income-tax rate λ. Since a larger λ makes the last subtracted term in the renter user-cost formula larger, the user cost itself falls, shifting

---

12. When $\tau = 0$, the owner's user cost equals $(i + h + d - g)v$, which is larger than the renter's user cost. When $\tau = 1$, the owner's user cost is $(d - g)v$, which is smaller than the renter's user cost provided $(i + h)v - \lambda ev/(1 - \lambda)$ is less than 0, a condition that is assumed to hold.

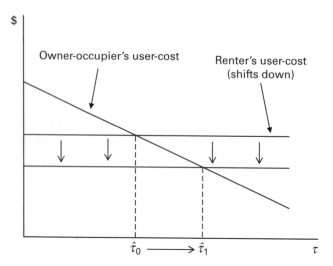

Figure 6.2
Effect of a higher landlord tax rate.

the horizontal line in figure 6.1 downward, as shown in figure 6.2. As a result, the cutoff tax rate $\hat{\tau}$ rises, decreasing the share of households that are homeowners.[13] Intuitively, a higher tax rate makes the excess depreciation deduction worth more to landlords, and this larger benefit is passed on to consumers in lower rents. The result is an increase in the renter share, or equivalently, a decline in the homeownership rate. Sonstelie and Narwold (1994) provide empirical confirmation of this prediction.[14]

The model can also predict how other economy-wide changes, such as higher property taxes or a more liberal excess depreciation, will affect the rate of homeownership. In addition, a large empirical literature explores how household characteristics, including the crucial income-tax rate variable, affect the choice between renting and owning. Such variables also include family size and age of head of household.[15]

---

13. Exercise 6.1 provides a numerical example illustrating this effect.
14. Sonstelie and Narwold assume that the landlord's tax in a state is equal to the sum of the maximum marginal state and federal rates. With their sample consisting of households from many states, the relevant landlord tax rate thus varies across households, which allows its effect to be measured.
15. For representative studies, see Goodman 1988 and Haurin and Gill 2002. Another literature investigates whether homeowners "make better citizens" than renters, being more likely to vote, know their neighbors, and so on. Related studies investigate whether educational outcomes (high school graduation, for example) are more favorable for children raised in owner-occupied dwellings. See Dietz and Haurin 2003 for a survey.

6.4.3 Some other factors affecting tenure choice

A number of other factors not considered in the model may also affect tenure choice.

Expected mobility Consumers incur substantial transaction costs in buying and selling houses, including closing costs and commissions for real-estate salespeople. Although these costs are worth bearing occasionally when changing residences, their burden becomes more significant with frequent moves. Therefore, homeownership may be the wrong choice for a consumer who expects to relocate relatively soon.

Pride of ownership Consumers often take pride in being able to own, rather than rent, the dwelling they occupy, and this feeling can affect tenure choice. In the context of the model, pride of ownership would appear as a negative cost, which would lead to a downward shift in the owner-occupier's user-cost curve in figure 6.1. This shift would reduce the cutoff tax rate $\hat{\tau}$, with the result that the homeownership rate would rise relative to a situation in which pride of ownership is absent. This psychological effect is probably a significant determinant of homeownership, along with purely economic forces.

Risk Although homeownership involves a risky investment, the risk can be amplified in some situations. For example, a consumer whose wage income is positively correlated with housing prices in her city of residence is exposed to more risk than if income and prices were uncorrelated. Such a consumer might work in a "company town" such as Detroit, where bad times in the auto industry translate into both downward pressure on incomes and capital losses on real estate. If they are aware of this kind of double jeopardy, residents of company towns may display less inclination toward homeownership, or buy smaller houses, than consumers whose incomes aren't correlated with their city's house prices. On the other hand, some risk considerations can favor homeownership. For example, locking in housing costs by purchasing a home with a fixed-rate mortgage insulates the consumer from the risk of year-to-year rent changes under the renting option.[16]

---

16. For evidence on these two effects, see Davidoff 2006 and Sinai and Souleles 2005.

Dislike of home-maintenance tasks It is sometimes argued that people who dislike home-maintenance tasks, such as mowing the lawn, will choose to rent rather become owner-occupiers. Renting shifts responsibility for unpleasant household tasks to the landlord. This argument may seem reasonable at first, but it doesn't make economic sense. The reason is that an owner-occupier can always pay to have someone else perform maintenance tasks. Since landlords implicitly charge for maintenance costs anyway as part of rent, a homeowner's cash outlay to maintenance providers (in lieu of spending personal time) wouldn't tip the balance away from ownership.

6.5   Down-Payment Requirements, Tenure Choice, and Mortgage Default

6.5.1   Down payments and tenure choice

Traditionally, a home buyer was required to make a substantial down payment. This requirement was weakened during the period of the recent housing bubble, but down-payment requirements have been stiffened again since the collapse of the housing market. Although a down-payment requirement constitutes an important barrier to homeownership, it plays no role in the model developed above. The model simply looks at the annualized costs of owning versus renting, portraying the consumer as taking the cheaper option without acknowledging that an important hurdle to homeownership (the down payment) must be cleared. Even though homeownership may be preferred on the basis of annualized costs, a consumer lacking the funds for a down payment will not be able to act on this preference, so that renting is the only option.

Although young home buyers sometimes acquire down-payment funds as a gift from their parents, accumulating a down payment usually requires saving. Economic analysis of consumer saving shows that a major factor influencing the willingness to save is an individual's "impatience." In an economic context, "impatience" refers to the strength of the consumer's desire for current as opposed to future consumption, as captured by a subjective "discount factor." Since an impatient person values current consumption highly relative to future consumption, such an individual will not be inclined to save. For such a person, the act of saving boosts less-valued future consumption in return for an unattractive sacrifice of highly valued current consumption. A patient individual, who values current and future consumption more nearly equally, will be more inclined to save.

Since impatience affects saving, and since saving is needed to accumulate the down payment required for homeownership, impatience and tenure choice are linked. An impatient consumer will be reluctant to save enough to become a homeowner, whereas a patient consumer will find it easier to overcome the down-payment hurdle by saving the required amount.

With the model amended to include a down-payment requirement, the following conclusions emerge. Consumers with income-tax rates below the cutoff level $\hat{\tau}$ will still be renters. Consumers with tax rates above $\hat{\tau}$ would like to be owners (based on annualized costs), but only the patient individuals in this group will be able to accumulate the required down payment. Among this high-tax-rate group, impatient consumers will not save enough for a down payment and will end up renting even though homeownership is preferable on the basis of annualized costs.[17]

6.5.2 Mortgage default

Although the analysis so far presumes that consumers who become homeowners will keep that status, an involuntary return to renter status is likely when an owner-occupier defaults on the mortgage used to purchase a house. "Default" means that the consumer stops making the required monthly payments to the mortgage lender. The act of default usually leads to foreclosure, under which the lender evicts the resident, takes possession of the house, and sells it to a new buyer. After defaulting, a consumer cannot get a mortgage on another house for a number of years, which makes renting the only tenure option.

The down-payment requirement discussed in subsection 6.5.1 is in fact meant to reduce the likelihood of default. To see how the incentives work, consider a simple setup in which the consumer buys a house at the beginning of a period for an amount V and then lives in it until the end of the period. To make the purchase, the consumer borrows M from a mortgage lender and makes a down payment D using his or her own funds, so that $M + D = V$. The new homeowner vacates the house at the period's end, at which time the mortgage amount M must be repaid.[18] The funds for this payment would come from sale of the house at the end-of-period price, equal to V^*.

---

17. For formal analysis of a tenure-choice model that incorporates these ideas, see Brueckner 1986 and Artle and Varaiya 1978. Also see exercise 6.2.

18. For simplicity, suppose that mortgage is of the interest-only type, and that the interest rate is 0. Then, aside from repaying the borrowed amount, there is no actual mortgage payment to be made.

The price V^* could lie below the initial purchase price V, and this outcome raises the possibility of default. To see how, note that if the consumer sells the house and pays back the mortgage M, the amount of money left over is $V^* - M$, which equals his "equity" in the house. If the consumer instead defaults on the mortgage, failing to pay back the balance M and letting the lender seize the house, he is left with nothing. If $V^* - M < 0$, so that the sale price V^* is less than the mortgage amount (and equity is negative), the homeowner ends up "in the hole" when paying off the mortgage, having to contribute out-of-pocket funds to do so. He would thus be better off defaulting, in which case he would come out even. This negative-equity default rule is modified slightly when the consumer incurs "default costs," denoted by C, which capture the cost of an impaired credit rating, the costs associated with moving out of the house, and the psychic costs (guilt) that defaulting on a mortgage might bring. In this case, default will occur only when $V^* - M < -C$, or when equity is more negative than $-C$. This rule again minimizes out-of-pocket costs when leaving the house.

A down payment makes default less likely because it reduces the mortgage amount M (recall $M = V - D$), making it less likely that equity $V^* - M$ is less than $-C$. More specifically, let $V^* - M$ be rewritten as

$$V^* - (V - D) = D + (V^* - V).$$

Thus, $V^* - M$ equals the down payment D plus the change in the house's value (which is negative when $V^* < V$). The default condition is then

$$\text{equity} = V^* - M = (V^* - V) + D < -C.$$

If the house's value stays the same ($V^* = V$), then equity equals D, a positive value, so the consumer doesn't default and gets his down payment back after paying off the mortgage. If the house's value falls, then whether default occurs depends on the values of D and C. For a given value of D, default is more likely the smaller is C. Similarly, for a given value of C, default is more likely the smaller is D. Thus, for a given decline in the house's value, default is more likely to occur the smaller are the down payment and the default costs.

After the bursting of the recent housing bubble, mortgage default and foreclosure were widespread. As a result, hundreds of thousands of new homeowners returned to renter status, and the rate of home-ownership declined. Many of the post-bubble defaults were driven by the incentives captured by the three factors in the above default condition. The first of these factors was the severity of the decline in the prices of houses, which made $V^* - V$ negative and large. The second was the existence of many low-down-payment mortgages, which made D small. The third factor was the presence of many borrowers with poor credit ratings, who became homeowners through the use of "subprime" mortgages that charged high interest rates (a new financial innovation). Such borrowers have little to lose from default since their credit is already bad, so they have small values of C. Given these three factors, the default condition was satisfied for huge numbers of homeowners, encouraging mortgage defaults.[19] Foreclosures followed these defaults, and attempts by the lenders to resell the large number of houses they seized flooded the market and further contributed to the post-bubble decline in housing values.

Subsection 6.5.1 showed that the down-payment requirement is an obstacle to homeownership, and that it must be overcome through saving or other sources of funds. But a down payment, once accumulated, gives the homeowner a financial stake in his property (thus discouraging default) by keeping equity positive even when prices decline, as long as the decline isn't too severe. Thus, although it represents a hurdle, a down payment preserves the incentive for owner-occupancy under adverse market conditions.

6.6   Property Abuse and Tenure Choice

Another factor omitted from the model is the potential for property abuse by renters. A renter may not have the same incentives as a homeowner to take care of a dwelling, and these differing incentives can affect tenure choice in a way not envisioned in the previous analysis. The following analysis will show that since rents must cover the cost of careless behavior by renters, they are high relative to the cost of owner-occupancy, making that option more attractive.

To understand the property-abuse issue, it is useful to develop a simple model that suppresses many of the previous features. As in the

---

19. Among many empirical studies on the determinants of default, a recent example is Foote, Gerardi, and Willen 2008. Such studies show that adverse events like unemployment of the borrower, which aren't connected to house values or down payments, can affect default, and the model explains this connection. Unemployment may necessitate moving to a cheaper dwelling, which effectively eliminates a portion of default costs since a move is necessary even in the absence of default. Thus, unemployment can cause a drop in C, leading to default.

default discussion, suppose that an owner-occupier buys a house at the beginning of a period for an amount V, lives in it during the period, and sells it at the end of the period. The individual pays cash for the house, so that no mortgage is used. While living in the house, the owner-occupier incurs an "operating cost," denoted by O, which could include property taxes. Income-tax considerations are suppressed, so that these costs are not tax deductible. Beyond operating costs, an additional potential cost is the cost of "caring" for the property. This cost is best viewed as the cost of responsible behavior (avoidance of wild parties, close monitoring of pets, and so on) that prevents damage to the property during occupancy. Let C now denote the dollar cost of exercising care.

The resale value of the house depends on whether care is exercised. With care, the resale value is V, equal to the purchase price (market conditions are assumed to be unchanged). When care isn't exercised, however, the resale value is $V - D$, where D now captures the damage to the house.

Now consider the homeowner's care decision. If care is exercised, the cost of owner-occupancy equals $V + O + C - V$, which captures the cost of the initial house purchase, the operating and care costs during occupancy, and the benefit from selling the house at the end of the period (which leads to a negative cost of $-V$). With the house's value staying the same, V cancels and the cost expression reduces to $O + C$, or operating cost plus the cost of exercising care. If care isn't exercised, the cost of owner-occupancy equals $V + O - (V - D) = O + D$, or operating cost plus the damage attributable to lack of care. Note that the care cost C is avoided, but the house sells for D less because care wasn't exercised.

The care decision thus affects the cost of owner-occupancy, which equals $O + C$ when care is exercised and $O + D$ when it isn't. Since the owner-occupier will make a care decision so as to minimize the cost, it follows that care will be exercised when $C < D$, and that care will not be exercised when $C > D$. In other words, if the cost of exercising care is less than the loss in a house's value from lack of care, the person will exercise care, and otherwise he will not. Suppose that $C < D$, so that the owner-occupier exercises care. The cost of owning is then $O + C$.

Now consider the behavior of renters. Letting P denote rent, the cost of renting is equal to P plus any costs associated with care. If the renter exercises care, the cost of renting is $P + C$, but if no care is exercised, the cost is P. Since the renter doesn't own the property, there is no resale penalty from failure to exercise care. As a result, the renter will not exercise care since this behavior leads to a lower cost of renting.

The rent P that the landlord charges reflects this lack of care by renters. To see how, note that a landlord's profit is equal to $-V + P - O + V - D$. This expression contains the cost of the initial outlay to buy the rental property ($-V$), the rental income P earned, net of operating cost O, plus the return $V - D$ from selling the property in a condition that reflects lack of care by the renter. This profit expression reduces to $P - O - D$. Since competition among landlords will reduce profit to 0, rent is then given by $P = O + D$. Therefore, rent covers operating cost plus the damage attributable to lack of care of the property.

Now consider the tenure-choice decision: should the consumer decide to be an owner, or a renter? From above, the cost of owning is $O + C$, while the cost of renting is just P, which in turn equals $O + D$. But since $C < D$, the owner-occupancy cost is lower. As a result, no one will choose to be a renter.[20] The logic of this argument is summarized in table 6.3.

This outcome arises because, under the maintained assumptions, renters have no incentive to take care of a dwelling. Therefore, landlords must charge for the resulting damage as part of rent. Owner-occupiers, however, do have an incentive to exercise care, since they

Table 6.3
Tenure choice with property abuse.

Owner costs as a function of care	Choice of care	Owner-occupier's cost
$O + C$ with care		
	Exercise care, since $C < D$	$O + C$
$O + D$ without care		

Renter costs as a function of care	Choice of care	Renter's cost
$P + C$ with care		P, equal to $O + D$
	Do not exercise care, since $C > 0$	with zero profit
P without care		

Tenure choice
Own, since $O + C < O + D$

20. For a more realistic model of this type, see Williams 1993.

bear the loss attributable to not doing so. But since the cost of exercising care is less than the damage resulting from failure to exercise care, the owner's cost is less than rent, which incorporates the larger damage amount. Owning is therefore cheaper.

The bad behavior of renters could be altered through the requirement of a damage deposit. If renters were required to pay a damage deposit of D, to be returned in the event that the property was vacated in good condition, then renters' incentives would match those of owner-occupiers, which would lead renters to exercise care.

However, damage deposits seem to fall short of the maximum damage renters can do, which means that a damage premium is still likely to be incorporated in rent. As a result, the logic of the analysis would still apply, capturing a force that favors owner-occupancy. This force may be especially strong in the case of high-quality dwellings, for which the cost of potential damage may be large. For such dwellings, the required damage-related rent premium would be high enough that no one would want to occupy one as a renter. By this logic, the rental market for high-quality dwellings should be thin.

6.7 Summary

Whereas the traditional model of housing demand assumes that housing consumption can be measured in a unidimensional fashion, the hedonic price model treats housing as a bundle of attributes. Estimation of a hedonic price function reveals the implicit prices of these attributes. In order to provide a more realistic picture of housing costs, which include mortgage interest and property taxes, a return to the traditional model is needed. Incorporation of these cost elements then yields user-cost expressions for owner-occupied and rental housing. By comparing user costs, a household can decide whether renting or owning is cheaper. The model predicts that high-income households, whose high tax rates make the tax benefits of owner-occupancy worth a lot, prefer to own. Low-income households prefer to rent, thus enjoying the tax benefits conferred on landlords. Other factors, such as pride of ownership and down-payment requirements, also affect tenure choice, as does the potential for property abuse by renters.

7 Housing Policies

7.1 Introduction

Previous chapters discussed a number of government policies that affect housing, including urban growth controls, zoning, and the tax subsidy to homeownership. This chapter focuses on several additional policies that involve government intervention in the housing market. The chapter starts by analyzing rent-control laws, under which a city government attempts to limit the rents that landlords charge to their tenants. Rent-control policies are in place in many cities throughout the world, and it is important to gain an understanding of their effects. Next, the discussion turns to housing-subsidy programs, another way governments try to make housing more affordable for consumers. Instead of limiting the rents that landlords can charge, the government undertakes expenditures that make housing more affordable for renters, typically paying part of their rent. The last section of the chapter focuses on the problem of homelessness and policies to correct it.

7.2 Rent Control

write on two.

7.2.1 How it works

Rent-control laws exist in many cities. The best-known U.S. example is New York City, where controls have been in place since World War II. Among other large cities, Los Angeles has a form of rent control. Many smaller cities also control rents.

Rent-control laws typically limit the rate of increase of rent for a dwelling during a tenant's period of residence. When a new tenant moves in, the law usually allows the rent to be raised to the free-market level. But the subsequent rate of increase is again restricted as long as the new tenant stays in the dwelling. New buildings are often exempted from rent control.[1]

Rent control generates large benefits for households living in controlled dwellings, who often pay much less for housing than occupants of buildings not covered by the law. These benefits are the source of political support for rent-control laws. But despite the existence of such support, rent control generates a host of negative effects that make it unpopular among economists. These effects include inadequate maintenance of dwellings, reduced incentives for new construction, and misallocation of households to dwellings.

Inadequate maintenance—a consequence of lower spending by landlords—is a natural result of attempting to limit the landlord's income via a rent-control law. Since lower rental income leads to reduced profit, the landlord will try to recoup his loss by cutting costs, and one cost that can be lowered easily is maintenance spending. By this argument, dwellings in rent-controlled buildings should be less well maintained than units in uncontrolled buildings. In effect, the housing market responds to rent limits by reducing the quality of the controlled units, so that tenants, to some extent, "get what they pay for." Striking empirical evidence illustrating this phenomenon is provided by Gyourko and Linneman (1990), who use data from New York to show that rent-controlled buildings are more likely to be "dilapidated" than uncontrolled buildings.

The second negative effect of rent control, reduced incentives for new development, may emerge even when newly constructed buildings are exempt. Despite such an exemption, housing developers may be wary of starting projects in rent-controlled cities, thinking that a future government may change the law, extending rent control to their buildings.

The third negative effect, misallocation of households to dwellings, is clear when it is recognized that households paying a low controlled rent are reluctant to move. Having given up a rent-controlled apartment, the household would have to start paying rent at the free-market level, either in an uncontrolled apartment or in another rent-controlled apartment vacated by its tenant. This reluctance to move may leave rent-controlled units in the hands of the wrong people, denying access to households who value the units most.

Although the second negative effect and the third are fairly clear intuitively, it is useful to analyze them in more detail using an explicit

---

1. For a useful overview of the economics of rent control, see Downs 1988.

model. The following analysis uses a "stock-flow" model of the housing market, which explicitly takes into account the fact that housing is a durable commodity.

7.2.2 The stock-flow model

Since housing is durable, lasting for decades before replacement, the existing stock of housing is much larger than the "flow" of new construction. In the United States, the stock of housing is around 100 million units, and the flow of new units is (in normal times) between 1 million and 2 million units per year. The stock-flow model captures this distinction between the stock of housing and the flow of new construction. The model assumes that all housing is rented, ignoring the owner-occupied side of the market for simplicity.

The left panel of figure 7.1 represents the stock side of the housing market. The quantity of housing, measured in square feet of floor space and denoted by H, is represented on the horizontal axis, with the price per square foot p on the vertical axis. The stock supply curve, labeled S_0, is a vertical line at a quantity $H = H_0$, which equals the size of the existing housing stock. This curve indicates a perfectly inelastic supply of housing from the existing stock. In other words, the line indicates that the entire existing stock of H_0 square feet will be rented out regardless of the price per square foot. The logic is that renting an

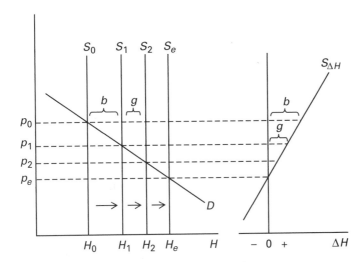

Figure 7.1
Stock-flow model.

existing unit is better for the landlord than leaving it vacant, which generates no rental income at all. In reality, a landlord might prefer a unit to be vacant when the rent is very low (not even covering occupancy costs), in which case the supply curve would bend toward the origin as p approaches zero. But this possibility has no effect on the analysis and can be ignored.

The left panel of figure 7.1 also shows the aggregate demand curve D for housing, which cuts the vertical supply curve S_0 at price p_0. At this price, the existing stock is just absorbed by the market, with the quantity demanded equal to H_0.

With the figure's left panel representing the stock side of the market, the right panel represents the flow side. The upward-sloping curve $S_{\Delta H}$ is the "flow" supply curve. It indicates the net flow of new housing into the market, which is denoted by ΔH and represented on the horizontal axis. When p is high, the $S_{\Delta H}$ curve indicates that the net flow ΔH is positive. But when p is low, the curve indicates a negative net flow, with ΔH negative. These different outcomes can arise because demolitions of existing housing as well as new construction determine the net change in the stock. When the price per square foot is high, few units are demolished and many new ones are constructed, so that the net change is positive. However, when the price is low, housing generates little rental income, making new construction unattractive and encouraging demolition of existing units, with the land converted to alternate uses. In this case, the net change in the stock is negative. At the price p_e, where the $S_{\Delta H}$ curve cuts the vertical axis, new construction just balances demolitions, and the stock remains unchanged.

The stock and flow sides of the market interact to generate a long-run equilibrium. When the housing stock starts at size H_0, the resulting price of p_0 is high enough to generate a net increase in the stock. Moving across from the stock side to the flow side of figure 7.1 at price p_0, it can be seen that the stock increases by the amount b. But this increase is then added to the pre-existing H_0 square feet in the market, yielding a new stock size of $H_1 = H_0 + b$ in the next period (and a new vertical supply curve, S_1). However, in order for this larger stock to be absorbed by the market, the price must fall to p_1. Again moving across to the flow side of the diagram, this price generates a positive, but now smaller, increase in the stock, equal to g. The resulting stock size, equal to $H_2 = H_0 + b + g$, generates a lower price, p_2, which in turn calls forth a yet smaller increase in the stock. This process stops when the price has fallen to p_e and the stock has reached a size H_e, which represent equilibrium values.

7.2.3 Demand shock and the imposition of rent control

To understand the motivation for imposition of rent control and its ultimate effects, consider a housing market that starts in equilibrium and is then subject to a demand shock. Such a shock, which shifts the demand curve to the right, could come from an increase in the population in the market. For example, the Miami housing market received such a shock after the Mariel boatlift in 1980, which added 125,000 Cuban refugees to the area's population in only a few months.

In the absence of rent control, the adjustment to such a demand shock can be traced using the stock-flow model, as in figure 7.2. Starting at D, the demand curve shifts rightward to D', and the price per square foot of housing shoots up to p'. This price increase indicates the increased scarcity of housing, a result of the presence of more demanders in the market. Note that the stock hasn't yet increased in response to the demand shock, which means that the new larger population must fit in the same total square footage as before. To achieve this outcome, some existing residents must reduce their consumption of housing, perhaps by moving in with relatives.

In response to the higher price, new construction surges, yielding a net increase in the stock equal to m, as in the right panel of figure 7.2. Further adjustments follow the path seen in figure 7.1, with the stock

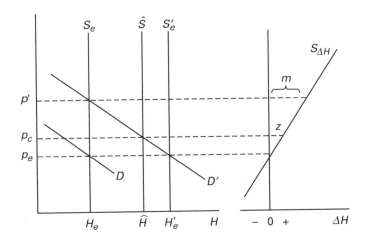

Figure 7.2
Effects of rent control.

growing through successive rounds of construction and the price falling until it again reaches p_e. In the new equilibrium, the stock achieves a size of H'_e. Thus, the housing market responds to the demand shock and the resulting price increase by successive bursts of new construction that eliminate the housing shortage, causing the price to fall back to its equilibrium level.

Existing residents, however, suffer from higher housing costs during the transition to the new equilibrium. The price surges to p' before eventually falling back to p_e, and the existing residents are unhappy with the resulting burden. As a consequence, anticipating what would happen in the absence of government intervention, the residents may persuade the local government to impose a rent-control law immediately after the demand shock, limiting the subsequent price increase. Accordingly, suppose that the government sets a maximum level for the rent per square foot equal to p_c, which is less than p' but a bit higher than p_e.[2] Suppose also that new construction isn't exempted from the law. This assumption leads to a more extreme picture of rent control's effects than may be justified, but it captures the view that exemptions may not fully ameliorate developers' concerns about future implementation of the law.

7.2.4 Effects of rent control on new construction

The market's response to the demand shock under rent control can be analyzed using figure 7.2 and can be compared with the response that would have occurred in the absence of rent control. Instead of increasing all the way up to p', the price immediately after the demand shock rises to p_c and increases no further, being limited by the rent control. Whereas the first-round increase in the housing stock was equal to m in the absence of rent control, the lower controlled price p_c elicits a smaller stock increase, equal to z in figure 7.2. Without rent control, the second-round stock increase would have been a bit smaller than m (equal to a magnitude like g in figure 7.1). But with rent control, the price is still stuck at the low p_c value, which leads to the same stock increase z as before, smaller than the one occurring without rent control. The upshot is that *rent control slows down the construction response to the demand shock*. In effect, rent control interferes with the market's signal

2. This view of rent control is slightly unrealistic because the control is portrayed as a limit on the price per square foot rather than on the rent charged for the entire dwelling. In addition, note that the law puts an upper limit on p rather than limiting the price's rate of increase. The latter restriction would be appropriate in a more realistic model.

of housing scarcity: the market price. By keeping the price artificially low under conditions of high demand, the market muffles the scarcity signal, preventing the developers from responding with an appropriately large burst of new construction.

Eventually, the slow-growing housing stock reaches a size of $\hat{H}$, at which point the rent-control law ceases to bite. In other words, when the stock size equals $\hat{H}$, the market generates a price of p_c independently of the rent control. From this point onward in the adjustment process, the path is the same as it would have been in the absence of rent control. The stock eventually reaches the same equilibrium size H'_e as it would have without rent control, and the price eventually falls to p_e. But, as was noted above, *it takes longer for the stock to grow up to size $\hat{H}$ than in the absence of rent control, which means that it takes longer for the market to ultimately reach the new equilibrium.*

This conclusion shows that the rent control is counterproductive. The problem caused by the demand shock is a housing shortage, and the solution is new construction. But rent control interferes with the solution, prolonging the time it takes for the market to eliminate the shortage.[3]

7.2.5 Misallocation of households to dwellings under rent control

Misallocation of households to dwellings, the third negative effect of rent control, can also be seen in figure 7.2. This misallocation arises from the existence of *excess demand for housing* during the period when the rent control is effective (when the stock is below $\hat{H}$ in size). Consider, for example, the situation immediately after the demand shock, when $p = p_c$ and the stock is still at size H_e. As can be seen from the figure, the quantity of housing demanded at price p_c equals $\hat{H}$, while the quantity of housing available is only H_e, so the excess demand equals $\hat{H} - H_e$.

Under conditions of excess demand, a commodity usually ends up being allocated among consumers in a capricious fashion, with those valuing the good most not necessarily getting it. To make this point concrete, imagine the Miami housing market after arrival of the Cuban refugees in 1980. Focus on two households: a little old lady (a long-time Miami resident) occupying a spacious three-bedroom apartment with her cats, and a Cuban refugee family with three children and ample financial resources. In the absence of rent control, the large increase in

---

3. Exercise 7.1 provides a numerical example of the adjustment process.

the price per square foot in the Miami market would push the rent for the lady's three-bedroom apartment beyond her ability to pay, and she would move into her daughter's house. The Cuban family would take over her vacated apartment, with their large household size and their ample resources making the high rent worth paying. In contrast, with rent control, the little old lady's rent would rise only a bit, straining her budget slightly. By cutting corners financially, she would be able to stay in her apartment. With many other existing Miami residents making similar decisions, the Cuban family would be unable to find any rental housing at all. As a result, the family would move into the basement of a house belonging to a relative (an earlier migrant from Cuba), living in cramped, uncomfortable conditions. This outcome indicates excess demand because the Cuban family would like to consume a substantial amount of housing at the controlled price p_c, but cannot do so.

The outcome reflects a misallocation of households to dwellings. The Cuban family, with a high demand for space and the ability to pay, consumes an inadequate amount of shelter, while the little old lady continues to occupy an amount of space that is inappropriately large in view of the true scarcity of housing after the demand shock. The problem is that rent control prevents the proper scarcity signal (a high market price) from being transmitted, which allows the lady to continue to inhabit an apartment that would more appropriately be occupied by the Cuban family.[4] The lady, of course, is better off as a result and would thus vote in favor of a rent-control law. But the outcome isn't the right one from society's point of view. Rent control is thus an example of a government policy that benefits a particular interest group (existing residents who would like to stay in their current dwellings) at the expense of society as a whole.

7.2.6   Other justifications for rent control?

It could be argued that if benefits from rent control accrue to a group that society would like to help, such as low-income renters, then the policy may still be worthwhile despite its broader negative effects. But Gyourko and Linneman (1989) show that rent-control benefits in New York City are distributed in a highly unsystematic fashion, not being concentrated among any particular social group. Gyourko and

---

4. On renters' unwillingness to move from rent-controlled dwellings, see Krol and Svorny 2005. These authors show that commute times are longer for individuals living in New Jersey census tracts subject to rent control than for individuals living in uncontrolled tracts.

Linneman conclude that rent control isn't narrowly enough focused to be useful as an instrument of targeted social policy. The implication is that if the government wants to reduce housing costs for a deserving group, it should provide direct subsidies to that group instead of relying on a rent-control law, which distorts the housing market in addition to being poorly targeted.

Another argument in favor of rent control is based on concerns about monopoly power in the housing market.[5] In a monopolized rental housing market, with a single landlord controlling all the dwellings, rents will be too high and the supply of housing will be too small. By forcing rents downward, a rent-control law in this situation would work just like price regulation of a natural monopoly (such as a public utility), and it would be in society's interest. The question, though, is whether monopoly power should ever be a concern in the housing market. Since ownership of rental housing is very diffuse in most markets, with holdings seldom concentrated in just a few hands, this concern seems misplaced. Therefore, imposing rent control as a response to concerns about market power is probably not justified.

7.3 Housing-Subsidy Programs

7.3.1 Overview

Rather than imposing rent control, an alternative way of reducing housing costs is to use government funds to explicitly subsidize consumption. Housing subsidies exist in various forms throughout the world, with the expenditures generally targeted to low-income groups. In the United States, subsidy programs are distinct from the federal tax subsidy to homeownership, which involves a "tax expenditure" (forgone tax revenue) rather than an explicit subsidy. Before discussing the actual form of U.S. programs, it is useful to present a general analysis of the forms that housing subsidies may take.

The analysis recognizes that housing-subsidy programs may serve two possible goals. The first is to raise the standard of living of the targeted group, low-income households. A second goal may be to reduce the negative externality associated with the existence of areas of substandard housing in the city. The existence of such areas, which will be referred to as "slums," is likely to reduce the urban quality of

---

5. Arnott (1995) argues that rent control may be helpful in an imperfectly competitive housing market.

life even for those individuals not living in them. Therefore, non-poor households may be willing to pay taxes in support of housing subsidies, recognizing that the resulting "slum-reduction" effect makes the city a nicer place to live. Given this twin focus, the analysis considers two effects of housing-subsidy programs: their effect on the standard of living (utility) of low-income households, and their slum-reduction effect. The magnitude of the slum-reduction effect depends solely on the increase in low-income housing consumption generated by the subsidy, whereas the utility effect depends on the consumption of both housing and bread (the non-housing good). As will be seen, the effects of housing-subsidy programs can differ along these two dimensions.

7.3.2 Analysis of housing-subsidy programs

Using the notation of chapter 3, let q denote housing consumption and let c denote bread consumption. The price per unit of housing is again p, and the income of a low-income household is denoted by y. With commuting cost suppressed for simplicity, the budget constraint of the low-income household is $c + pq = y$. Solving for q, the constraint can be rewritten as $q = y/p - c/p$. The resulting budget line is plotted in figure 7.3, which has q on the vertical axis and c on the horizontal axis. The

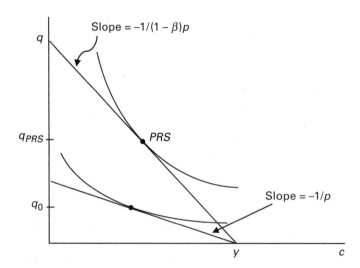

Figure 7.3
PRS program.

slope of the budget line is $-1/p$ and the c intercept is y.[6] The low-income household maximizes utility, achieving a tangency point between an indifference curve and the budget line. The resulting level of housing consumption, denoted by q_0, is low, corresponding to a slum dwelling. Note that q could be viewed as capturing the quality of a dwelling along with its size.

The first housing-subsidy program to be considered is a "Proportional Rent Subsidy" (PRS) program. Under this program, the government pays a fraction β of the household's rent bill, which equals pq. The budget constraint is now written as $c + (1 - \beta)pq = y$, with $(1 - \beta)pq$ representing the household's portion of its rental cost. The household is free to choose a different q under the PRS program, and to illustrate its choice, note that the program effectively reduces the price per unit of housing from p to $(1 - \beta)p$. In figure 7.3, the slope of the budget line then changes from $-1/p$ to $-1/[(1 - \beta)p]$, a more negative value, so the line gets steeper, rotating in the counterclockwise direction around its c intercept. The new level of housing consumption, denoted by q_{PRS}, is determined by a tangency between this rotated budget line and an indifference curve. Since housing is a normal good, the effective price reduction attributable to the PRS program must lead to an increase in housing consumption, which means that the new tangency must lie above the original tangency in figure 7.3, satisfying $q_{PRS} > q_0$. But the PRS consumption point could lie either to the right or to the left of the original point. Figure 7.3 illustrates the former case, with bread consumption thus assumed to increase along with housing consumption under the PRS program.

The PRS program increases the utility level of the low-income household, allowing it to reach a higher indifference curve. The program also achieves slum reduction by increasing the household's consumption of housing from q_0 to q_{PRS}. For each low-income household, the government's outlay under the PRS program is $\beta pq_{PRS} \equiv G$, its portion of the household's rent bill.

Now consider a different kind of program: one in which the government gives the low-income household an income grant, a fixed increment to its income not tied to the consumption of housing. Suppose that, under this income-grant (IG) program, the government sets the size of the grant so that it equals the outlay it would have made under

---

6. Note that, relative to the similar diagram in chapter 2 (figure 2.2), the housing and bread axes are reversed.

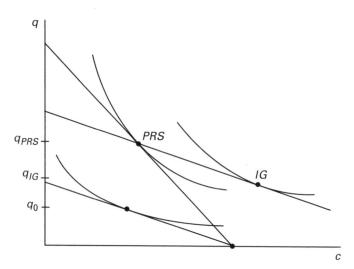

Figure 7.4
IG program.

the PRS program. The income grant thus equals G, so that the budget constraint of the household becomes $c + pq = y + G$.

Since it effectively increases the household's income, the IG program shifts the budget line outward in a parallel fashion, without changing its slope. But by how much does the budget line shift? Because the income grant equals the outlay under the PRS program, the consumption point chosen under that program must be affordable under the IG program. Thus, the IG budget line must pass through the PRS consumption point, as shown in figure 7.4.

The chosen consumption point under the IG program lies at the tangency between an indifference curve and the IG budget line. As seen in figure 7.4, this tangency point must lie downhill from the PRS consumption point on the IG budget line. The reason is that an indifference curve, being tangent to the PRS budget line at the PRS consumption point, necessarily cuts the flatter IG line at that point, so that the IG tangency must lie downhill. With housing and bread both normal goods, the IG tangency must also lie to the northeast of the original consumption point, with both bread consumption and housing consumption greater (so that $q_{IG} > q_0$). This outcome is illustrated in figure 7.4.

How do the effects of the PRS program and those of the IG program compare? As can be seen from figure 7.4, the IG program yields a higher utility level for the low-income household, which reaches a

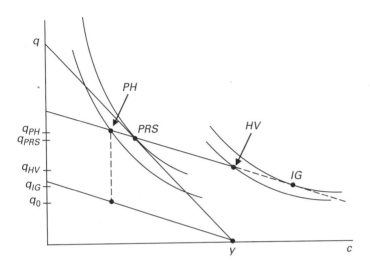

Figure 7.5
HV and PH programs.

higher indifference curve than under the PRS program. Conversely, the slum-reduction effect is greater under the PRS program, with q_{PRS} larger than q_{IG}. These differences reflect a general pattern that goes beyond the housing context: subsidizing consumption of a particular good always raises consumption of that good by more than an equivalent income grant, while leading to a smaller increase in utility.

A housing-voucher (HV) program, another type of housing-subsidy program similar to the IG program, would involve giving low-income households vouchers that would function like "reverse food stamps," being usable toward the purchase of housing but not toward the purchase of bread. The dollar value of the vouchers would match the cash amount G given under the IG program.

As shown in figure 7.5, the HV budget line consists of the upper portion of the IG budget line. The dashed portion of the line, which lies to the right of the intercept of the original budget line, is inaccessible. To see why, note that since housing vouchers can't be used to buy bread, the household can't buy more bread than the maximum amount it could acquire in the original pre-subsidy situation. That amount, equal to y, is consumed when the household spends all of its cash income on bread, acquiring housing only with vouchers. The resulting consumption point lies directly above the original bread intercept. But as long as the household is supplementing the vouchers with some of its own money (spending less than y on bread), the vouchers are indistinguishable from cash, making the upper portion of the IG line relevant.

In the situation illustrated in figure 7.5, the utility-maximizing point on the HV budget line is the corner solution corresponding to the lower endpoint. To see why, note that under the IG program the household would like to spend all of its original cash income y, and a portion of the income grant G, on bread, choosing a point on the dashed segment of the budget line. Under the HV program, the household can't use the vouchers to acquire bread and is thus prevented from moving onto the dashed segment. But it gets as close as possible to the IG tangency by consuming at the endpoint of the HV line.

As can be seen from figure 7.5, the HV program generates an outcome that lies between the PRS and the IG outcomes. The utility increase generated by the HV program is larger than the increase under the PRS program but smaller than that under the IG program. Since $q_{PRS} > q_{HV} > q_{IG}$, the slum reduction generated by the HV program is greater than that under the IG program but smaller than that under the PRS program.

In a different situation, the HV and IG programs could be equivalent. In particular, if the IG tangency point lay on the solid rather than the dashed part of the IG budget line, then the HV consumption point would coincide with it. Since in that case, the low-income household wouldn't have to use any of its income grant to buy bread, switching the grant to voucher form wouldn't affect its choice.

A fourth subsidy program relies on a "subsidy in kind" rather than an outlay of cash or vouchers. The program involves provision of "public housing": the government builds a housing unit larger than the original one and offers it to the household at a below-market rent. Thus, the household receives a dwelling, rather than a financial transfer, from the government.

A public housing (PH) program can be represented conveniently and fairly realistically by assuming that the household pays the same rent to the government as it paid for its original unit. The government takes the money and supplements it with additional funds in the amount G to build a larger dwelling, which is then offered to the household. With same rent paid, it follows that the household's bread consumption is the same as in the pre-subsidy situation, which means that its new consumption point lies directly above the original point. But how far above it? To answer this question, suppose that the government can produce housing at a cost per unit equal to the market price

Table 7.1
Rankings of housing-subsidy programs.

Increase in household utility	Extent of slum reduction
IG	PH
HV	PRS
PRS	HV
PH	IG

p (which equals the private-sector cost given zero profit). Then a government expenditure of G per household should be able to boost consumption of housing by the same amount as a grant G used to buy extra housing in the private market. As a result, under the PH program, the vertical movement upward from the original consumption point should get the household exactly to the IG budget line. The resulting PH consumption point is shown in figure 7.5. Note that if the government is an inefficient producer of housing (as many believe), the PH point would lie below the IG line.

As can be seen in figure 7.5, the PH program yields the largest slum-reduction effect of all the programs, with $q_{PH} > q_{PRS} > q_{HV} > q_{IG}$, while generating the smallest increase in utility.[7] Table 7.1 ranks all the programs on the increase in household utility and extent of slum reduction they generate. Note that the two rankings of the housing-subsidy programs are exactly the reverse of one another. For a given government outlay, the programs that do the best job of increasing household utility do the worst job of slum reduction and vice versa. Society's choice of a particular program would thus involve opposing interests. If low-income households themselves could dictate the chosen program, it would be IG or HV. But if the choice were to be made by non-poor households, who care most about the slum externality and are less attuned to the welfare of the slum residents, it would be PH or PRS. Since the non-poor households provide the tax revenue to pay for the subsidy program, they presumably would have the power to dictate the choice. Therefore, if the model is accurate, it seems likely that the housing-subsidy program(s) selected by the political process would the ones that do the best job of slum reduction: PH and/or PRS. As will be seen in subsection 7.3.3, this prediction is partly consistent with actual practice in the United States.

---

7. Note that the PH-PRS ranking would be reversed if the PRS point were located to the left, rather than to the right, of the pre-subsidy consumption point.

7.3.3 Actual housing-subsidy programs

In the 1950s and the 1960s, public housing was the most popular housing-subsidy program, with hundreds of thousands of units of public housing built by local governments. But public housing has since fallen into disfavor, and many of the housing projects are being demolished. The reason public housing has lost support is that, owing to the high concentration of poor households, public housing projects became breeding grounds for crime and other social problems. Instead of improving the quality of life of low-income households through better housing, the projects came to be viewed as offering a worse environment than the status quo.

The PRS program discussed above also has several real-world counterparts, although their rules are superficially different from those in the model. Under actual PRS programs, the government, instead of paying a fraction of household rent, pays a portion of a building's development cost, with the understanding that the units must be occupied by low-income households at reduced rents. The effect of such an arrangement, however, is identical to that of the model's PRS program. In earlier years, the Section 236 program subsidized developers' costs, but more recently, the Low-Income Housing Tax Credit (LIHTC) program has been the source of these subsidies.

Aside from the LIHTC program, the other important current source of housing subsidies is the Section 8 program. This program is often referred to as a "housing voucher" program, but it works differently than the model's food-stamp-style vouchers. Under Section 8, the government pays a portion of a low-income household's rent, with the payment going directly to the landlord. To compute the payment, the "fair market rent" for a dwelling large enough to accommodate the household is determined on the basis of local market conditions. The subsidy is then equal to the difference between this rent and 30 percent of the household's income. Thus, the household receives adequate housing in return for only 30 percent of its (low) income.

The Section 8 program limits the household's freedom of choice somewhat, preventing government funds from being spent on bread. Therefore, although it doesn't match up exactly with any of the programs in the model, Section 8 is similar to the PH and PRS programs in its effects, yielding substantial slum reduction rather than allowing the household greater freedom in use of the subsidy. Therefore, the main current housing-subsidy programs (PH, LIHTC, and Section 8) appear to put the highest priority on slum reduction, paying less attention to raising the utility levels of low-income households.

7.3.4 Effects of housing subsidies on neighborhoods

The poor performance of public housing in the United States is partly a consequence of the negative "neighborhood effects" caused by spatial concentration of poor households. An experimental program called Moving to Opportunity (MTO) tried to overcome these effects by relocating some public-housing residents to subsidized dwellings in non-poor neighborhoods. Because the residents were chosen randomly, the effects of a better neighborhood on various household behavioral outcomes (mental health, risky youth behavior, economic self-sufficiency of adults) can be measured without concerns about self-selection. These concerns would be present, for example, if only those households with the strongest capacities to achieve better outcomes had signed up for the relocation program. According to Kling, Liebman, and Katz (2007), the effects of living in a better neighborhood aren't as pronounced as might have been expected.

Many other studies have attempted to measure of the strength of neighborhood effects by relating household outcomes to neighborhood characteristics without the benefit of MTO's experimental approach. But they must contend with the self-selection problem, which arises because people choose the neighborhoods where they live instead of being assigned under an experimental program.[8]

7.4 Homelessness and Policies to Correct It

Homelessness has become a serious problem in the United States and in Europe.[9] Homeless individuals do not own or rent a dwelling, instead living on the streets and perhaps spending time in free shelters provided by charitable organizations. Like other housing decisions, homelessness can be analyzed by means of an economic model.

When living on the street, a homeless person effectively chooses zero housing consumption, setting $q = 0$. Figure 7.6 illustrates this decision, using a diagram like those used to analyze housing-subsidy programs. The homeless individual maximizes utility subject to a budget constraint, and for homelessness to be chosen, the highest indifference

---

8. See, for example, Aaronson 1998 and Oreopoulos 2003.
9. For an extensive analysis and discussion of homelessness, see O'Flaherty 1996.

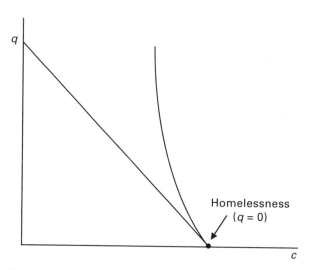

Figure 7.6
Homelessness.

curve must touch the budget line at its bottom endpoint, where $q = 0$. This outcome requires that the person's indifference curves be steep and that they intersect the horizontal axis.[10]

Steep indifference curves indicate that the consumer is very reluctant to give up bread, requiring large compensation in the form of extra housing to do so. This reluctance could be due to addiction, with "bread" now defined to include substances (alcohol or crack cocaine, for example) to which the person is addicted. The physiological difficulty of reducing consumption of alcohol and/or drugs prevents the individual from using any of his or her limited funds to purchase housing. The connection between homelessness and substance abuse is clear to anyone with street experience in a big city.

Mental illness is also associated with homelessness, often in tandem with addiction. But steep indifference curves like those in figure 7.6 may also simply indicate dire poverty, with housing consumption a lower priority than getting enough food to eat when funds are severely limited.

As long as indifference curves aren't vertical, a reduction in the price of housing may entice a homeless person to raise q above zero. Figure 7.7 illustrates the effect of a clockwise rotation of the budget line, as

10. For a similar diagrammatic analysis, see Colwell and Trefzger 1992.

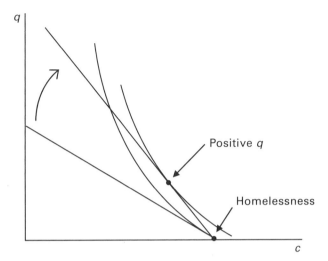

Figure 7.7
Housing subsidy eliminates homelessness.

would result from a PRS program. Since the highest indifference curve is now reached at an interior point where $q > 0$, a homeless person can thus be encouraged to purchase some shelter if housing is made cheap enough. Targeting such a subsidy so that only previously homeless individuals use it would probably not be feasible, however.

Some commentators argue that housing regulations can exacerbate the problem of homelessness, and that homelessness may therefore be partly a result of government policy. The culprit, it is argued, is building-code regulations that require rental units to provide a minimum level of housing consumption. For example, building codes may require that every dwelling unit have a private bathroom, ruling out dormitory-style housing in which bathrooms (and perhaps kitchens) are shared. It is argued that allowing such single-room-occupancy (SRO) housing to be provided at very low rents might encourage many homeless people to leave the streets.

Figure 7.8 illustrates this argument. When regulations require housing consumption to exceed a minimum level q_{min}, the lower dashed part of the budget line becomes inaccessible. Even though, in the absence of the regulation, the low-income individual would choose to rent a very small dwelling of size q^*, the q_{min} threshold essentially leaves two choices: rent the smallest available dwelling, of size q_{min} (larger dwellings are dispreferred), or become homeless, setting $q = 0$. In the

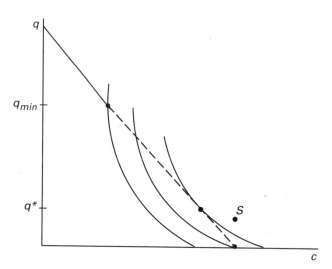

Figure 7.8
The effect of a minimum dwelling size.

situation illustrated, the homeless choice lies on a higher indifference curve than the minimum-size dwelling, so that homelessness is the outcome. However, if the minimum-size requirement were eliminated, say by legalizing SRO housing, the individual would chose to rent a small unit of size q^*, moving off the streets into appropriate shelter.[11]

As the above analysis shows, apparently well-meaning policies such as a minimum dwelling size can backfire to produce unintended harmful effects. The government wants to help consumers by requiring developers to provide "proper" dwellings, but by making housing unaffordable for individuals with very low incomes, such a policy drives them into homelessness. Evidently, this possible link between housing regulations and homelessness is becoming more widely appreciated, and policies are changing accordingly.

Charitable shelters can address homelessness by accommodating people who are homeless either because of substance abuse or because of the unaffordability of the smallest available dwellings. A charitable shelter allows an individual to consume a small positive amount of housing at zero cost, generating a consumption point like S in figure 7.8, which lies directly above the horizontal intercept of the budget line. S is preferred to homelessness, and in the situation illustrated, it is also

---

11. Exercise 7.2 provides a numerical example based on figure 7.8.

better than the minimum-size dwelling. In the substance-abuse case, S will also be preferred to homelessness. Therefore, charitable shelters are one remedy for homelessness, although their reliance on limited private donations may constrain their capacity.

Some cities have more homelessness than others. Quigley, Raphael, and Smolensky (2001) show that there is more homelessness in cities where rents are high and housing vacancy rates are low. A temperate climate also encourages homelessness.[12]

7.5 Summary

Rent-control laws, which limit the rents that landlords can charge, are a common type of government intervention in the housing market, but they have negative effects. Rent control leads to undermaintenance of existing dwellings and reduces the incentives to construct new ones. By making tenants reluctant to move out of cheap rent-controlled housing, rent control also distorts the allocation of households to dwellings. Housing-subsidy programs also are meant to make housing more affordable, and their effects differ depending on the design of the subsidy. Public housing and proportional rent subsidies lead to a larger increase in housing consumption by low-income households than other programs. This effectiveness in slum reduction may lead higher-income taxpayers (who finance subsidy programs) to favor programs of these kinds. Homelessness can be addressed by subsidies and by the availability of charitable shelters, but elimination of housing regulations that limit the availability of small dwelling units can also help.

---

12. See also Honig and Filer 1993.

8 Local Public Goods and Services

8.1 Introduction

In the United States, most of the public goods and services that people consume are provided by local jurisdictions, not by the federal or state governments. The federal government provides national defense, interstate highways, national parks, and some other less visible public goods and services. State governments provide highways, parks, and higher education through systems of public universities. But it is local governments that provide elementary and secondary education, police and fire protection, mass transit, city streets, recreational facilities, public health facilities, sewers and sanitation, and other goods and services. These goods play a bigger role in people's daily lives than the goods provided by higher levels of government. As a result, the economics of local public goods and services constitutes an important segment of urban economics.

There are many types of local governments in the United States. The most important are cities, counties, and school districts. Another type of government is the "special district," which provides a particular public good (say, sewage and sanitation) over an area that doesn't necessarily match up with the boundaries of cities or counties. This complexity of local governmental structures isn't fully captured in the present chapter. But the analysis focuses on the most crucial feature of the local public sector: the fact that there are "many" local governments, in contrast to the existence of a single federal government and relatively few (fifty) state governments.

The multiplicity of local governments means that people can change their consumption of public goods and services by changing the jurisdiction in which they live. For example, within a given metropolitan area, a family can move from a school district with poorly funded schools to one with well-funded schools, or from a city with few poorly maintained parks, to one with many well-maintained parks. Such freedom of choice through location is not so easily available when it comes to public goods and services provided by the federal or state governments. Getting affordable access to better public higher education, for example, may require a major move to another state,[1] and a different level of national defense isn't available at all unless one is willing to move to another country.

Moving from one local jurisdiction to another in order to get a different level of public goods and services is called "voting with one's feet," and it plays a major role in the economics of the local public sector. To develop this theme, the chapter starts with an analysis of "socially optimal" provision of a particular public good: police protection. The crucial feature of a public good is that consumption of the good (the protection offered by a policeman) is "shared" among consumers. Given this property, the "social" benefit from an added unit of the public good is found by summing the additional benefit from the extra unit across all the residents, who share consumption of the unit. The social benefit is then compared with the cost of the extra unit. When the two are equal, the level of provision of the public good is socially optimal.

In Western countries, the democratic process guides the provision of public goods, but the process need not lead to a socially optimal outcome. The voting process is likely to lead to the wrong level of the public good, one either higher or lower than the socially optimal level. But this conclusion can be overturned by voting with one's feet. When people are free to move across jurisdictions in search of their desired levels of public goods, the right outcome emerges. Each jurisdiction ends up providing a public-good level that is socially optimal for its population. Indeed, according to the theory, voting with one's feet should lead to very simple jurisdictional population compositions. Jurisdictions end up being homogeneous in the strength of individual demands for the public good, with each resident desiring the same level of that good. Some jurisdictions will be populated entirely by higher demanders of the public good and others entirely by low demanders.

This view of the local public sector, which is based on a famous article by Charles Tiebout (1956), is developed in sections 8.2–8.4, which

---

1. A family could send a child to an out-of-state university without itself moving, but at a much higher cost than attending an in-state university.

also discuss various elaborations and refinements of the theory. Section 8.5 discusses another method beyond majority voting for choosing a jurisdiction's public-good level: property-value maximization. Section 8.6 discusses tax and welfare competition.

The ideas developed in this chapter apply to an economy in which local jurisdictions have substantial autonomy, being fully free to set taxes and choose the levels of public goods. Such autonomy exists in the United States, in Canada, and in a few other countries, but elsewhere local governments have less freedom. For example, localities may receive much of their revenue from higher levels of government, which may also dictate the public-good levels that are to be provided.[2] Although a desire to follow the U.S. model has spurred some movement toward fiscal decentralization in countries around the world, it should be borne in mind that in most countries, local governments still have less autonomy than the ones depicted in this chapter.

8.2   The Socially Optimal Level of a Public Good

To illustrate the choice of the socially optimal level of a public good, a stylized example is useful. Suppose that the public good in question is police protection, and let the level of the good be represented by the number of policemen on the force, denoted by z. As z increases, the level of police protection (and hence public safety) rises. Suppose that the jurisdiction contains only three people, with consumer A living in a large house, consumer B in a medium-size house, and consumer C in a small house. Suppose that all three consumers worry about burglary, which generates a loss that depends on the size of one's house. Big houses contain more things that can be stolen.

By reducing potential burglary losses, additional policemen generate dollar benefits for the consumers (table 8.1). The first policeman added to the force generates a $19,000 (annual) benefit for consumer A, a $16,000 benefit for consumer B, and a $13,000 benefit for consumer C, with the differences due to the different sizes of the consumers' houses. This policeman patrols the entire city, passing by each house and thus deterring burglars at each location.

Adding a second policeman to the force allows a higher frequency of patrols, reducing the chances of burglary and generating additional benefits. But since the second policeman just adds to existing

---

2. See Ter-Minassian 1997 for a survey of local fiscal arrangements in a broad set of countries.

Table 8.1
The socially optimal number of policemen (policeman's salary = $24,000).

Number of policemen (z)	Marginal benefit for consumer A	Marginal benefit for consumer B	Marginal benefit for consumer C	Marginal social benefit
1	$19,000	$16,000	$13,000	$48,000
2	$17,000	$14,000	$11,000	$42,000
3	$15,000	$12,000	$9,000	$36,000
4	$13,000	$10,000	$7,000	$30,000
5	$11,000	$8,000	$5,000	$24,000
6	$9,000	$6,000	$3,000	$18,000
7	$7,000	$4,000	$1,000	$12,000

protection, these benefits are $2,000 smaller than those from the first policeman, amounting to $17,000, $14,000, and $11,000 for consumers A, B, and C, respectively. Additional policemen beyond two generate further benefits for each consumer, but the previous pattern persists, with the "marginal" benefits becoming smaller as policemen are added.

Since an additional policeman protects all three houses, he generates a marginal social benefit equal to the sum of the marginal benefits across the three consumers. Thus, the first policeman generates a marginal social benefit of $19,000 + $16,000 + $13,000 = $48,000, and the second generates a marginal social benefit of $42,000. These marginal social benefits are shown in the last column of table 8.1.

Suppose that a policeman's salary is $24,000. Then, adding another policeman to the force is desirable as long as the marginal social benefit is at least $24,000. According to table 8.1, the socially optimal size of the police force is equal to five officers. The fifth policeman generates benefits of $24,000, exactly equal to his salary, which makes him just worth hiring.

The marginal-benefit numbers in table 8.1 generate demand curves for the public good. In figure 8.1 these demand curves are labeled D_A, D_B, and D_C. The height up to a demand curve at a particular z value shows the marginal benefit from an increase in z, starting at that value. Marginal social benefit, equal to the sum of the individual marginal benefits, can be represented by a curve equal to the vertical sum of the individual demand curves. The resulting curve is labeled D_Σ in the figure (Σ denotes summation), and its height at a particular z equals the sum of the heights of D_A, D_B, and D_C at that z value.

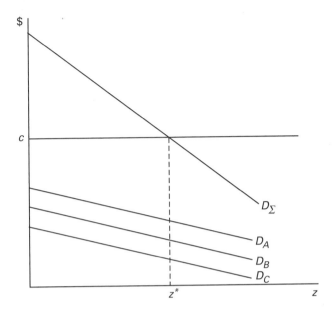

Figure 8.1
Socially optimal z.

Let the cost per unit of the public good (in the above example, a policeman's salary) be denoted by c. This cost is represented by the horizontal line in figure 8.1, whose height is c. Then the socially optimal level of z, denoted by z^*, lies at the intersection between the D_Σ curve and the c line. At z^*, the marginal social benefit from an additional unit of z (the height up D_Σ) is just equal to its cost, c. This diagram generalizes to a jurisdiction containing an arbitrary number of consumers. The D_Σ curve is then the vertical sum of a larger number individual demand curves, but z^* is again given by the intersection with the c line.

8.3   Majority Voting and Voting with One's Feet

8.3.1   Majority voting
Whereas an omnipotent social planner would set the public good at the socially optimal level, democratic societies choose z through a voting process. To analyze this process, suppose that consumers pay a uniform tax to cover the cost of the public good. If the jurisdiction contains three consumers, the total cost of a public good (equal to cz) is divided three ways, yielding a tax of $cz/3$ for each consumer. The cost per unit of z for each consumer is then $c/3$. In the police

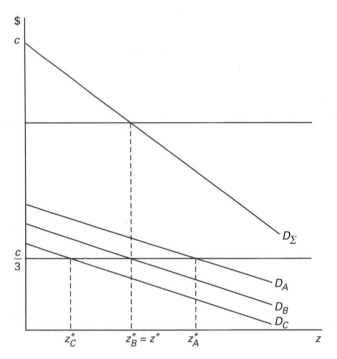

Figure 8.2
Majority voting.

example, each consumer would pay one-third of a policeman's salary: $24,000/3 = $8,000. In figure 8.2, this per capita cost is represented by the horizontal line at height $c/3$.

A consumer's preferred level of z (the preferred size of the police force) lies at the intersection between his demand curve and the $c/3$ line. In figure 8.2, these preferred levels are denoted by $z_A{}^*$, $z_B{}^*$, and $z_C{}^*$. At $z_A{}^*$, for example, consumer A's marginal benefit from an additional unit of z (the height up to D_A) equals the per capita cost of a unit of z ($c/3$), which indicates that no further increase is desirable for consumer A.

When consumers prefer different levels of z, a voting process is needed to reduce this disparity of views to a single choice. The model used by economists and political scientists to represent the voting process is known as the "median voter model." It portrays elections within a two-party system, with two candidates competing for votes by promising to provide particular levels of the public good if elected. Since a consumer votes for the candidate promising the z level closest to his preferred level, a candidate can attract more votes by moving to the "center," advocating a z in the middle of the range of preferred levels. In fact, a candidate who promises to provide the median among the preferred z levels is unbeatable in a two-way contest. The model thus predicts that the median preferred level is the one chosen under the voting process. In figure 8.2, the voting process thus leads to a public-good level of z_B^*, the median preferred level among the three voters. Thus, the "median voter" determines the outcome.

To judge the performance of the voting process, this median value must be compared with the socially optimal level, z^*. In the situation depicted in figure 8.2, the two levels happen to be the same. The reason is that the individual demand curves happen to be evenly spaced, with the vertical gap between D_C and D_B equal to the vertical gap between D_B and D_A. As a result, the height up to the D_Σ curve is exactly 3 times the height up to the median voter's demand curve, D_B. Therefore, the z value where the D_B curve intersects the $c/3$ line (chosen under the voting process) is the same as the value where the D_Σ curve (which is 3 times as high) intersects the c line. When these two values, z_B^* and z^*, are identical, the voting outcome is socially optimal.

This outcome, however, is just an accident. Suppose, for example, that the D_A curve were higher than in figure 8.2—an outcome that could be generated in the police example by adding, say, $2,000 to each of the marginal-benefit numbers in the second column of table 8.1. With the D_A curve higher, vertical summation would also lead to a higher D_Σ curve and a larger z^*. In figure 8.3, the new curves are labeled D_A^+ and D_Σ^{+} and the new z^* value is $z^{+\cdot}$ Since the lack of change in D_B leaves the median preferred z level unchanged at z_B^*, while socially optimal level rises to z^{*+}, the voting process now leads to *underprovision* of the public good.

The opposite outcome, *overprovision* of z, can also occur. For example, if the lower demand curve, D_C, were shifted downward (by reducing consumer C's marginal-benefit numbers in table 8.1), then the socially optimal level z^* would fall while z_B^* would again remain the same. Then, $z^* < z_B^*$ would hold, indicating that the voting process provides too much of the public good.[3]

The problem with the voting process is that it *fails to register the intensity of preferences for non-median voters*. The social planner, in contrast, takes the preferences of all voters into account in determining z^*.

---

3. Exercise 8.1 provides a numerical illustration of these possibilities.

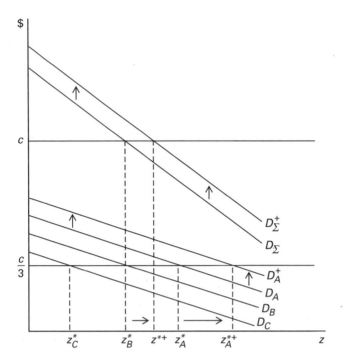

Figure 8.3
Inefficiency of majority voting.

As in the first situation above, this failure isn't problematic when the pattern of demands is symmetric, in which case the high and low intensities balance one another. But when the pattern is asymmetric, as in the latter two cases, the failure to properly register demand intensities distorts the outcome. Stated differently, voting works fine when the median demand for z is equal to the *mean demand*, which occurs when the demand pattern is symmetric. But when the median demand differs from the mean demand, as in the latter two cases, the voting process goes astray.[4]

8.3.2 Voting with one's feet
Under the voting outcome, consumer C gets more public good than he wants and consumer A gets less than he wants. These disparities

---

4. Formally, the mean demand curve in the three-person case is $D_\Sigma/3$, a curve with one-third the height of the D_Σ curve. When this curve coincides with the median demand curve, the voting outcome satisfies $D_\Sigma/3 = c/3$. But this condition reduces to the social optimality condition, which is $D_\Sigma = c$. For a general analysis of the inefficiency of the voting process, see Bergstrom 1979.

provide the motivation for voting with one's feet. If a dissatisfied consumer could move to another jurisdiction that provided his preferred amount of z, he would do so, in the absence of other impediments to relocation.

As an illustration of this point, consider a situation with only two types of consumers: high-demand type-A consumers and low-demand type-C consumers. Suppose there are two jurisdictions, each with population of 100 but with different mixes of type-A and type-C consumers. Whereas jurisdiction I has 10 A-types and 90 C-types, jurisdiction II has 90 A-types and 10 C-types. Given the 100-person sizes, the per capita cost per unit of z equals $c/100$ in each jurisdiction.

Figure 8.4 illustrates the situations in the two jurisdictions. In jurisdiction I, the median voter is a C-type, so that the jurisdiction's public good, z_I, equals z_C^*. In jurisdiction II, the median voter is an A-type, so that $z_{II} = z_A^*$. The D_Σ curves in the two jurisdictions aren't shown, but since the higher type-A preferences don't register in jurisdiction I's voting outcome (since C-types are the majority), the public good is *underprovided*. Conversely, since the lower type-C preferences don't register in jurisdiction II, where the median voter is an A-type, the public good is *overprovided*.

In this situation, the incentives for voting with one's feet are clear. The type-A voters in jurisdiction I can increase their consumption level

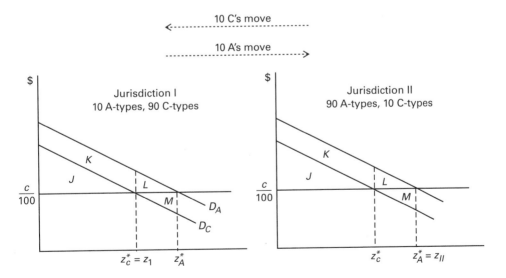

Figure 8.4
Voting with one's feet.

from $z_I = z_C^*$ to their preferred level of z_A^* by moving to jurisdiction II. The C-type voters in jurisdiction II can reduce their consumption level from $z_{II} = z_A^*$ to their preferred level of z_C^* by moving to jurisdiction I. Thus, 10 voters of each type will trade places, and the two jurisdictions will end up homogeneous, with jurisdiction I containing 100 C-types and jurisdiction II containing 100 A-types. Note from the figure that the consumer-surplus level of the relocating A-types rises from $J + K$ to $J + K + L$, and that the surplus level of the relocating C-types rises from $J - M$ to J.

In each of the new homogeneous jurisdictions, all consumers agree on the level of z. In addition, the level of the public good is socially optimal in each jurisdiction. The reason is that, with homogeneous demands for z, the mean and median demands are necessarily the same, so that the voting process generates an optimal outcome. Put differently, there are no non-median demands that fail to register in the voting process, making it efficient. It is interesting to note that a socially optimal outcome has been achieved not by changing the z levels in the jurisdictions, but instead by *changing their population compositions* so that the existing z levels exactly match the demands of the residents.

8.3.3   Observations on the outcome under voting with one's feet

Under the majority-voting process, individuals in some sense lack freedom of choice, since they may have to settle for a public-good level different from their preferred one. But voting with one's feet creates freedom of choice, mimicking a market outcome. In other words, even though a consumer cannot usually satisfy his or her preferences as a voter, a consumer can "shop" for the public-good level he or she prefers through choice of a place to live, as if z were being bought in a market.

The theory says that this "shopping" process should end up creating homogeneous jurisdictions, each filled with individuals whose public-good demands are identical. If demand differences are due to differences in consumer incomes, then the prediction is that jurisdictions should be homogeneous by income, with some jurisdictions poor and some rich. Rich jurisdictions would provide high levels of the public good, and their residents would pay high taxes. Poor jurisdictions would provide lower levels of z, and they would levy lower taxes, in keeping with their residents' lesser ability to pay.

Is this strong prediction of the theory accurate? On the one hand, cities do tend to differ in incomes, being viewed as high-income, middle-income, or low-income places. But this separation is by no means sharp, with most cities containing a diversity of income levels.[5]

Since the model is highly stylized, leaving out many aspects of reality, an imperfect match between its predictions and real-world patterns is to be expected. For example, the model assumes that public goods are the only factor determining locational choice, when in fact many other considerations matter. A consumer's job location, for example, may make moving to another city impractical even though that city offers a preferred public-good level. This obstacle is especially relevant when the urban areas in question are relatively isolated and not especially large, as in the case of cities dispersed across an agricultural region. Job considerations, however, may be less of an obstacle to voting with one's feet in a large metropolitan area. If a consumer works in central business district of the metropolitan area, he could alter his public-good consumption while keeping the same job by simply moving from one suburban bedroom community to another, which would only require changing the commute trip to work. Other obstacles to voting with one's feet may exist, including family ties that restrict mobility or preferences for amenities (a peaceful rural environment, or a view of the ocean) that may be lost after a move.

Despite these obstacles, public goods and services appear to play a substantial role in location decisions for many households. Families with school-age children, for example, often pay close attention to school quality when selecting a place to live in a large metropolitan area, choosing a school district with the best possible schools (subject to the affordability of taxes and housing). Thus, even though real-world patterns do not match the model's homogeneity predictions closely, the notion of voting with one's feet seems to contain a strong element of truth.

8.3.4 Voting with one's feet under a property-tax system

The analysis so far assumes that consumers pay a "head tax" of cz/n that is equal to their per capita share of the cost of the public good. This tax is the same for all residents of a jurisdiction, rich or poor. In reality, however, much of the funding for public goods at the local level comes from the property tax, with the tax payment depending on the size of the consumer's house and thus ultimately on his or her income.

---

5. Real-world evidence on the homogenization of jurisdictions is mixed. See, for example, Strumpf and Rhode 2003; Pack and Pack 1978.

Does voting with one's feet work the same way under a property tax as it did under a head tax? In particular, do rich and poor consumers still have an incentive to form homogeneous jurisdictions? Under a head tax, poor consumers did not want to move into a rich jurisdiction, even though its high public-good level is attractive, because the tax burden is too large for their low incomes. The property tax changes this picture by giving poor consumers a tax break when moving into a rich jurisdiction. Because they live in small houses, the poor end up paying *less than their per capita share of public-good costs* after the move. Even though they lose their majority status, thus having to settle for the rich consumers' public-good choice, this tax break may make the move worthwhile.

To analyze these incentives, suppose that the rich (R) and the poor (P) live in homogeneous jurisdictions of size 100, as in figure 8.4. If a jurisdiction is homogeneous, it doesn't matter whether a head-tax system or a property-tax system is in place since taxes are equal to $cz/100$ in both cases. Thus, in these two communities, the per capita cost per unit of z is $c/100$ under a property tax, just as in figure 8.4. The chosen levels of public goods are given by z_R^* and z_P^*, as shown in figure 8.5.

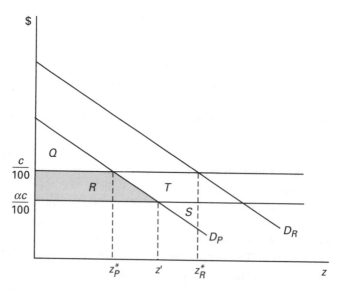

Figure 8.5
Voting with one's feet under a property tax.

Now suppose that a single poor person contemplates moving into the rich jurisdiction. With some algebra, it can be shown that the cost per unit of z for this poor consumer would be $\alpha c/100$, where α is the ratio of the house sizes of the poor and the rich (equal to $q_P/q_R < 1$). Thus, the poor consumer, because his house is smaller, would pay less than his per capita share of the public good's cost. This lower cost is represented by the lower horizontal line in figure 8.5. Although the rich would be subsidizing this poor consumer's tax break, the increase in their per capita cost would be negligible, since only one poor person would have arrived. Therefore, a rich household's cost per unit of z would remain at $c/100$.

Now consider whether the poor household would benefit from such a move to the rich community. His surplus level in the original homogeneous poor community, where $z = z_P{}^*$, equals Q. In the rich community, the poor consumer would get the public-good level $z_R{}^*$ chosen by the rich, but he would pay only $\alpha c/100$ per unit. As a result, the poor consumer's surplus level would equal Q + R − S. Because of the cost break, the consumer would enjoy a surplus gain of R on all the units of z up to z' but would suffer a loss of S on the units between z' and $z_R{}^*$. But since R > S holds in the situation shown in the figure, the consumer would come out ahead, enjoying a surplus greater than the original level of Q. Therefore, the poor consumer has an incentive to move into the rich jurisdiction, and the original homogeneous pattern would break down. If the head-tax system were in place instead, the consumer would lose by moving to the rich jurisdiction. His surplus level would fall from Q to Q − (T + S), making the move undesirable.[6]

It is easy to see that, if the difference between the house sizes of the poor and the rich narrows, so that α rises and the two horizontal lines in figure 8.5 get closer, then the S area grows and the R area shrinks. By reducing the poor consumer's tax break, this change may create a surplus loss, eliminating the incentive to move.[7] The same outcome could happen if the rich demand curve were to move outward, indicating a relatively stronger demand for the public good among rich households. Then, although the R area would stay the same, the S area would grow, potentially creating a surplus loss for the poor consumer. Because the rich now would demand more of the public good, having to settle

---

6. Note that, in contemplating his move, the poor resident ignores his effect on the population of the rich jurisdiction, which would increase from 100 to 101.

7. Exercise 8.2 offers a numerical example illustrating these different outcomes.

for their z choice would create a bigger downside for the poor than before, potentially eliminating the incentive to move.

This analysis shows that under a property-tax system, voting with one's feet may no longer lead to the formation of homogeneous jurisdictions.[8] The poor may have an incentive to move into rich communities in order to benefit from the resulting tax break. However, rich jurisdictions may take steps to prevent this entry, thus enforcing separation of the two income groups.[9] These steps involve the imposition of "fiscal zoning," which effectively restricts the minimum allowable house size in a jurisdiction. By forcing poor consumers to live in bigger houses than they can afford, fiscal zoning eliminates their incentive for entry. In practice, fiscal zoning is implemented through minimum-lot-size restrictions, which make conforming houses unaffordable for lower-income consumers.

8.3.5   Equity issues under voting with one's feet

Although separation of the rich and poor into homogeneous jurisdictions is "efficient," with each consumer type getting exactly its preferred level of the public good, the outcome may seem inequitable. For example, if the public good in question is education, the poor end up living in jurisdictions with low taxes and correspondingly poor schools, matching their low incomes. Society may view this outcome as unfair and undesirable.

One widely practiced remedy for this inequitable educational outcome is state aid to local school districts. Under such an arrangement, some state tax revenue (collected through state income and sales taxes) is distributed to school districts, with poor districts getting more aid than rich ones. The goal is to even out differences in school quality, so that low-income children aren't penalized in educational access by the low tax bases in their areas of residence. However, differences in school quality typically remain despite the existence of state-aid systems, so that incentives to vote with one's feet are still present.

8.3.6   Voting with one's feet and urban sprawl

The incentives for consumers to separate into homogeneous jurisdictions may have spatial implications. As consumers vote with their feet,

---

8. For a formal counterpart to this analysis, see Wheaton 1993.

9. Although the first poor entrant has a negligible effect on the rich residents in the above analysis, subsequent entry will end up raising cost per unit of z for the rich, making them worse off.

an existing central city containing both rich and poor households is likely to lose its rich residents, who will coalesce into homogeneous rich jurisdictions. Where will these jurisdictions be located? Most likely, they will emerge on the urban fringe, in the form of new suburban communities. But the emergence of these communities will expand the spatial size of the metropolitan area, contributing to urban sprawl. Thus, voting with one's feet may be a culprit in the sprawl phenomenon.[10]

As rich households leave the central city, their departure is likely to create fiscal distress. The previous public spending level in the central city, which probably reflected a compromise between rich and poor demands, becomes unsustainable in the absence of high-income residents. A painful process of cutting the central city's budget must then ensue.

One remedy for such fiscal distress is aid from a higher level of government. Although state-aid systems can help central cities cope with the loss of rich households, another often-suggested remedy is the creation of a metropolitan-area-wide governmental structure, which would allow resources to be transferred from the suburbs to the central city. However, political support for this remedy may be lacking, given that it cancels some of the gains that rich households reap by forming their own homogeneous jurisdictions.

8.3.7   Voting with one's feet and peer-group effects

Voting with one's feet may reduce the benefits from "peer-group effects"—neighborhood effects (see chapter 7) that usually arise in an educational context. In the classroom, disadvantaged students from low-income households typically perform better if their peers include higher-income students, who benefit to a greater extent from costly extracurricular activities (tutoring, computer access, music lessons, and so on) that may raise their level of general knowledge and make them more receptive to learning.[11] But since voting with one's feet tends to divide income groups into separate homogeneous jurisdictions, these peer-group benefits for low-income students may be reduced. Group separation may also reduce peer-group effects not directly related to education, such as the role-model benefits that come from residential intermixing of lower-income workers and successful higher-income employees.[12]

---

10. Nechyba and Walsh (2004) argue this point.
11. For recent empirical evidence, see Hanushek et al. 2003.
12. For theoretical analyses of such losses, see de Bartolome 1990 and Benabou 1993.

8.4 Public-Good Congestion and Jurisdiction Sizes

8.4.1 Basics

In the three-person jurisdiction considered above, a public-good level of z could be consumed at a per capita cost of $cz/3$, whereas the same level would cost only $cz/100$ per capita in a jurisdiction of size 100. This dramatic cost saving reflects the implicit assumption that z is a *pure public good*, which means that a fixed spending level can be spread over more and more people as the population grows without any loss in consumption of the good. This assumption is unrealistic for most public goods, since spending usually must increase as the jurisdiction's population grows in order to maintain public consumption.

In order to understand this point, consider the police example that was used above. In the three-person jurisdiction, imagine that the houses of the three consumers are far enough apart that it takes an hour for a single police patrol to pass by each house. Thus, if the jurisdiction has one policeman, he passes each house once per hour. If it has two policemen on staggered patrols, each house is passed by two patrols per hour, and so on. The number of patrols per hour (a natural measure of police protection) is then equal to the number of policeman on the force.

Now suppose that the jurisdiction doubles in size to six consumers, and that its spatial area doubles as a result. Now one policeman has farther to travel and can pass by each house only once every 2 hours instead of hourly. Thus, with one policeman, patrols per hour would equal 1/2, and with two policemen, patrols per hour would equal 1. To maintain a given level of police protection, say one patrol per hour, the number of policemen on the force therefore must double from 1 to 2 when the community population doubles. To keep patrols per hour constant at 2, the police force again must double (from two to four officers), and a similar doubling is required for other target values of patrols per hour.

Alternatively, the city might become denser as its population doubles, so that its spatial area would less than double. Then, to maintain a particular number of police patrols per hour as the city population doubles, the size of the police force could *less than double*.

When additional resources are needed in this fashion to keep public consumption constant as a jurisdiction's population grows, the public good is said to be *congested*. To represent the cost of providing a congested public good, let n denote the jurisdiction's population size.

Then, the cost parameter c from above is replaced by an increasing function $c(n)$ that depends on n. The cost of providing a public consumption level z to the jurisdiction's n residents is then equal to $c(n)z$. In the police example, z would be patrols per hour, and $c(n)$ would be proportional to n in the case in which the city's spatial area doubles when population doubles.[13] The function would increase less than proportionally with n in the rising-density case.

Whereas the above discussion considered several different arbitrary jurisdiction sizes ($n = 3$, $n = 100$), an *optimal* jurisdiction size usually emerges when the public good is congested. The optimal size is the value of n that minimizes the per capita cost of the public good. The cost per capita is $c(n)z/n$, and for any z, this cost is lowest at the n value that minimizes $c(n)/n$. Figure 8.6 shows the graph of $c(n)/n$, which is depicted as U-shaped, and the resulting optimal jurisdiction size, denoted by n^*. Consumers will be best off if they live in jurisdictions of size n^*, getting the public good as cheaply as possible.

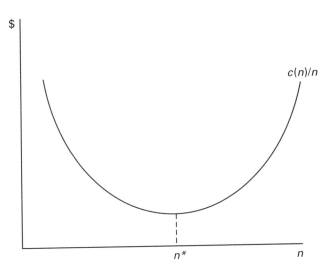

Figure 8.6
Optimal jurisdiction size.

13. Since the cost of providing one patrol per hour to three residents is $24,000 (one policeman's salary), the cost of providing one patrol per hour to n residents is $(n/3)24,000$. The cost of providing z patrols per hour is then equal to $(n/3)24,000z = 8,000nz$. Hence, in this case $c(n) = 8,000n$. Whereas the above formulation requires cost $c(n)z$ to be proportional to z, a more general approach would express the cost of providing consumption z to n residents as $C(z,n)$ without imposing proportionality. In this case, the optimal jurisdiction size (discussed below) may depend on z.

Two distinct forces exactly balance one another at the optimal jurisdiction size: congestion and cost sharing. As n increases, congestion causes the cost of providing any given z to rise, as captured by the increase in $c(n)$. But the cost of the public good is also spread over more residents, a beneficial effect captured by the n in the denominator of the ratio $c(n)/n$. At the optimal jurisdiction size n^*, these forces just balance, with the loss resulting from additional congestion just canceling the gain from wider cost sharing.

The graph of $c(n)/n$ could have a different shape than the U-shaped form shown in figure 8.6. It could be decreasing over the entire range of population sizes (in which case the largest possible jurisdiction size would be best), or it could be a horizontal line (in which case all jurisdiction sizes would be equally good).[14] Empirical evidence surveyed by Hirsch (1970, chapter 8) suggests that these possibilities are all relevant for particular public goods: $c(n)/n$ is U-shaped in some cases, flat or decreasing in others, and decreasing over an initial range and then flat thereafter in yet other cases. One study cited by Hirsch shows that fire protection is in the last of these categories, the flat range being reached at a population of 300,000. For a more recent study of fire protection, with a finding that is broadly consistent with this latter conclusion, see Brueckner 1981.[15]

8.4.2   Relevance to voting with one's feet

The discussion of figure 8.4 showed that voting with one's feet would lead to the homogenization of the two jurisdictions. The high-demand and low-demand residents who are initially in minorities in their jurisdiction end up switching places, creating homogeneous jurisdictions of size 100. That population size was arbitrary, however, and the argument must be amended to recognize that some jurisdiction sizes are better than others. To make the homogenization story work in general, *all jurisdictions must have the optimal size n^*.*

To see why, suppose that n^* were equal to 500, so that smaller jurisdictions of size 100 would have much higher per capita costs, as in

---

14. The first case arises for a pure public good, where the function $c(n)$ is just a constant independent of n, as in figures 8.1–8.3. Then $c(n)/n$ is decreasing in n. The second case, in which $c(n)/n$ takes a constant value, arises when $c(n)$ is proportional to n, as in the police case considered in note 13. There, $c(n) = 8,000n$, so $c(n)/n = 8,000$. In this case, the public good is said to be a "publicly provided private good."

15. Brueckner's empirical specification allows $c(n)/n$ to be either flat, increasing, or decreasing, and the estimates are consistent with the decreasing case. Brueckner's results would be generated by the data if the per-capita-cost curve initially falls and then flattens out.

figure 8.6. Then suppose that, in addition to the two homogeneous 100-person A-type and C-type jurisdictions in figure 8.4, there existed an optimal-size 500-person jurisdiction inhabited solely by A-types. Would the residents of the two smaller jurisdictions be happy in their homogeneous communities in the presence of this alternative place to live? The A-types would certainly like to move to the larger jurisdiction, since they get the z level they prefer and enjoy lower per capita costs. What about the C-types? They would no longer get their preferred z level (being in the minority in the big community), but the public good they do get would be provided much more cheaply on a per capita basis. Thus, the C-types might also want to move into the big community. But this outcome would overturn the previous story, in which voting with one's feet creates homogeneous jurisdictions with efficient levels of public goods.

For the earlier portrayal of voting with one's feet to be robust, all jurisdictions must be kept at an optimal size. Then there would never be an incentive for the C-types to move in with the A-types just to benefit from a better-sized jurisdiction with lower costs. With each jurisdiction homogeneous and of the optimal size n^*, no consumer would want to leave and move in with the other type. Thus, as long as there is some force pushing populations toward n^*, voting with one's feet will create homogeneous jurisdictions via the logic described above.[16] This outcome, in which the population is divided into homogeneous optimal-size jurisdictions where the z values match the residents' preferences, represents the overall social optimum. It is the best possible economic arrangement for the consumption of local public goods and services.[17]

8.4.3   Multiple public goods and special districts

As was explained earlier, the spatial organization of local governments in the United States is complex, with various levels of overlapping jurisdictions. The concept of optimal jurisdiction size can give some

---

16. Tiebout (1956) made this very argument. The modern literature formalizing Tiebout's idea sketches a more specific institutional structure leading to such an outcome. In this literature, each jurisdiction is run by a competitive, profit-maximizing "community developer" who controls the jurisdiction's population, sets its public-good level, and collects taxes. Voting with one's feet is still present in the sense that consumers are free to move between jurisdictions. But with the developer controlling z, the majority-voting process is no longer operative. For a summary of this literature, see Wildasin 1986 and Scotchmer 1994.

17. Exercise 8.3 provides a numerical illustration of this point. Exercise 8.4 entails calculating the losses when the economy is organized into jurisdictions of the wrong size.

insight into these patterns. Consider figure 8.7, which gives hypothetical $c(n)/n$ graphs for two public goods: police and sewage/sanitation. The optimal jurisdiction size for police is n_P^* and the larger optimal size for sewage/sanitation is n_{SS}^*. In fact, the n_{SS}^* value in the figure is exactly three times n_P^*. In view of this difference, the optimal jurisdictional organization within a large metropolitan area would be the one illustrated in figure 8.8. Whereas police protection would be provided by cities (in effect, "police protection districts"), sewage/sanitation would be provided by "sewage/sanitation districts" which are three times as large. Thus, each of these districts would cover three cities, as shown in the figure. This example is stylized and unrealistic, but it provides the crucial insight that existing patterns of overlapping local governments are a response to differences in the optimal sizes of jurisdictions that provide different public goods.

In some cases, multiple public goods are provided by a single type of jurisdiction. For example, police and fire protection are usually

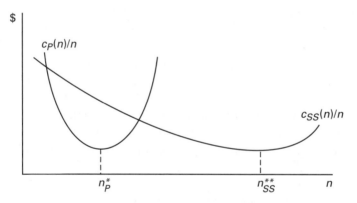

Figure 8.7
Optimal jurisdiction sizes for police and sewage/sanitation.

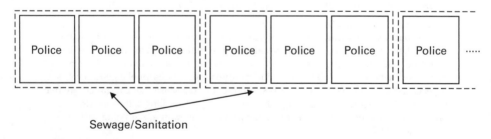

Figure 8.8
Optimal jurisdictions.

both provided by a city government over a common spatial area. However, if these public goods were instead provided by separate jurisdictions, their n^* values probably would be different. Therefore, to explain the existing city-level pattern, some benefit must arise from constraining the provision of police and fire protection so that a common population is served. This kind of benefit could arise from economies of scope, which exist when two different products (here, public goods) can be provided more cheaply by a single firm than by separate firms. Economies of scope in fire and police protection would appear to exist, a consequence of the efficiencies from sharing a common communications network and the greater ease of coordinating police and fire emergency responses over a common spatial area. While these benefits presumably help explain the city-level provision of police and fire protection, the provision of other public goods in separate, single-purpose jurisdictions with different spatial coverages may testify to the lack of economies of scope among these goods.

8.5   Capitalization and Property-Value Maximization

8.5.1   Capitalization

The analysis of voting with one's feet under property taxation in subsection 8.3.4 drew a connection between public goods and the housing market. This connection has been a major focus of research in public economics, with much attention directed to the phenomenon of *capitalization*. This term refers to the link between house prices and public-good levels, which comes from a compensating differential like that in the urban model of chapter 2. The idea is that a renter household should be willing to pay a higher rent in a jurisdiction with a high public-good level than in a community that provides a lower z. The higher rent payment leaves less money for bread, ensuring that utility is the same in the high-z and low-z jurisdictions. Although capitalization thus might appear to undercut the incentive to vote with one's feet, homogeneous communities are still predicted to emerge when it occurs.

Sonstelie and Portney (1980) provide evidence that capitalization indeed affects rents. They use a hedonic rent regression like those discussed in chapter 6, with the regression including measures of public-good levels along with housing characteristics. The public-good coefficients are positive, showing that rents are indeed higher in high-z jurisdictions, with housing characteristics held constant.

Rather than focusing on rents, most empirical research on capitalization studies the link between house values and public goods. House values are linked to rents in a simple fashion. The value of a rental house is just the present discounted value of the net income that flows to its owner. If there are no operating costs, then value is just the present value of the rent flow. With R_j denoting the rent earned by house j and θ denoting the interest rate, the value of house j then equals R_j/θ.[18] But the owners of rental properties face various operating costs, a major one being the annual property-tax payment. If T_j is the property-tax payment for house j, the net income equals $R_j - T_j$, so that the value of the house is equal to $(R_j - T_j)/\theta$.

Since rent still depends on public-good levels, house value as given by this formula also depends on those levels. But the formula shows that another public-sector variable, property taxes, also affects house values. Higher taxes leave less income for a house's owner, thus depressing the house's value.

Since the capitalization effect now includes both property taxes and public-good levels, the Sonstelie-Portney-style hedonic regression must be altered. The regression now uses house value rather than rent as the dependent variable, and the house's property-tax payment (or the jurisdiction's property-tax rate) now appears along with z as an explanatory variable. Following the pioneering work of Oates (1969), dozens of empirical studies have estimated such regressions, finding the predicted positive z effect as well as a negative effect of property taxes.

8.5.2 Property-value maximization

Subsection 8.3.1 established the inefficiency of the majority-voting process and showed that voting with one's feet was one possible remedy. But might there be some other solution that doesn't rely on a wholesale reshuffling of the population? The capitalization phenomenon in fact provides a way for local governments to set public-good levels in a socially optimal manner.

This approach makes use of information that is readily available to the government: property values in the jurisdiction, which are needed to compute individual property-tax bills. Under this approach, the government sets z so as to maximize the jurisdiction's aggregate property value. In other words, the government chooses the z value that

---

18. Note that R denotes total rent, not rent per square foot.

leads to the highest total value of all the jurisdiction's houses. This property-value-maximizing z value turns out to be the same as the socially optimal level, z^*.

To establish this conclusion, suppose that all the houses in a jurisdiction are occupied by renters (an equivalent argument could be made with owner-occupied houses). Then recall that the value of house j equals $(R_j - T_j)/\theta$, where θ is the interest rate. Since the interest rate plays no role in the analysis, let it be set equal to 1, so that the value of house j is $R_j - T_j$. Aggregate property value is then

$$V = \sum_{j=1}^{n}(R_j - T_j) = \sum_{j=1}^{n}R_j - \sum_{j=1}^{n}T_j = \sum_{j=1}^{n}R_j - c(n)z.$$

To get the last expression, note the individual property-tax payments must add up to the cost of the public good, $c(n)z$. The formulas thus show that aggregate property value equals aggregate rent in the jurisdiction minus the cost of the public good.

As was explained earlier, house rents should rise as a jurisdiction's z level increases, reflecting a higher willingness-to-pay to live there. To see this connection using table 8.1, suppose that house A (the one inhabited by consumer A) would command a rent of G_A if there were no police protection at all in the jurisdiction. Since the first policeman generates a benefit of $19,000 for the house's resident, annual rent should then go up by an amount equal to this benefit, rising from G_A to $G_A + 19,000$ if one policeman were hired. Since the second policeman generates $17,000 of additional benefits, rent should rise to $G_A + 36,000$ when a second policeman is added to the force, and so on. The second column of table 8.2 gives the resulting rent levels for house A at different values of z. The next two columns, using the numbers from table 8.1, similarly give the rents for houses B and C at different values of z, with G_B and G_C denoting their "base rents." Aggregate rent is shown in the next column, and the total cost of the public good is shown in the second-to-last column of the table. Aggregate property value, again equal to aggregate rent minus the cost of the public good, is given in the last column.

Aggregate property value is maximized, reaching $60,000, when $z = 5$. The police force then consists of five officers, so that z equals the socially optimal value z^* from table 8.1.[19] Thus, the property-value-maximizing

---

19. Aggregate value also equals $60,000 when $z = 4$, but the larger z value of 5 is chosen. This outcome also occurs in table 8.1, where the gain from hiring the fifth policeman is actually zero, given that the marginal social benefit equals the policeman's cost.

Table 8.2
Property-value maximization.

z	Rent for house A $G_A + \cdots$	Rent for house B $G_B + \cdots$	Rent for house C $G_C + \cdots$	Aggregate rent $G_A + G_B$ $+ G_C + \cdots$	Cost of public good 24,000z	Aggregate property value
1	$19,000	$16,000	$13,000	$48,000	$24,000	$24,000
2	$36,000	$30,000	$24,000	$90,000	$48,000	$32,000
3	$51,000	$42,000	$33,000	$126,000	$72,000	$54,000
4	$64,000	$52,000	$40,000	$156,000	$96,000	$60,000
5	$75,000	$60,000	$45,000	$180,000	$120,000	$60,000
6	$84,000	$66,000	$48,000	$198,000	$144,000	$54,000
7	$91,000	$70,000	$49,000	$210,000	$168,000	$42,000

level of z is socially optimal.[20] The reason for this coincidence is easy to see. The crucial observation is that the increase in aggregate rent caused by hiring another policeman is just equal to the sum of the marginal benefits from the policeman, as can be seen in the construction of table 8.2. Since the change in aggregate property value equals the aggregate-rent change minus the policeman's salary (the change in public-good costs), it follows that aggregate property value goes up only if the sum of marginal benefits exceeds the policeman's salary. But this is the very condition that makes the policeman worth hiring from society's point of view. Thus, when aggregate property value stops rising, reaching a maximum, the sum of the marginal benefits (the marginal social benefit) has become equal to the cost of another policeman, and the level of z is socially optimal.

This analysis shows that if the jurisdictional government were granted authority to set the public-good level, with voters relinquishing their right to set it, then the social optimum could be achieved through property-value maximization. Given that voters cherish their right to decide public issues, such an abandonment of control may seem implausible. But local governments do have the power to make some spending adjustments without direct voter approval, and property-value maximization could guide them to good decisions. More generally, the analysis shows that it is reasonable to pay attention to changes in property values when evaluating the desirability of public policies. In many cities, local Chambers of Commerce often seem to argue this point, and they are right.

20. See Brueckner 1982 for a formal demonstration of this point.

8.6   Tax and Welfare Competition

8.6.1   Tax competition

So far, the existence of many jurisdictions that offer different public-good levels and compete for residents (so as to achieve an optimal size) has been portrayed as beneficial, leading to a socially optimal outcome. But economists have also recognized that interjurisdictional competition has a downside, resulting from particular effects of taxation that have not been considered so far. These effects emerge when jurisdictions rely on a property tax rather than using a head tax to finance public spending.

A property tax leads to unequal tax burdens that may encourage intermixing of the rich and poor (as was seen in subsection 8.3.4). But the tax may also affect the extent of investment in housing in a jurisdiction. A high property tax reduces the return that developers earn from housing investments, and this effect may cause the developers to move their housing capital (the building materials used to produce structures) to a lower-tax jurisdiction where a better return can be earned. Thus, jurisdictions with a high property-tax rate may end up with a low tax base (low investment in housing) as developers move their projects elsewhere. Aware of this reaction, local governments will be reluctant to charge high property-tax rates, and each government will therefore tend to keep its tax rate low. In doing so, each jurisdiction is engaging in what is known as "tax competition." But since property-tax revenue pays for the public good, these low tax rates translate into low levels of z. Each jurisdiction may realize that the resulting public-good level is lower than the one consumers would prefer, but it knows that raising its tax rate so as to raise z would just lead to a counterproductive loss of tax base.

If jurisdictions could somehow agree to raise their tax rates simultaneously, in which case no housing capital would move, then a socially desirable increase in public-good levels could be achieved. But since this kind of tax coordination usually isn't feasible, the outcome with low public-good levels will persist. Tax competition thus leads to underprovision of public goods, according to the theory.[21]

Thus, although local control of public-good provision generates benefits through the possibility of voting with one's feet, it also opens the door to tax competition and its undesirable effects. This trade-off raises an interesting question: Would it be better to eliminate local autonomy

---

21. See Wilson 1999 for a survey of the large theoretical literature on tax competition.

in the provision of public goods, and have the national government dictate a uniform level of z across all jurisdictions along with a uniform property-tax rate? With the resulting centralization of control, voting with one's feet wouldn't be possible, but tax competition would stop. Brueckner (2004) addressed this question and showed that the answer is "It depends." Centralization may be better than local autonomy under some circumstances and worse under others.

8.6.2 Welfare competition

Welfare competition is similar to tax competition. To see how, first note that the welfare system in the United States, which supports poor households with children, is administered at the state level. Each state is free to set the level of its welfare benefits, with the resulting expenditures partly supported by federal grants. As a result, some states offer generous welfare benefits and others are less generous.

Differences in welfare benefits across states may lead to "welfare migration," a phenomenon in which poor households move to generous states in search of a better standard of living. This possibility creates a situation very much like tax competition, with the mobile poor now playing a role like that of housing capital. In particular, with welfare migration, a state will attract a larger poor population if it raises its welfare-benefit level. This inflow creates an extra burden for taxpayers, given that the higher benefit must be paid to the newcomers as well as to the current poor residents. As a result, states will be reluctant to raise welfare-benefit levels, being less generous than they would be if welfare migration didn't occur. Thus, welfare benefits are underprovided, in the same way that public goods are underprovided under tax competition.

A remedy for the resulting underprovision can be implemented through the structure of federal grants. If grants take a "matching" form, with the federal government paying a *percentage* of the state's chosen welfare-benefit level, then the perceived marginal cost to the state of a dollar's increase in welfare benefits will be lower. With the matching rate set correctly, welfare benefits will rise to a socially optimal level despite the drag imposed by welfare migration. Until the mid 1990s, the welfare system did include federal matching grants. But welfare reform replaced this structure with a system of block grants that fails to generate the correct incentives for states.[22]

---

22. See Brueckner 2000c for a survey of the issues related to welfare competition.

8.6.3   Interjurisdictional competition as a disciplinary device

Although local governments have so far been portrayed as acting in the best interests of their residents, other types of behavior are possible. Local governments could produce public goods inefficiently as a result of inattention or laziness. Alternatively, local governments could be efficient producers, but they could engage in "rent seeking," in which some tax revenue is diverted to uses that benefit local officials (nice offices, generous pensions, and so on) without helping consumers.

Competition between jurisdictions might help to limit such undesirable behavior. Jurisdictions in which inefficiency or rent seeking leads to excessive taxes relative to the public goods provided will fail to attract residents who are voting with their feet. They will also fail to attract housing developers, who will build projects in jurisdictions with lower tax burdens. These losses will tend to punish and thus eliminate undesirable governmental behavior, reinforcing the positive side of interjurisdictional competition.[23]

8.7   Summary

At the socially optimal level of a public good, the marginal social benefit of an additional unit is equal to the unit's cost. Majority voting, which often determines the level of public spending, unfortunately doesn't generally lead to socially optimal levels of public goods. But voting with one's feet, in which consumers "shop" across jurisdictions for their preferred public-good levels, can generate the social optimum. Ideally, this process should lead consumers to separate into homogeneous jurisdictions of optimal size, with the residents of each jurisdiction having the same demand for public goods. But real-world frictions prevent this idealized prediction from being perfectly realized. Property-value maximization by local governments offers another way of achieving optimal provision of public goods, though it is not likely to replace the voting process. As jurisdictions worry about the loss of housing investment, tax competition may keep local taxes too low, offsetting the benefits of voting with one's feet. Welfare competition may similarly lead to inadequately generous welfare benefits.

---

23. For a recent contribution to the literature that attempts to measure such competitive effects, see Hoxby 2000.

9 Pollution

9.1 Introduction

Pollution has reduced the quality of life in cities for hundreds of years, especially since the dawn of the Industrial Revolution. Some pollutants affect air quality, and others compromise the quality of groundwater and the water in rivers. Beyond the local effects of pollution, the greenhouse gases produced by all types of combustion contribute to global warming, with potentially harmful long-term effects on the environment.

In developed countries, urban air pollution has become less severe as factories, power plants, and automobiles have gotten cleaner. In addition, rivers and streams are less polluted than they once were. But serious air-quality problems remain in some cities in developed countries (Los Angeles, for example), and severe air pollution continues to afflict many cities in the developing world (Mexico City, for example).

Since air pollution should thus be high on anyone's list of urban problems, it is important to gain an understanding of policies that are designed to reduce it. This chapter serves that goal by analyzing the generation of pollution and policies that attempt to limit it. Section 9.2 considers a simple, stylized setting in which a single factory pollutes a neighborhood, causing harm to the residents. The analysis shows that the air pollution generated by the factory is higher than the socially optimal level. Direct regulation of the factory's pollution level is one way of eliminating excess pollution, and imposition of a pollution tax is another. Section 9.3 considers a different solution: bargaining between the firm that owns the factory and the neighborhood's residents. The analysis derives the famous Coase Theorem, which shows that, under some circumstances, bargaining between the polluter and the affected parties leads to the socially optimal pollution level. Section 9.4 considers a more realistic setting in which many factories contribute to the pollution in an area. In this setting, a "cap-and-trade" system for reducing pollution may be desirable.

9.2   Pollution from a Single Factory and Governmental Remedies

9.2.1   The marginal-damage and marginal-benefit curves

Consider the situation illustrated in figure 9.1: a single factory producing smoke that harms the residents of a surrounding neighborhood. Let the level of pollution from the factory, measured in some fashion, be denoted by P. The neighborhood's residents are harmed by the pollution, which causes health problems, soils their houses, gardens, and cars, and is visually unappealing. Although putting a value on impaired health can be difficult, suppose nevertheless that the damage resulting from the pollution can be measured in dollars. Let the damage resulting from a pollution level of P be denoted by $D(P)$, which is an increasing function of pollution. The damage from an additional unit of pollution is given by the "marginal damage" function, $MD(P)$. This function, plotted in figure 9.2, is also increasing in P, realistically indicating that additional units of pollution are increasingly harmful as the level of pollution grows. The area under the MD curve up to any pollution level P' equals the total damage attributable to that level of pollution, $D(P')$. That area sums the incremental damages from all the successive units of pollution, which are represented by the heights up to the MD curve between zero and P'.

Figure 9.1
Pollution from a factory.

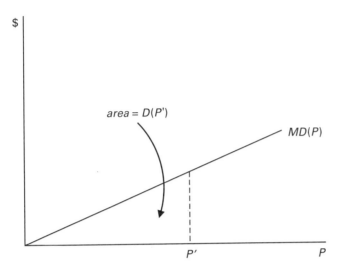

Figure 9.2
Marginal-damage curve.

Although additional pollution is harmful for the residents, it is beneficial for the firm that owns the factory. The reason is that cleaning up pollution is costly. Thus, additional pollution allows the firm to spend less on pollution abatement, which leads to an increase in profit. This profit gain is captured by the "marginal benefit" curve, denoted by $MB(P)$ and plotted in figure 9.3. The height up to the MB curve at a particular P shows the benefit (increase in profit) to the firm from being able to generate an additional unit of pollution starting at the given P, a benefit that comes from lower pollution-abatement costs. Note that the height up to MB also gives the *loss* to the firm from going in the other direction—that is, from reducing P rather than increasing it. If P were reduced rather than increased, the previous benefit would be taken away, abatement costs would rise, and profit would fall. Thus, MB gives both the benefit from additional pollution when P rises and the loss of profit from a reduction in pollution when P falls.

The second interpretation helps to explain the shape of the MB curve in figure 9.3. $\bar{P}$ is the level of pollution generated when the firm spends nothing on pollution abatement. Starting from $\bar{P}$, the first units of pollution reduction are easy to achieve, entailing little cost. Thus, the MB curve has a height of 0 at $\bar{P}$, and its height rises above 0 but stays low as P drops below $\bar{P}$. But as P becomes smaller, further reductions in pollution are increasingly difficult and costly to achieve. Thus, the

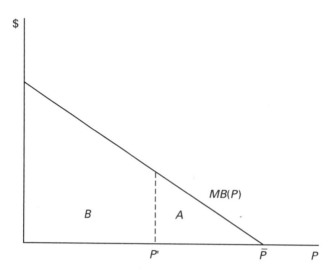

Figure 9.3
Marginal-benefit curve.

height of the *MB* curve continues to rise, reaching an appreciable magnitude, as *P* becomes smaller.

How much does it cost, in abatement expenditures, to reduce pollution all the way from $\bar{P}$ to *P'* in figure 9.3? This cost is equal to the area
A in the figure, which equals the sum of the costs of all the incremental
reductions between $\bar{P}$ and *P'* (that is, the sum of the heights up to *MB*
over this range). Conversely, the area A also shows the total *benefit*
when the factory increases pollution from *P'* up to $\bar{P}$. This benefit
(reflected in higher profit) equals the total abatement cost that no longer
must be incurred.

By this logic, the cost of a complete pollution cleanup, which reduces
P from $\bar{P}$ to zero, is equal to the area A + B. It can be argued, however,
that no amount of money spent on abatement could reduce pollution
all the way to zero, in which case the *MB* curve is misdrawn. To capture
this case, the *MB* curve should increase at an increasing rate as *P* falls,
diverging to infinity as *P* approaches zero (indicating the impossibility
of a complete cleanup). However, since none of the analysis changes
when the curve is instead drawn with the simpler linear form shown
in figure 9.3, that form will be used instead.[1] Under this assumption,
the benefit to the firm of going from a complete cleanup to pollution
level $\bar{P}$ (a result of eliminating all abatement expenditure) is A + B.

---

1. Similarly, it could be argued that the marginal damage from pollution should increase
at an increasing rate. This possibility has no effect on the analysis.

9.2.2 The socially optimal level of pollution

If there were no penalty for polluting, the firm would keep increasing pollution until the marginal benefit from an additional unit was zero. Thus, the firm would choose the "free pollution" level $\bar{P}$, where MB falls to zero and no money at all is spent on abatement. This pollution level is not socially optimal, because the firm considers only its own profit, ignoring the damage to the neighborhood residents. This total damage equals the area under the MD curve up to $\bar{P}$, or C + E + F in figure 9.4. Thus, as is typically the case with negative externalities, the externality-generating activity occurs at too high a level.

To find the socially optimal level of pollution, the interests of both the firm and the residents must be considered. An additional unit of pollution is "desirable" from society's point of view as long as the benefit to the firm from the additional unit exceeds the damage to consumers. This relationship holds as long as the MB curve is higher than the MD curve. Thus, starting at $P = 0$, pollution should be increased up to the point where the MB and MD curves intersect. The resulting pollution level, P^* in figure 9.4, is socially optimal because the benefit from an additional unit of pollution just equals the damage it causes. The socially optimal level of pollution thus lies well below the free-pollution level.

The social loss attributable to over-pollution can be seen in figure 9.4. The damage to the residents when pollution increases from P^* to

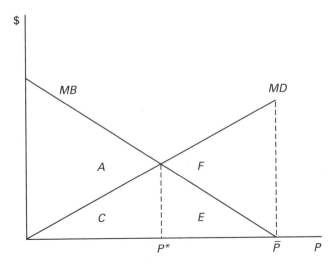

Figure 9.4
Socially optimal level of pollution.

$\overline{P}$ is equal to E + F, while the benefit to the firm is E. Therefore, the damage exceeds the benefit by the area F, which represents the loss of "social surplus" in moving from the social optimum to the free-pollution level.

Social surplus also motivates the choice of P^*. Starting from a pollution level of zero, P should be increased as long as the surplus is rising, which happens as long $MB > MD$. The highest surplus, achieved at $P = P^*$, equals A. It is the difference between the firm's total benefit level at P^* (that is, A + C) and the total damage incurred by the residents (C).

One might ask why the firm and the residents should get equal consideration in determining the social optimum. Shouldn't limiting pollution damage to the residents be society's main consideration? If this approach were adopted, the optimal level of pollution would be zero.

There are two ways of seeing that this approach is wrong. One way is simply to note that the last few units of pollution are very costly to clean up (the MB curve is high when P nears zero), and that these units cause little damage anyway (the MD curve is low in this range). As a result, it makes sense *not* to clean up these units, implying that it is optimal to tolerate some pollution. The second way to see why zero pollution is wrong is to suppose that all the shareholders in the firm that owns the factory live in the neighborhood, and that the firm pays out all of its profits in dividends. Then, starting from $P = 0$, an increase in pollution raises the firm's profits (as captured by MB), and thus raises the residents' dividend income, at the same time that it generates dollar damages. The residents will accept the damage from an additional unit of pollution as long as the increase in their income exceeds the dollar cost of the damages—that is, as long as $MB > MD$. Thus, P^* will be the optimal pollution level from the perspective of these shareholder-residents. This logic applies more broadly insofar as polluting factories are usually publicly owned, so that the owners are victims of the pollution created.

9.2.3   Achieving the social optimum

Whereas industrial factories polluted the environment wantonly through much of the industrial era, it could be argued that nowadays firms pay attention to their corporate images, which can be hurt by unrestrained pollution. Although this point could be used to argue that factories will no longer pollute at level $\overline{P}$, it is almost certainly the case that the socially optimal level, P^*, cannot be achieved without government intervention or some other type of action.

Government intervention could come in either of two forms. On the one hand, the government could regulate pollution directly by imposing a "pollution standard" (a maximum allowable level) equal to the socially optimal level, P^*. A firm seeking to minimize its abatement costs would then choose the largest allowable P, which would equal P^*. In order to implement direct regulation, the government would have to know P^*, and thus it would have to know both the MD curve and the MB curve. To get that knowledge, the government would have to hire medical experts to compute the health damage caused by pollution, and it would have to hire engineers to compute the abatement costs required to achieve different levels of P. With that information, the government could derive the two curves and thus find P^*.

Alternatively, the government could use a tax mechanism to correct the pollution externality, thereby generating the social optimum. One approach would rely on what is known as a Pigouvian tax, after the British economist Arthur Pigou. Under such a tax, the firm would be charged a tax denoted by t per unit of pollution, so that a pollution level of P would generate a tax liability of tP. The government would once again acquire the information needed to compute P^*, and then it would set t equal to the common height of the MB and MD curves at P^*, as illustrated in figure 9.5. The firm would then be free to choose its level of pollution, as long as the appropriate tax was paid.

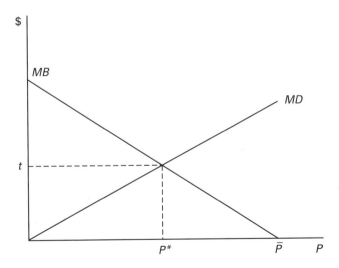

Figure 9.5
Pigouvian tax.

Now, the benefit of an additional unit of pollution to the firm will be lower than before, since a tax of t must be paid on each unit. In particular, the marginal benefit of a unit of pollution, net of tax, is $MB(P) - t$ at pollution level P. In the absence of a tax, the firm would set MB equal to 0 in choosing P, but now it will instead set $MB - t$ equal to 0, which means that it sets MB equal to t. But in view of the derivation of t in figure 9.5, MB equals t only at P^*. Thus, the firm voluntarily sets P at the socially optimal level under the Pigouvian tax.

The government's information requirements for computing the Pigouvian tax are exactly the same as under direct regulation of pollution. It must know the MD and MB curves, so that P^*, and thus the height up to the curves at P^*, can be computed. Another tax scheme, however, has a lower information requirement. Under that scheme, the government announces a tax-liability schedule, which specifies the total tax liability at each level of P. The tax liability is set equal to total damages, so that the liability at pollution level P equals $D(P)$, the area under the MD curve up to P. Under this method, the additional tax owed when an additional unit of pollution is generated is just equal to the marginal damage, $MD(P)$. Therefore, the firm's marginal benefit from an additional unit of pollution, net of tax, is $MB - MD$. The firm keeps increasing pollution until this net marginal benefit equals zero, which happens when $MB = MD$. But since this is the condition defining the social optimum, the firm chooses pollution level P^*.

The information requirements are lower under this tax scheme than under the Pigouvian scheme since the MD curve tells the government all it needs to know. The government doesn't have to hire any engineers to estimate the MB curve, requiring only the health experts' estimates of the damages from pollution (which still aren't easy to compute). Note that, since the total tax collected from the firm equals the residents' pollution damage, their losses from pollution would be exactly canceled if the revenue were transferred to them. In addition, the gain to the firm relative to the zero-pollution case equals its net-of-tax benefit, which in turn equals the gross benefit area A + C in figure 9.4 minus the tax liability, C. Thus, the firm gains A, an amount equal to the social surplus at the optimum.

The information advantages of the non-Pigouvian approach are magnified when there are different types of factories, some "clean" and some "dirty." The cost of a complete pollution cleanup would be lower for a clean factory (indicated by a subscript c) than for a dirty one (subscript d), so that the clean factory's MB curve would be lower, as

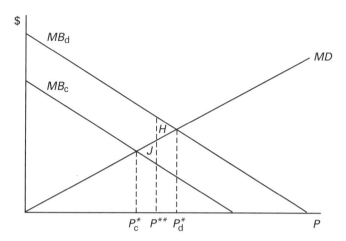

Figure 9.6
Common pollution standard.

shown in figure 9.6. Assuming that the factories are located in identical neighborhoods, with common MD curves, a different P^* exists for each one (P_c^* and P_d^* in the figure). With Pigouvian taxation, knowledge of both MB curves and of MD is required to compute the separate taxes, t_c^* and t_d^*. Under the non-Pigouvian scheme, however, only the MD curve must be known, amplifying its information advantage.

An alternate approach is to set separate pollution standards for clean and dirty factories. But since this approach must confront the same Pigouvian information burden, the government might instead use some rule of thumb to produce a common pollution standard (a uniform maximum level of pollution) for all neighborhoods, denoted by P^{**}, rather than imposing the optimal neighborhood-specific standards, P_c^* and P_d^*. Even if the rule of thumb worked well, so that it fell between these levels, it would still generate a surplus loss relative to a system that imposed correct individual standards. In figure 9.6, the surplus loss would be H + J, where H is the loss from suboptimal pollution from the dirty factory and J is the loss from higher-than-optimal pollution from the clean factory.[2]

Although the discussion has shown that pollution standards and Pigouvian taxes are equivalent in the simple cases depicted in figures 9.4 and 9.5, this equivalence disappears when the MD and MB curves are both stochastic, varying randomly from period to period as a result

2. Exercise 9.1 illustrates this outcome.

of some underlying economic shocks. Then one type of regulation may be better than the other, with the identity of the preferred approach depending on the nature of uncertainty (does it affect MD more than MB or vice versa?) and the shapes of the curves. However, the relevant analysis, first offered by Martin Weitzman (1974), isn't easily illustrated in simple diagrams.

The model developed so far greatly oversimplifies the problem of controlling pollution. In actuality, many polluters (not just a single factory) typically contribute to the pollution that affects consumers in a given neighborhood. In addition, real-world measurement of the MD and MB curves is fraught with difficulty. Section 9.4 discusses pollution policies in a more realistic setting.

9.3   Bargaining as a Path to the Social Optimum: The Coase Theorem

In a famous and influential article published in 1960, Ronald Coase argued that bargaining between the party generating an externality and those affected by it could, under some circumstances, lead to the social optimum. As a result of bargaining, the externality-generating activity would be set at the socially optimal level.

Coase argued that two conditions must be satisfied for this outcome to occur. First, the costs of engaging in the bargaining process must be sufficiently low. If only a few individuals are affected by an externality and only a single party generates it, a bargaining session can be arranged with little cost. But if thousands of people are affected by the externality, it will be difficult and costly to organize a bargaining session in which the interests of all the victims are represented. Bargaining then may not be feasible. In the simple case presented in this chapter, in which a factory pollutes a surrounding neighborhood, suppose that the affected population is small enough that bargaining costs are negligible, satisfying the first of Coase's requirements.

Coase's second requirement is that "property rights" must be assigned. This requirement sounds abstract, but it is easily understood in the context of the factory-and-neighborhood example. In this example, there are two possible assignments of property rights. Under the first assignment, the firm has the right to pollute. Under the second assignment, the neighborhood residents have the right to clean air. Assignment of property rights is necessary because it sets the status quo, the starting point for the bargaining process.

When the firm has the right to pollute, the status quo will be the free-pollution level, $\bar{P}$. To achieve a lower level of pollution, the residents must induce the firm to reduce P, an outcome that requires a cash payment to the firm in order to make the reduction worthwhile. In contrast, when the residents have the right to clean air, the status quo is $P = 0$. In order to avoid having to perform a costly complete cleanup of the pollution, the firm must induce the residents to accept a higher pollution level. It does so by making a cash payment to them.

To understand the role of property rights, imagine the situation if there were no clear assignment of such rights. The firm might then choose the free-pollution level, but the residents would contest its right to pollute that much. While recognizing that a cash payment would make the firm reduce P, the residents, not accepting the legitimacy of the status quo, would not be willing to make such a payment. A property-rights assignment favoring the firm would provide this legitimacy, yielding an unambiguous starting point for bargaining.

To analyze the bargaining process, suppose that the firm has the right to pollute, so that $\bar{P}$ is the status quo, and see figure 9.7. To eliminate one unit of pollution, the residents would be willing to pay an amount up to the height of the MD curve at $\bar{P}$, which represents their dollar gain from lower damages. Conversely, to reduce pollution by one unit, the factory would require a payment at least as large as the height of the MB curve at $\bar{P}$, which equals the abatement cost of eliminating the unit. Since at $\bar{P}$ the minimum amount the factory requires

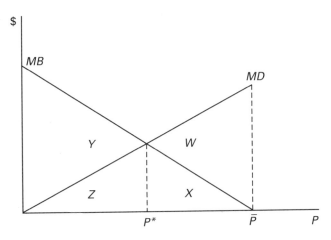

Figure 9.7
Bargaining over pollution.

Table 9.1
Bargaining outcomes when firm has right to pollute (status quo: $P = \bar{P}$).

	Residents' payment to firm	Residents' gain	Firm's gain	Social gain
Firm strong, residents weak	W + X	W + X – (W + X) = 0	W + X – X = W	W
Firm weak, residents strong	X	W + X – X = W	X – X = 0	W

to eliminate a unit of pollution (the *MB* height) is less than the maximum amount the residents are willing to pay to do so (the *MD* height), some payment will occur and pollution will be reduced. Further reductions in pollution are possible as long as the *MD* curve remains above the *MB* curve. However, once *P* has reached *P**, the *MD* and *MB* heights are equal, and the residents will not be willing to pay the firm enough to induce further reductions in pollution. The bargaining outcome is thus a pollution level of *P**, the social optimally level.

The amount of money actually paid to the firm by neighborhood residents depends on the parties' bargaining strengths. It is illuminating to consider several different possibilities, as represented in table 9.1. Suppose that the firm is a strong bargainer while the residents are weak, as shown in the second row of the table. Then, the firm will be able to extract from the residents the maximum amount they would be willing to pay for each unit of pollution eliminated, an amount equal to the height up to the *MD* curve. In moving from the status quo down to *P**, the residents would then end up transferring to the firm an amount equal to the area W + X. Since this amount is just equal to the reduction in total damages in moving from $\bar{P}$ to *P**, the residents gain nothing from the lower pollution, as can be seen in the table. The firm, however, spends only X on pollution abatement in reducing P to *P**, and since it receives a payment of W + X, it gains W. The sum of these gains is thus W, which is just the gain in social surplus from the reduction. This social-surplus gain is captured entirely by the firm.

Now suppose that the firm is a weak bargainer and the residents are strong, as represented in the bottom row of table 9.1. The residents will then pay the minimum amount that the firm requires to eliminate each unit of pollution: the height up to the *MB* curve. The residents will then end up transferring an amount X to the firm as pollution is reduced from $\bar{P}$ to *P**. The firm will gain nothing, as this payment will just cover

Table 9.2
Bargaining outcomes when residents have right to clean air (status quo: $P = 0$).

	Firm's payment to residents	Residents' gain	Firm's gain	Social gain
Firm strong, residents weak	Z	$Z - Z = 0$	$Y + Z - Z$ $= Y$	Y
Firm weak, residents strong	$Y + Z$	$Y + Z - Z$ $= Y$	$Y + Z - (Y + Z) = 0$	Y

its abatement costs. The residents gain W, an amount equal to the reduction in their damages (W + X) minus their payment to the factory firm (X). In this case, the social-surplus gain resulting from lower pollution is captured entirely by the residents.

Table 9.2 represents the bargaining process when the residents have a right to clean air. The status quo is now $P = 0$, and the firm must pay the residents in order to be allowed to raise P. An increase in pollution is feasible as long as the height up to the *MB* curve (the firm's profit gain from an additional unit and thus the most it will pay) is greater than the height up to the *MD* curve (the minimum the residents require to accept incremental damage). Bargaining thus raises pollution to P^*, where the two curves intersect.

If the firm is a strong bargainer and the residents are weak, then the firm pays Z to the residents in moving from $P = 0$ to P^*. The residents gain nothing, and the firm captures the social surplus gain of Y, which equals the reduction in its abatement costs $(Y + Z)$ minus the payment Z. If instead the firm is weak and the residents strong, the firm pays $Y + Z$, gaining nothing, and the residents capture the surplus gain of Y, equal to the payment they receive minus damages Z.[3]

The important observation is that, in each of the four cases represented in tables 9.1 and 9.2, bargaining leads to the socially optimal level of pollution. The amount of the payments between the parties and the direction in which they flow depends on the assignment of property rights and on the parties' relative bargaining strengths, but a pollution level of P^* is always achieved. For the current example, this conclusion is a reflection of the Coase Theorem, which says that, when an externality is present and property rights are assigned, feasible bargaining generates the social optimum.

---

3. Exercise 9.2 generates a numerical example based on tables 9.1 and 9.2.

9.4   Cap-and-Trade Systems

9.4.1   Background

Unfortunately, the stylized pollution scenario discussed so far isn't an accurate depiction of the real-world contexts in which most pollution occurs. For example, in the Los Angeles metropolitan area, air pollution mainly comes from the millions of cars, trucks, and buses using the area's streets and freeways. Thus, rather than emanating from a single source, pollution is generated by a multitude of small sources and a few large polluters. In addition, rather than affecting a single neighborhood, the pollution affects millions of residents over hundreds of square miles of land area. Similarly, the acid rain that affects a wide portion of the Eastern Seaboard of the United States is the result of pollution from a large number of coal-burning power plants and factories scattered across the eastern half of the country. In such situations, bargaining between polluters and victims is obviously not practical as a remedy for the pollution externality.

To control pollution from automobiles, the U.S. government instead relies on direct regulation. Automobile emission standards have greatly reduced the amount of pollution generated by cars in the United States, and fuel-economy standards have compounded these gains by reducing the amount of gasoline burned.

In principle, pollution from large stationary sources (power plants and factories) can be limited by imposing Pigouvian taxes. Government regulators would measure the source's pollution output and levy a tax on each unit of pollution generated. As was explained above, the tax would provide an incentive to install abatement equipment such as smokestack scrubbers, which would reduce pollution and thus reduce the source's tax liability.

Despite the feasibility of pollution taxes, a different system for controlling pollution from stationary sources is used in the United States and Europe. The system has some elements in common with the pollution standard discussed above, and it is known as a "cap-and-trade" system. Under such a system, certificates called "pollution rights" must be acquired in order for a factory or power plant to emit pollution. One pollution right entitles the holder to emit one unit (say, a ton) of pollutants, so that a factory or power plant must acquire a number of pollution rights that exactly matches its pollution output.

Under a cap-and-trade system, the government first decides how much total pollution it will tolerate from polluters in a given area. Then, it distributes (for free) a corresponding total number of pollution rights among these factories and power plants. With this step, total pollution is "capped" since its volume cannot exceed the number of distributed pollution rights. The second feature of the system is that it allows trade. The distributed pollution rights can be "traded" among the holders, a process that would actually rely on a market in which pollution rights are bought and sold. This system would allow dirty pollution sources, for whom cleanup is very costly, to buy more pollution rights than they received under the government distribution. Clean sources, who may have gotten more pollution rights than they need, would sell some of their allocation on the market. Under a variant of the cap-and-trade system, there would be no initial distribution of pollution rights. Instead, the government would simply sell a fixed number of rights, adjusting the price so that demand by polluters equals the fixed supply.

9.4.2 Analysis
A cap-and-trade system has desirable properties, and to understand them, more analysis is needed. Accordingly, consider a region that contains n stationary pollution sources, say factories or power plants. The level of pollution from polluter i is denoted by P_i, where $i = 1, 2, \ldots, n$. Pollution from all these sources stays within the region, and it combines to generate a total pollution level of $P = \sum_{i=1}^{n} P_i$, which is experienced throughout the region (possibly by millions of people). As before, the marginal damage from pollution, which captures the impact on all those affected, is given by $MD(P)$. Each polluter has a marginal-benefit function, which again captures the increase in profit from an additional unit of pollution. Some pollution sources are dirty, with high marginal benefit curves, and some are clean, with low curves (as in figure 9.6). Polluter i's marginal benefit function is $MB_i(P_i)$.

In this setting, the social optimum has a more complicated description than in the previous simple model. Now the optimum is characterized by a total pollution level P^* and by a *distribution* of this total across the n polluters. Each polluter has an individual optimal pollution level, denoted by P_i^* for polluter i, with $\sum_{i=1}^{n} P_i^* = P^*$.

· The social optimum is found in two steps. First, for any given total pollution level P, the optimal distribution of this total across polluters must be found. This distribution is the one that makes total abatement costs as small as possible, holding total pollution fixed at P.

To see what the optimal distribution of pollution requires, suppose that individual pollution levels P_i have been assigned to the polluters, and that they add up to P. Also, suppose that for two polluters, k and j, marginal benefits are different, with $MB_k > MB_j$. The assignment of pollution levels can't be optimal when this inequality holds for any two polluters. To see why, suppose that polluter k is allowed to pollute one more unit while polluter j must reduce pollution by one unit, so that total pollution stays constant at P. Then, polluter k's abatement costs go down by MB_k, while the abatement costs of polluter j rise by MB_j. But since $MB_k > MB_j$, k's cost decrease is larger than j's cost increase, so that total abatement costs fall. This conclusion means that any assignment of pollution levels that leaves marginal benefits unequal between any pair of polluters cannot be optimal. Thus, marginal benefits must be the same for all polluters:

$$MB_1 = MB_2 = \cdots = MB_{n-1} = MB_n.$$

With pollution assigned to equate marginal benefits, the second step is to choose the optimal *total* level of pollution, P^*. This total is chosen using the previous approach: at P^*, the polluters' common MB level is equal to MD.

As before, a substantial amount of information would be needed to compute P^* along with the P_i^* values for the individual polluters. Each polluter's MB curve must be known along with the MD curve. If this information were available, the government could generate the social optimum either by using pollution standards, with maximum pollution levels set for individual polluters, or by using a Pigouvian tax system.

In practice, governments do not have access to all this information. As a result, they make no attempt to compute the optimal total level of pollution. Instead, a government will, in effect, "guess" as to the correct level of P, deciding in some fashion about the total pollution level it will tolerate. But after making such a guess, the next challenge is to distribute the chosen total amount of pollution across polluters in an optimal fashion, leading to the lowest possible abatement cost. The beauty of the cap-and-trade system is that it achieves this goal.

To see how, suppose that the government decides on a total pollution level of $\hat{P}$. It then allocates R_i pollution rights to polluter i, with $\sum_{i=1}^{n} R_i = \hat{P}$, so that the total number of rights allocated equals the chosen level of total pollution. A pollution right market comes into being, so that polluters needing more rights than they were allocated can buy them, and polluters with excess rights can sell them. Let the market price of a pollution right be s.

Initially, each polluter can only pollute up to a level equal to the number of pollution rights it has been allocated. If polluter i wants to set P_i above R_i, then it must buy more pollution rights on the market at the price s. The polluter's benefit from an additional unit of pollution (its profit increase) is MB_i, but it has to pay s for the additional pollution right required to generate an additional unit. Thus, the net benefit of the additional unit of pollution is $MB_i - s$. The polluter will increase its pollution level P_i up to the point where this net benefit equals zero, or $MB_i = s$.

What if a polluter j has too many pollution rights and wants to sell some? In this case, the polluter gets s for selling an additional pollution right, but it then has to reduce its pollution, incurring MB_j in additional abatement costs. The net benefit from selling the pollution right is then $s - MB_j$, and the firm will stop selling rights when this net benefit is zero, or when $MB_j = s$. Thus, regardless of whether a polluter buys or sells pollution rights, it equates its marginal benefit to s in setting its level of pollution.

But if the MB's of all the different polluters are equal to s, then they all equal to one another, just as required under the socially optimal distribution of pollution from above. Therefore, the cap-and-trade system generates a socially optimal outcome, conditional on the government's choice of P. In other words, the cap-and-trade system ensures that the chosen total pollution level will be generated with the lowest possible total abatement costs.[4]

Note that the operation of the pollution-rights market will ensure that sales and purchases of rights exactly balance, an outcome that requires a market-clearing level for the price s. Another observation is that the (conditional) social optimum will also emerge if polluters start out with no pollution rights and must buy them from the government. Then every polluter will be a buyer, and each will set MB equal to the price s in choosing its level of pollution (and its purchase of pollution rights). As before, all the MB's are equal in the end.

A final point is that, when pollution rights are distributed for free, the pattern of distribution can enrich some polluters while putting burdens on others. In particular, firms who are allocated more pollution rights than they need will earn windfall profits from selling the excess, while firms on the buying side, who were initially allocated too few pollution rights, will see their profits depressed by the required outlays.

---

4. Exercise 9.3 illustrates the operation of a market in pollution rights.

9.4.3   Real-world cap-and-trade systems

The 1990 Clean Air Act created the Acid Rain Program, a cap-and-trade system for regulating the emissions of sulfur dioxide (SO_2) from U.S. power plants using fossil fuels (coal, oil, and natural gas). At its outset, the program required 261 power plants in 21 states to cut emissions, with the goal of reducing acid rain in the eastern part of the United States. The plants were given "emission allowances" (pollution rights), and the total allotment decreased over time in order to generate the desired emission reductions. By 2007, the program had reduced SO_2 emissions by 50 percent relative to 1980 levels (Environmental Protection Agency 2009).

The European Union in 2005 instituted a similar cap-and-trade system focusing on emissions of greenhouse gases (carbon dioxide). The system caps emissions from large sources such as power plants and factories, and it covers a substantial share of CO_2 emissions in the EU.

9.5   Evidence on Air Pollution and Property Values

While the harm from air pollution could in principle be measured by asking health experts to estimate it, another approach relies on information from the housing market. If urban residents are harmed by air pollution, then they will not pay as much for a house in a polluted area as for one in an area with clean air. Thus, following the principles of chapter 2, a compensating price differential will emerge between houses in areas with good and bad air quality. This differential can, in turn, be measured using a hedonic price regression like those discussed in chapter 6. The estimated house-price differential is then a measure of the dollar value of good air quality to consumers.

The earliest hedonic air-quality study was by Ridker and Henning (1967), and it used data on average sales prices, property characteristics and neighborhood air quality for census tracts in the St. Louis metropolitan area. Following this study, a large literature developed, and its results are summarized by Smith and Huang (1995). Their overview shows that the estimated value of air quality tends to vary widely across different studies and that it is sometimes small in numerical magnitude. More recently, Chay and Greenstone (2005) took an atypical approach by using county-level data, including the average value of houses in the county, average air quality and other variables, instead of using more disaggregated data.[5] These authors use better statistical procedures than previous studies, which control for the possibility of consumer self-selection across counties on the basis of air quality.[6]

Their results show a larger air-quality impact on house values than most earlier studies, with an estimated elasticity of –0.20 to –0.35 (implying that a 1 percent increase in air pollution reduces the value of a house by between 1/5 and 1/3 of a percent). Using the estimates, the authors calculate that tougher enforcement of U.S. air-quality standards over the 1970s generated an aggregate property-value increase of $45 billion, which represents the dollar benefit to consumers of the resulting air-quality improvement.

9.6   Summary

Since pollution affects urban areas worldwide, it is important to understand the workings of policies that are designed to attack excessive pollution. One remedy for overpollution by a single stationary source like a factory is a pollution standard, which imposes a pollution limit equal to the socially optimal level. Another approach relies on a Pigouvian tax, under which the polluter pays a tax per unit of pollution generated. Although the information requirements for pollution standards and Pigouvian taxes are high, a simpler approach is to use a non-Pigouvian tax, under which the tax liability for any level of pollution is just equal to the total damage it generates. When the costs of bargaining are low and property rights over the pollution externality have been assigned, excess pollution can be eliminated through bargaining between the parties involved. This conclusion (the Coase Theorem) means that government intervention may not be required to reduce pollution. In more complex and realistic situations involving multiple pollution sources, computing the socially optimal level of pollution may be difficult. However, the government can arbitrarily pick a target level of total pollution and, by using a cap-and-trade system, can ensure that this target is achieved with the lowest possible total abatement cost.

---

5. Their air-quality measure is "total suspended particulates" (TSP), a main component of air pollution along with ozone.

6. Recall from chapter 4 that self-selection is an issue in measuring the effect of urban sprawl on obesity. In the air-quality context, the problem is that people who strongly dislike air pollution may choose not to live in polluted counties, which will instead be populated by people who don't mind pollution as much. The measured effect of air pollution on house values may then mainly reflect the preferences of the pollution-insensitive consumers, thus being small and unrepresentative.

10   Crime

10.1   Introduction

Like pollution, crime reduces the quality of life in cities, where it is usually concentrated. In addition to imposing large losses on victims, crime affects the patterns of daily living for everyone in cities where it is high. Residents avoid certain dangerous areas, and they may be reluctant to go out at night. Much crime is related to theft of property (cars, wallets, household goods, and so on) or to protection of economic interests (as when a drug lord is killed by a competitor). Other crimes (assault or murder committed in the heat of anger, or rape), yield no economic benefit to the perpetrator.

Property crime arises partly from the inability of potential criminals to earn adequate livelihoods in legitimate activities, a limitation that may be a consequence of their low abilities and education levels or perhaps antisocial tendencies. This insight is the foundation of the economic theory of crime, which is the main focus of this chapter. Although property crime requires the presence of a disadvantaged group, it also is spurred by the availability of "loot": property owned by a separate prosperous segment of the population, which can be stolen by criminals. Thus, along with poverty, wealth plays a role in the generation of property crime. A society's standards of behavior may also matter. Criminal activity may bring scorn on an individual from his or her peers, which may reduce the incentives to carry it out.

The level of crime also depends on the likelihood and the severity of punishment. These factors, in turn, depend on the size of a city's police force (which determines the likelihood that a criminal will be caught) and on the money spent on prisons (which determines the capacity to impose long jail sentences on convicted criminals). Crime is also made easier when criminals have access to guns. When guns aren't easy to obtain, crimes that involve the intimidation of victims (store or bank robbery, for example) are harder to commit.

The economic theory of crime incorporates all of the above factors: the existence of a disadvantaged group, the presence of wealth, the likelihood and severity of punishment, the ease with which crimes can be committed, and society's behavioral standards. The theory, originated in a paper published in 1968 by Gary Becker, is explained in section 10.2. It is extended in section 10.3, which also discusses a more recent approach to the analysis of crime that focuses on neighborhood effects and social networks. Extending the public-sector analysis of chapter 8, section 10.4 addresses a crime-related resource allocation problem: how to divide a city's police force between its rich and poor neighborhoods.

10.2 The Economic Theory of Crime

10.2.1 A simple model

In order to develop a clear picture of how economic factors determine the level of crime in a city, a simple model is useful. This model builds on the work of Gary Becker (1968) but uses elements of a framework sketched by Edward Glaeser (1999). The approach is to focus on the "occupational choices" of individuals, asking whether they become legitimate workers or criminals. After making an occupational choice, criminals also decide on the "intensity" of their criminal activity (the number of crimes to commit per period). For simplicity, the model doesn't consider the latter choice, assuming instead that each criminal commits a single crime per period. In addition, the model initially focuses on property crime, although it can be altered to apply to other types of crime.

Suppose that the city has $\bar{n}$ residents, indexed by $n = 1, 2, \ldots, \bar{n}$, each of whom would earn a different income in legitimate employment as a consequence of differences in skills, education, and sociability. Suppose that the index is chosen so that legitimate incomes increase as the index number rises, with individual 1 having the lowest income and individual $\bar{n}$ the highest. Figure 10.1 shows the curve that relates legitimate income to the individual's index (the curve is increasing). The height up to this "legitimate-income curve" at $n = k$ equals the legitimate income for individual k.[1]

---

1. This indexing is analogous to the labeling of commuters according to their alternate cost, discussed in chapter 5.

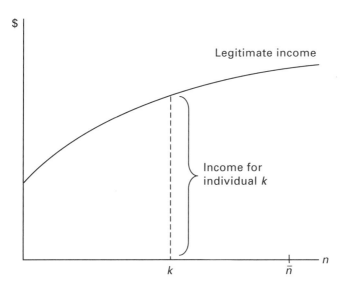

Figure 10.1
Legitimate-income curve.

Whereas the legitimate-income curve shows what someone can earn in legitimate employment, the alternative is to earn income as a criminal. For simplicity, suppose that all individuals have identical skills in criminal activity even though their legitimate incomes differ. Criminal income is thus the same for everyone, and it depends importantly on how much "loot" a criminal can steal per period. Let this loot be denoted by L. The amount of loot that a criminal is able to acquire may depend on the city's characteristics, as will be explained below.

Criminals might be apprehended during or after commission of a crime, in which case their loot is lost. If a denotes the probability of apprehension, the expected value of the criminal's loot is then $(1 - a)L$. In addition to losing their loot, apprehended criminals go to jail (they are all assumed to be convicted). Suppose that a jail term imposes a dollar cost of J on a criminal, which is best thought of as capturing the psychic cost of being incarcerated. Then the expected cost of punishment is aJ, the probability of being apprehended times the cost of incarceration.

The apprehension probability a will depend on size of the city's police force. In addition, the incarceration cost will depend on the length of the prison sentence and thus on prison expenditures, which determine the capacity of the prisons. These dependencies of a and J are considered further below.

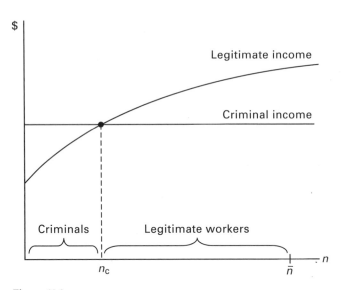

Figure 10.2
Occupational choice.

Criminals will also incur costs in the commission of a crime. These costs depend on the amount of effort involved, and they may also include the cost of social stigma, which arises if the criminal's peer group disapproves of such activity. Crime-commission costs, denoted by e, could thus depend on the ease of gun acquisition (since guns make crimes easier to commit) as well as on social standards. Combining all the above elements, the expected net income from crime is equal to

$$(1 - a)L - aJ - e.$$

Since this criminal income doesn't depend on the identity of the individual, it appears in figure 10.2 as a horizontal line that intersects the legitimate-income curve at $n = n_c$.

Occupational-choice outcomes can be seen clearly using figure 10.2. Individuals with index values above the intersection value n_c earn more income in legitimate employment than in criminal activity. These individuals will thus choose to be legitimate workers. Individuals with index values below n_c earn higher incomes through criminal activity than as legitimate workers, and thus choose to be criminals. Since the index value n_c also gives a count of the number of individuals choosing criminal activity, the city has $\bar{n} - n_c$ legitimate workers and n_c criminals. With each criminal committing one crime, the city's level of crime is also equal to n_c.

The model thus predicts that the city's criminals are its most disadvantaged residents—individuals whose poor skills and low education levels (and perhaps antisocial tendencies) prevent them from earning good incomes as legitimate workers. These individuals do the rational thing: they choose a criminal occupation, in which better incomes can be earned.

10.2.2 How a city's characteristics affect crime

The model predicts that the number of criminals in a city, and thus the amount of crime, depends on the city's characteristics. First, suppose that the city's disadvantaged individuals become more disadvantaged. In other words, suppose that skills and education levels among the city's disadvantaged population fall, so that the legitimate-income curve shifts down over its lower range, as illustrated in figure 10.3. If this shift encompasses the previous intersection point, as shown in the figure, then the intersection point moves to the right, now occurring at an index value of $n_c' > n_c$. Therefore, if the city's disadvantaged residents become more disadvantaged, the number of criminals and the amount of crime rise.

Changes in a city's characteristics can also reduce criminals' incomes, with attendant affects on the number of criminals and the amount of crime. Suppose first that the police force grows in size. Then the

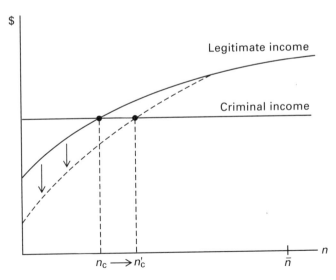

Figure 10.3
The effect of a more disadvantaged population.

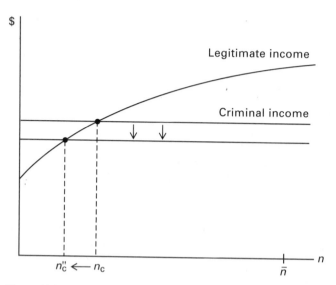

Figure 10.4
The effect of a large police force.

apprehension probability a increases, and the previous formula shows that criminal income falls. The horizontal criminal-income line in the figures thus shifts downward, and its intersection point with the income curve moves leftward to $n_c'' < n_c$, as shown in figure 10.4. Thus, by reducing the returns to crime through a greater chance of apprehension, a larger police force reduces the number of criminals and the amount of crime in the city. The same outcome happens if the city spends more on prisons, allowing longer sentences to be imposed. Then, the incarceration cost J rises, and the formula shows that criminal income again falls, with n_c again declining. Stricter gun controls would have the same effect. They would reduce criminal income by increasing the effort e required to commit a crime, since criminals must then rely on less effective weapons. The horizontal criminal-income line would again shift down, reducing n_c and the level of crime. The same effect (a rising e and falling n_c) would arise if community standards were to tighten, increasing the stigmatization of criminal activity.

Suppose that the loot stolen by criminals comes from the city's highest-income residents, who are legitimate workers. If the incomes of these individuals increase, two things happen. First, the legitimate-income curve shifts upward over its upper range. By itself, this shift has no effect on the intersection point, as can be seen in figure 10.5. But

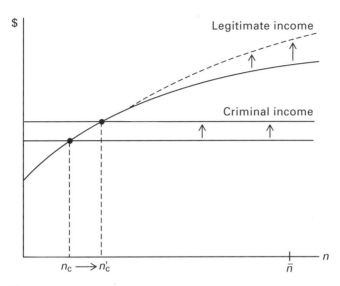

Figure 10.5
The effect of greater wealth.

with crime victims now richer, the loot variable L also increases, which raises the criminal-income line, thus shifting the intersection point to the right, to n_c'. Thus, the model predicts that greater wealth in a city will increase the number of criminals and the amount of crime.

All these effects make intuitive sense, and they show the usefulness of the economic theory of crime. But do the model and its predictions apply to other types of crimes, in which loot isn't acquired by the criminal? In fact, a modified version of the model applies to crimes of passion, and to rape and other non-economic crimes. The first required modification concerns the interpretation of the L variable. Instead of representing loot, L now represents whatever benefit the criminal gets from the particular crime. In the case of crimes of passion, this benefit may be the satisfaction gained by inflicting harm on a certain person. Since this benefit is gained even when the criminal is apprehended, the L variable need not be multiplied by the apprehension probability a.

More importantly, since the crimes in question aren't economic, the notion of criminal income and occupational choice is no longer relevant. Instead, the previous formula, rewritten as $L - aJ - e$, now captures the net benefit of crime, not criminal income. If this net benefit is positive, then the individual has an incentive to commit the non-economic crime. Otherwise, the benefit will not be worth the cost. As before, more police, more prison spending, and a higher crime-commission cost all reduce the net benefit of the crime, making it less likely to happen. Although it may seem implausible that crimes of passion will be deterred by a larger police force, an individual who is spurred to commit such a crime may nevertheless consider his chance of getting arrested before acting.

10.2.3   Optimal spending on crime prevention

The model shows that increasing the size of the police force reduces the number of criminals and the amount of crime. This effect yields an inverse relationship between crime, denoted by C, and the cost of the city's police force, as shown in figure 10.6.[2] This "crime-prevention cost curve" is downward sloping, indicating that higher values of C are associated with fewer police and thus lower costs. The figure also shows that the curve rises at an increasing rate as the number of crimes falls. This pattern indicates that successive reductions in crime are increasingly difficult and costly to achieve, requiring successively larger increments in the size of the police force. The second curve in figure 10.6 illustrates the cost of crime to its victims, representing their

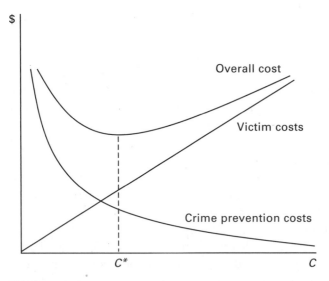

Figure 10.6
The socially optimal level of crime.

---

2. Recall that, in the model, the amount of crime is the same as the number of criminals.

dollar losses from being victimized. This "victim-cost curve" curve is drawn as linear, indicating that an additional crime always entails the same incremental cost to victims.

With these two curves, the socially optimal level of crime can be determined. This level isn't zero, as intuition might suggest, but is instead equal to C^*, the level associated with the smallest overall cost. In other words, C^* is the level of crime that minimizes the sum of crime-prevention costs and victim costs. This level is found by plotting the vertical sum of the crime-prevention and victim-cost curves, which yields a third curve showing the overall costs at different levels of crime. The socially optimal crime level corresponds to the minimum point on this curve, as shown in figure 10.6.

It is easy to understand why tolerating some crime is optimal for society. Although less crime is always better for potential victims, reducing crime toward zero requires large increases in police expenditures, which may not be justified by the resulting benefits. This conclusion is analogous to a point that was made in chapter 9: reducing pollution to zero is never optimal given the high costs involved.

Even though this analysis focuses only on police expenditures as a means of preventing crime, spending on prisons could also be considered. The first step then would be to find, for each level of crime, the cheapest combination of spending on police and prisons that achieves it. The second step would again be to determine the level of crime that minimizes overall cost, now equal to victim cost plus combined police and prison costs.

10.3 Additional Aspects of the Theory

10.3.1 Multiple crime equilibria

The spatial concentration of criminal activity is occasionally puzzling. Some neighborhoods of a city may experience little crime while otherwise similar neighborhoods experience high crime levels. Why do such concentrations of crime arise? Why isn't crime distributed evenly?

The simple model of crime used here can explain these spatial concentrations when some additional factors are incorporated. These factors are closely related to the concept of public-good congestion introduced in chapter 8. To make the required additions, suppose first that the model can be applied to individual neighborhoods within a city, so that it determines the crime level in each neighborhood separately. Then, note that "congestion" may arise as criminals compete for loot. In other words, if each neighborhood has a fixed total amount of loot for criminals to steal, then the amount of loot that each one gets will be lower when more criminals are active. Since L then falls as the number of criminals n_c rises, criminal income (equal to $(1 - a)L - aJ - e$, as before) will tend to be lower when there are more criminals.

But an opposite congestion phenomenon affects the police as they try to apprehend criminals. With more criminals present, the probability of catching any single criminal is lower. Thus, as n_c rises, the apprehension probability a falls. This effect works in the opposite direction to the loot congestion effect, tending to make criminal income higher, not lower, as n_c rises.

Although the net effect of these two opposing congestion effects is unclear, suppose that the apprehension effect dominates when the number of criminals is low, so that criminal income initially rises with n_c. Ultimately, the loot congestion effect wins out, so that criminal income starts to falls once the number of criminals becomes large enough. Suppose that the two effects generate the S-shaped criminal-income curve shown in figure 10.7.[3]

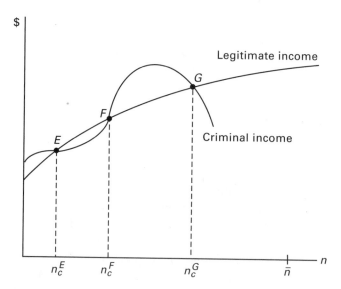

Figure 10.7
Multiple equilibria.

---

3. Note that the horizontal axis of figure 10.7 now plays two roles. It indexes individuals, but to capture congestion effects, it also counts the number of criminals, moving rightward on the axis. See Freeman et al. 1996 and Conley and Wang 2006.

Instead of the single previous intersection, the criminal-income curve now intersects the legitimate-income curve three times. The three different intersection points (E, F, and G) represent different possible equilibrium divisions of the neighborhood's population into criminals and legitimate workers. However, the middle intersection point (F) isn't of interest, because it is an "unstable" equilibrium. To see why, and to better understand the workings of the modified model, suppose that the neighborhood is at equilibrium F. It thus has n_c^F criminals, consisting of individuals numbered from 1 through n_c^F. Each criminal is happy with his choice since his income (equal to the height h up to the criminal-income curve at $n = n_c^F$) is larger than what he could earn in legitimate employment (equal to the height up to the legitimate-income curve at the appropriate leftward point corresponding to his index value). Similarly, each legitimate worker is happy with his choice, earning a legitimate income (equal to the height up to the legitimate-income curve at his index value) that is higher than the criminal income h. But suppose that, even though everyone is content with his or her occupational choice, a few workers with index values just above n_c^F were to mistakenly switch to criminal activity. Since the criminal-income curve lies above the legitimate-income curve just to the right of F, these individuals would discover that they were happy with their mistaken switch, and more legitimate workers would then switch as well. The criminal group would keep growing in size until the intersection point G was reached.

Although the equilibrium F is thus unstable to a small perturbation, the same conclusion doesn't apply to G, where individuals 1 through n_c^G are criminals. At G, everyone is again content with his or her occupational choice. But suppose that some legitimate workers with index values just above n_c^G again mistakenly switch to criminal activity. These workers will regret their move. The reason is that, to the right of G, the legitimate-income curve is higher than the criminal-income curve, so that switchers see that they would be earning higher incomes in their original legitimate occupation. They will thus return to that occupation, restoring the equilibrium point G. The same stability property also applies to point E. The crucial feature of points E and G is that the criminal-income curve cuts the legitimate-income curve from above. At the unstable equilibrium F, the criminal-income curve instead cuts from below.

The upshot is that the neighborhood has two stable crime equilibria, representing very different levels of criminal activity. Equilibrium E has relatively few criminals and little crime, whereas equilibrium G has many criminals and lots of crime. Apparently, a neighborhood could end up in either of these equilibria. As a result, two separate neighborhoods with identical characteristics (and thus identical income curves) could have dramatically different levels of crime, mimicking the puzzling pattern sometimes observed in reality.

The remaining question is how the two neighborhoods would end up reaching these different equilibria. A "shock" to one neighborhood could provide the impetus. For example, suppose that both neighborhoods are in the low-crime equilibrium C. Suppose that in one neighborhood some legitimate workers become friendly with criminals, who persuade them to try a life of crime even though there is no current gain from doing so. If enough legitimate workers were to try this experiment, the number of criminals could be pushed to the right of F, at which point even more legitimate workers would (according to the stability arguments discussed above) have an incentive to switch.

10.3.2 Neighborhood effects, social networks, and crime

Chapter 7 argued that when disadvantaged households can escape the negative neighborhood effects felt in poor areas by moving, the result may be better labor-market outcomes for adults and better educational outcomes for children. The Moving to Opportunity program provided experimental evidence partly confirming such improvements. Conversely, for poor households that remain in place, negative neighborhood effects may contribute to bad life outcomes.

Criminal behavior is such an outcome, and it can be generated through neighborhood effects. Social networks in a neighborhood may link individuals to other people who are criminals, and these linkages may lead to criminal activity instead of legitimate employment. The mechanism could be criminal "tutoring," in which established criminals teach people in their social networks the skills needed for success in criminal activity. In the context of the model, the better skills learned through tutoring would reduce the effort e needed to commit crimes, raising the incomes of criminals and making criminality more attractive. In addition, by putting individuals in touch with criminal role models, social networks might reduce the perception of social stigma from criminal activity, which also would reduce e.

The criminal networks that develop through social ties often rely on an individual known as a "key player." Although many criminals in the network may know him, they may not know one another directly, being connected only indirectly through their links to the key player. Thus, if the police can identify the key player and arrest him, the criminal network may collapse, thereby reducing crime in the city. Using network theory, Ballester, Calvó-Armengol, and Zenou (2006) show how to identify the key player by using a measure that computes an individual's "centrality" in the network.

The effects of social networks can also help explain the large differences in crime that are sometimes observed between otherwise identical neighborhoods, reinforcing the multiple-equilibria explanation. The logic is presented by Zenou (2003). Relying on the more complex model of Glaeser, Sacerdote, and Scheinkman (1996), Zenou shows that the likelihood of either a very high or a very low crime level is greater when people mimic the criminal behavior of others (which is observed via social networks) than when they make decisions about criminal behavior in isolation. In the isolation case, suppose that there are two potential criminals, each of whom flips a coin to decide whether or not to engage in criminal activity. In the mimicking case, suppose that one person flips a coin and the other person then mimics his occupational choice. Although the expected number of criminals is one in each case, mimicking behavior ends up putting greater probability weight on the extreme outcomes, in which the number of criminals is either two or none. Therefore, mimicking behavior fostered by social networks can produce large disparities in crime across neighborhoods.

10.3.3   Interjurisdictional competition in the context of crime

Chapter 8 analyzed tax and welfare competition, in which concern about the loss of business investment or the attraction of poor migrants kept spending on public goods and welfare payments inefficiently low. A related outcome emerges in the case of spending on crime prevention if criminals are mobile across jurisdictions. With criminal mobility, if one jurisdiction increases its crime-prevention expenditures, then criminals, spurred by a greater likelihood of arrest or longer imprisonment, will relocate to other jurisdictions. The result will be an increase in crime in the receiving jurisdictions. But since the original jurisdiction doesn't take this negative effect into account, thinking only about the reduction in its own crime, it will tend to set crime-prevention expenditures at too high a level.[4] Thus, when criminals are mobile across jurisdictions, jurisdictions will overspend on crime prevention.

---

4. See Lee and Pinto 2009 for a recent analysis of such a model.

Interestingly, this conclusion is the reverse of the underspending outcome that emerges under tax and welfare competition.

10.3.4   Does crime-prevention spending actually reduce crime?

As the preceding discussion showed, a fundamental assumption in the economic theory of crime is that the amount of crime falls as expenditures on crime prevention rise. Although this assumption seems uncontroversial, empirical evidence supporting it has been hard to generate. Over the years, many studies have shown no effect of police spending on crime, or a counterintuitive positive association. The problem, however, was failure to account for the endogeneity of such spending. In other words, cities will put lots of police into crime-prone areas as they attempt to reduce crime, which can generate a positive rather than a negative correlation between crime and police presence.

Steven Levitt (1997) was the first to control for this endogeneity. He did so by recognizing that police spending rises before elections as incumbent politicians, seeking to improve their reelection chances, try to reduce crime. Levitt used data on the timing of elections to isolate the part of police spending that isn't a response to fundamental crime levels. Levitt found that spending on police, measured in this way, does indeed lead to the expected reduction in crime.

Levitt (2004) also attempts to isolate the factors underlying the decline in crime that has occurred in the United States over the last 20 years. He identifies several factors already captured in the model as helping to explain the decline in crime between 1990 and 2000. One factor is an increase in the sizes of police forces. Two others are the increase in the capacity of prisons and the increase in the number of inmates. As was seen above, these factors are captured in the model by increases in the apprehension probability a and the incarceration cost J. Levitt argues that neither gun control (which raises e) nor an improvement in the labor market (which would raise the legitimate-income curve in figure 10.3) has been an important factor. But he makes the controversial claim that legalization of abortion in the 1970s helped reduce crime 20 years later. He argues that, with fewer unwanted babies coming of age, the young adult population in the 1990s was better adjusted socially and thus better able to earn income in legitimate activities. This change can be represented by an upward shift in the legitimate-income curve in figure 10.3, which reduces crime.

10.4   How to Divide a Police Force Between Rich and Poor Neighborhoods

10.4.1   Basics

It was argued in chapter 8 that one important feature of public goods is their uniform provision to all residents of a jurisdiction. Although the nature of some public goods (national defense, for example) makes it impossible to provide a higher level to some people than to others, many public goods can be provided unequally. Crime prevention is one such good. Even though cities try to provide a level of police protection that is fairly uniform across neighborhoods, it is possible in principle to withhold police from one neighborhood while providing frequent police patrols in other neighborhoods. In view of this possibility, it is interesting to study the police allocation problem in some detail, drawing on elements of the economic theory of crime.[5]

Suppose that a city consists of two neighborhoods, one rich and one poor, and that these neighborhoods are equal in population. The city has a fixed total number of police, $\bar{P}$, who can be divided between the two neighborhoods in any fashion. If P_r and P_p denote the number of police in the rich and the poor neighborhood, respectively, it follows that $P_r + P_p = \bar{P}$. The question of interest is how to allocate the police between the neighborhoods.

To allow a simple analysis, suppose that all crime in a neighborhood is "internal"—that is, crimes are committed by residents of the neighborhood against other neighborhood residents. Thus, in the poor neighborhood, crimes involve poor criminals attacking poor victims, and in the rich neighborhood, crimes involve rich criminals attacking rich victims. This pattern rules out the case where poor criminals commit crimes (such as house burglary) in the rich neighborhood. Without this kind of crossover crime, what kind of crimes will occur in the rich neighborhood? These crimes, where rich criminals prey on rich victims, might consist of offenses like teenage vandalism and bank embezzlement. The poor neighborhood's crimes probably will include armed robberies, drug-related killings, and other more serious offenses. Although some "crossover crimes" occur in the real world, the internal-crime assumption isn't grossly unrealistic.

With crime internal to a neighborhood, its level of crime depends only on the number of police allocated to that neighborhood. It is thus

5. This analysis builds on work by Shoup (1964). For an empirical study that makes use of the same kind of framework, see Behrman and Craig 1987.

independent of the number of police allocated to the other neighborhood. Crossover crime would eliminate this simplification: poor-neighborhood police could reduce rich crime, for example, by catching poor crossover criminals (who burglarize rich people's houses) when they are at home asleep in bed. In the absence of crossover crime, however, poor crimes (denoted by C_p) depend on only P_p, and rich crimes (denoted by C_r) depend on only P_r. These simple relationships, which allow an easy analysis, are both inverse in nature, with more police in a neighborhood reducing the number of crimes there.

The two downward-sloping relationships are plotted in figure 10.8, with the upper panel showing the "crime curve" for the poor neighborhood and the bottom panel showing the crime curve for the rich neighborhood.[6] In analyzing these curves, the requirement that P_r and P_p must add up to $\bar{P}$ is ignored for the moment, being reintroduced later.

Several features of the crime curves deserve note. First, the curves are convex, with crime decreasing at a decreasing rate as the number of police increases. This property indicates that the "productivity" of an additional policeman (the drop in crime he causes) declines as more police are added. When the neighborhood has few police, one additional policeman provides significant additional deterrence, reducing crime appreciably, but when many police are already present, the crime reduction from an extra policeman isn't as large.

The second notable feature is that the poor crime curve is higher than the rich crime curve at a common level of P_p and P_r. Thus, if the two neighborhoods have the same number of police, then $C_p > C_r$, so that there is more crime in the poor neighborhood. The reason is that members of a disadvantaged population are more likely to commit crimes, holding the level of police deterrence constant, as was seen in section 10.2.

The third feature of the crime curves is that the poor curve is flatter than the rich curve. In other words, comparing the slopes of the curves at a common level of P_p and P_r, the poor curve has a flatter slope. This difference indicates that, starting with equal numbers of police, the productivity of an additional policeman is lower in the poor neighborhood than in the rich neighborhood. In other words, with the number

---

6. Note that the crime curves are mirror images of the crime-prevention cost curve in figure 10.6. That curve showed crime-prevention cost (which is proportional to the number of police) as a function of crime. The curves in figure 10.8 instead put crime on the vertical axis and police on the horizontal axis.

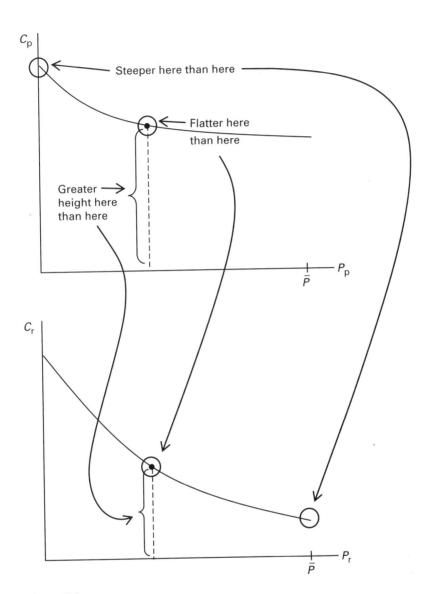

Figure 10.8
Crime curves.

of police set equal at the start, the crime reduction from an additional policeman is smaller in the poor neighborhood. This difference again reflects the weaker effect of police deterrence in the poor neighborhood. With criminal activity more necessary as a means of securing adequate incomes in the poor neighborhood than in the rich one, crime is both more plentiful in the poor neighborhood and harder to reduce through the allocation of additional police.

The fourth feature of the crime curves is that the poor curve at $P_p = 0$ is steeper than the rich curve at $P_r = \bar{P}$. In other words, the productivity of the *first* policeman allocated to the poor neighborhood is greater than the productivity of the $\bar{P}$th policeman allocated to the rich neighborhood. Thus, although an additional policeman is less productive in the poor neighborhood starting at equal numbers of police, the comparison is reversed at these other, unequal starting points. Starting with no police at all in the poor neighborhood, the first policeman reduces crime by an appreciable amount—more than the crime reduction from putting the $\bar{P}$th policeman into the rich neighborhood.

10.4.2 The transformation curve

The fact that the police allocated to the rich and poor neighborhoods must add up to $\bar{P}$ generates a trade-off between crimes in the two neighborhoods. In other words, a reduction in C_p, which requires an increase in the number of police in the poor neighborhood, means an increase in C_r, a consequence of the offsetting loss of police in the rich neighborhood. This trade-off is summarized in the "transformation curve" in figure 10.9. The curve is downward sloping (reflecting the crime trade-off) and convex (mirroring the convexity of the underlying crime curves).

To see how the crime curves are used to generate the transformation curve, consider first the curve's endpoints. At the upper endpoint, where C_p is as small as possible, all the police are in the poor neighborhood, so that $P_p = \bar{P}$ and $P_r = 0$. The endpoint's C_p value is thus equal to the poor crime level at the bottom of the poor crime curve in figure 10.8, where $P_p = \bar{P}$. Conversely, the endpoint's C_r value is equal to the crime level at the top of the rich crime curve, where $P_r = 0$.

In contrast, at the lower endpoint of the transformation curve, where C_r is as small as possible, all the police are in the rich neighborhood, so that $P_r = \bar{P}$ and $P_p = 0$. The coordinates of this lower endpoint are read off the crime curves in figure 10.8 in the same way as before. At the

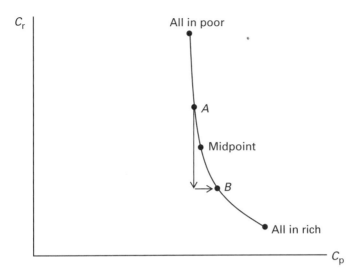

Figure 10.9
Transformation curve.

midpoint of the transformation curve, the police are equally divided between the two neighborhoods, with $P_r = P_p = \overline{P}/2$. Since, with equal numbers of police, crime is higher in the poor neighborhood, $C_p > C_r$ holds at the midpoint, as can be seen in figure 10.9.

While convex, the transformation curve is also steep over most of its range. This property reflects the fact that an additional policeman is typically more productive in the rich neighborhood than in the poor one. To see the logic, suppose that the police are divided in a way that generates point A on the transformation curve in figure 10.9. Since A is above the curve's midpoint, where the police force is equally divided, $P_p > P_r$ holds. Now suppose that a group of police is moved from the poor neighborhood to the rich one. This movement reduces crime in the rich neighborhood, as indicated by the vertical arrow in the figure. It also increases crime in the poor neighborhood, as indicated by the horizontal arrow in the figure, leading to the new point B on the transformation curve. The important observation is that, since the police are more productive in the rich neighborhood, the reduction in its crime due to the added policemen is greater than the increase in crime in the poor neighborhood due to its loss of police. In other words, the vertical arrow in the figure is longer than the horizontal arrow. But this difference simply means that the transformation curve is steep over the range between point A and point B.

Recall from above that the first policeman allocated to the poor neighborhood is assumed to be more productive than the last policeman allocated to the rich neighborhood. This assumption means that the police-productivity comparison is reversed near the bottom of the transformation curve, where the police are concentrated in the rich neighborhood. Over this range, an additional policeman is more productive in the poor neighborhood than in the rich one. Thus, if the starting point of the movement from point A to point B were nearer the bottom of the transformation curve, the lengths of the arrows in figure 10.9 would be reversed. The transformation curve thus flattens out near its bottom, with the slope becoming less than one in absolute value.

10.4.3 Choosing the police allocation

The transformation curve, redrawn in figure 10.10, shows the feasible combinations of crime in the city's two neighborhoods, given the fixed total size of its police force. The question, then, is which crime combination (along with an associated police allocation) should be chosen.

Three possible allocations seem reasonable. The first of these allocations is, in some sense, the most natural, and it corresponds to the midpoint of the transformation curve, where the police force is divided equally between the neighborhoods. In figure 10.10, this midpoint allocation is called the "equal-police allocation." As was noted above, the

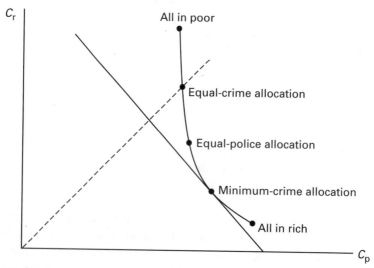

Figure 10.10
Allocating the police.

poor neighborhood has more crime than the rich neighborhood under this allocation.

Another natural allocation also relies on the notion of equality, but the focus is on crimes rather than on the number of police. Under this "equal-crime allocation," the police are allocated to equalize the number of crimes between the rich and poor neighborhoods. Since $C_r = C_p$ holds along the 45° line, this allocation corresponds to the intersection of that line with the transformation curve, as in figure 10.10. With the equal-crime allocation lying uphill from the equal-police allocation, it follows that $P_p > P_r$ holds under this allocation. Given the greater crime proclivity of the residents of the poor neighborhood, more police must be allocated there to equalize crime.[7]

These two equality-based allocations exhibit a fundamental difference. The equal-police allocation yields "equal opportunities," in the sense that the neighborhoods enjoy the same "opportunity" for protection against crime in the form of identical numbers of police. In contrast, the equal-crime allocation yields "equal outcomes," in the sense that the level of crime experienced in the neighborhoods is the same. Equal outcomes, however, mean unequal opportunities, since more police must be allocated to the poor neighborhood to equalize crime. Conversely, equal opportunities yield unequal outcomes, since an equal division of the police leads to more crime in the poor neighborhood.

The choice between equal opportunities and equal outcomes is often faced in discussions of public policy. For example, affirmative-action rules, which give minority job applicants an advantage in hiring, represent an attempt to generate equal outcomes via unequal opportunities. Liberals and conservatives have argued for decades about whether society should attempt to offer equal outcomes or equal opportunities (with liberals tending to favor the former), but there is no right answer in this debate.

Beyond these two equality-based allocations, another possible approach is to allocate the police using some measure of social welfare. Total crime is a natural welfare measure, and in this case, the goal would be to allocate the police so as to minimize total crime.

This problem can be solved graphically by borrowing from the theory of cost minimization for a firm. Whereas a firm focuses on iso-cost lines (recall the housing production example in chapter 2), the

---

7. Crime equalization may be impossible, an outcome that would arise if the poor neighborhood still has higher crime when it contains all the police. In this case, the upper endpoint of the transformation curve would lie below the 45° line.

relevant construct in the crime case is an "iso-crime line." This is a line along which total crime is constant, representing the graph of the equation $C_r + C_p = k$, for some constant k. Since this equation can be rewritten as $C_r = k - C_p$, iso-crime lines are parallel and downward sloping, with a slope equal to -1.

To minimize crime, the goal is to find the point on the transformation curve that lies on the lowest iso-crime line. Since the curve is convex, the resulting point will be a point of tangency between the curve and an iso-crime line, as in figure 10.10. Since the transformation curve is steep over most of its range, this "minimum-crime allocation" lies near the bottom of the curve, at a point where its slope is -1, matching the slope of the iso-crime line. At this point, the productivities of the police are equal in the rich and poor neighborhoods (the previous arrows then have the same length).

To achieve equal productivities, the productivity of police in the rich neighborhood must be pushed down to the lower poor level by putting nearly all of the police in that neighborhood. Thus, the minimum-crime allocation is near the "all in rich" endpoint of the transformation curve. In effect, this skewed outcome emerges because crime is easier to stop in the rich neighborhood, which means that most of the police should be allocated there if the goal is to minimize total crime.

The assumed ease with which crimes can be stopped in the rich neighborhood may be due to the less serious nature of these crimes. But once this difference is recognized, the goal of minimizing total crime, which treats all crimes as equal, may have to be altered. Accordingly, suppose that crimes in the poor neighborhood can be viewed as twice as serious as those committed in the rich neighborhood. Then, instead of minimizing total crime, the proper goal would be to minimize a weighted sum of crimes, equal to $C_r + 2C_p$. The graphical solution would make use of "iso-weighted-crime lines," which come from the equation $C_r = k - 2C_p$. These lines, whose slopes are equal to -2, are steeper than the iso-crime line shown in figure 10.10. The tangency point on the transformation curve would then occur at a point where the curve's slope equals -2, a point that lies uphill from the minimum-crime allocation, as in figure 10.11. This solution yields a more nearly equal allocation of police between the two neighborhoods, overturning the seemingly peculiar favoritism toward the rich neighborhood seen in the minimum-crime allocation.

The problem of allocating public spending across neighborhoods in the presence of productivity differences arises in contexts other than

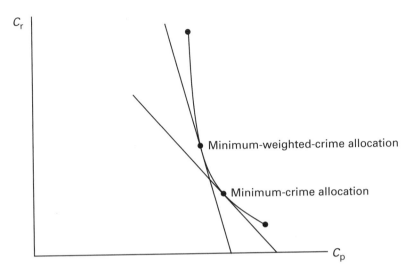

Figure 10.11
Minimum-weighted-crime allocation.

crime prevention. For example, a city may have a fixed education budget that must be allocated between rich and poor neighborhoods, with the productivity of school spending in raising test scores differing between the neighborhoods.[8] Or the city may have a fixed health budget to allocate between the neighborhoods, with the neighborhoods showing different health improvements in response to additional spending. The principles exposed in the previous analysis will again emerge.

10.5   Summary

The economic theory of crime depicts individuals as choosing between criminal activity and legitimate employment to secure the best income. Disadvantaged individuals, who would earn low incomes in legitimate employment, thus tend to become criminals. Therefore, the number of criminals in a city grows as the disadvantaged population rises, and it falls with an increase in crime-prevention spending (which reduces criminals' incomes). When congestion effects are added to both the criminal and police sides of the model, the possibility of multiple

---

8. For a numerical example illustrating the allocation of school spending, see exercise 10.1.

equilibria emerges. In this case, otherwise-identical neighborhoods may exhibit dramatic differences in crime, matching occasionally observed patterns. Imitation behavior within social networks, in which individuals mimic the criminal behavior of others, can also produce big swings in crime across neighborhoods. Building on the economic theory of crime, the problem of allocating a fixed police force across neighborhoods can be analyzed. Different solutions are possible, depending on society's objectives.

11 Urban Quality-of-Life Measurement

11.1 Introduction

Amenity effects play a prominent role in popular discussions of real-estate markets in the United States. For example, it is often argued that the high housing prices on the West Coast are due in part to amenity advantages, including a temperate climate and ocean access. More generally, many commentators seem to view any West-Coast or East-Coast location as superior to one in the interior of the country, thereby justifying a bicoastal housing-price premium.

The claim that the coasts are superior might be challenged by many Americans, especially those happily living in the nation's heartland. But if the claim is granted, its implications for variation in the price of housing would seem to be logical, relying on a compensating-differential argument like that developed in chapter 2. In other words, consumers living in a desirable region must pay for the privilege with higher housing costs, while those residing in undesirable places must be compensated via cheaper real estate. Housing prices would thus appear to be a direct indicator of the quality of life in a region. Comparing the prices of a standardized house (same square footage, lot size, and so on) in two different regions would indicate which region is a nicer place to live.

Although this logic is appealing, the conclusion is premature. The reason is that compensation in an interregional context can occur on more dimensions than within a single city, where housing prices must do all the work. To understand this point, recall that in the basic urban model of chapter 2, in which everyone earned the same income, price differences served to compensate for locational disadvantages (high commuting costs in the suburbs). But since incomes can differ from city to city, housing prices by themselves need not do all the work in compensating for amenity differences *across* cities. Both housing prices *and* incomes can vary to compensate consumers for intercity or interregional differences in the quality of life.

Once this possibility is admitted, the simple logic from above appears to unravel. Although it was argued that housing should be expensive in nice places, couldn't incomes be the compensating factor? In other words, couldn't high-amenity regions instead have low incomes, which would cancel their amenity benefits and leave consumers equally well off in all places? Without additional information, the answer is unclear.

The key to resolving this ambiguity is to recognize that interregional differences in real-estate prices and incomes affect economic agents other than consumers. In particular, business firms care about real-estate prices, which reflect the cost of an important input, floor space, and firm costs also depend on consumer incomes, which represent the cost of labor. As was seen in chapter 2, compensating differentials serve to equate profits across locations within a single city (recall low suburban land rents). Thus, in an interregional context, variation in real-estate prices and incomes should equalize firm profits across regions while also ensuring that consumers are equally well off everywhere.

As will be seen below, this double compensation requirement is sufficient to pin down the theoretically permissible variations in housing prices and incomes across regions with differing amenities, eliminating the ambiguity identified above. One possible pattern is intuitively sensible: A high-amenity region should have both high housing prices and low incomes, so that both compensating factors work in tandem. But other patterns are also theoretically possible. The analysis of these patterns, presented in section 11.2, follows the seminal 1982 paper of Jennifer Roback.

Once it is recognized that both regional housing prices and incomes are likely to vary with amenities, an obvious market-based measure of the quality of life is no longer apparent. Housing prices no longer may be a perfect indicator of the desirability of a location since incomes are varying as well. The question, then, is how to use market information to determine which places are nicest. The theoretical answer is provided by Roback (1982) and implemented by Blomquist, Berger, and Hoehn (1988) and others. Section 11.3 discusses this approach and presents the actual quality-of-life ranking that it generates.[1] Section 11.4 discusses additional issues.

---

1. For an overview of the theory and its uses similar to the one presented in this chapter, see Blomquist 2006.

11.2 Theory: The Roback Model

11.2.1 Consumer analysis

In the urban model of chapter 2, consumer utility depended on consumption of bread and housing, denoted by c and q. When the focus is extended to include urban amenities, the utility function also depends on an amenity variable, denoted by a. Although a will generally be a vector, including average temperature, rainfall, crime, and other variables, it will be treated as a single index for simplicity in developing the amenity model.

In a given location, consumers will choose c and q to maximize utility, now written as $u(c, q, a)$. The utility level they achieve will depend on the income they earn (y), on the price they pay per square foot of housing (p), and on the amenity level. This dependence is summarized in an "indirect utility function," written as $V(y, p, a)$. Since the achieved utility level is high when income is high but low when the housing price is high, the V function is increasing in y and decreasing in p. If amenities are measured positively (capturing, for example, the pleasantness rather than unpleasantness of the climate), the indirect utility function is increasing in a.

As in the urban model of chapter 2, a fundamental equilibrium requirement is that consumers be equally well off in all locations. If this requirement did not hold, consumers would move to locations offering higher utility, bidding up housing prices or pushing down incomes until utilities are equalized everywhere. With $\bar{u}$ denoting the uniform utility level, the equal-utility requirement is written $V(y, p, a) = \bar{u}$.

As an illustration of the compensating-differential argument made in the introductory section, suppose that incomes were somehow constrained to be equal in all locations. Then the housing price p would have to do all the work in equalizing utilities between high-amenity and low-amenity places. Since a higher a raises utility (as given by the V function) whereas a higher p lowers it, a price increase of just the right amount will keep $V(y, p, a)$ constant between high-amenity and low-amenity locations, ensuring that utility equals $\bar{u}$ in both places. But the incomes will not necessarily be the same in the two locations, so further investigation is needed.

A useful tool in this investigation is a type of indifference curve, which shows the different combinations of p and y that yield the same utility, conditional on a given amenity level. Figure 11.1 shows two such indifference curves. The lower curve corresponds to amenity level

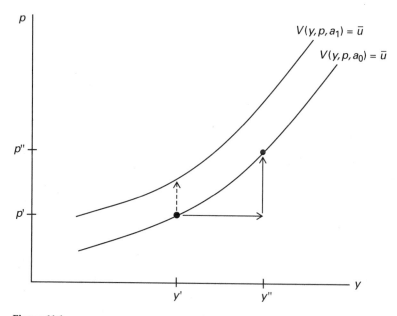

$V(y, p, a_1) = \bar{u}$

$V(y, p, a_0) = \bar{u}$

Figure 11.1
Indifference curves.

a_0 and reflects the requirement that $V(y, p, a_0) = \bar{u}$. To understand why the curve is upward sloping, start with a situation where $p = p'$ and $y = y'$, and suppose that income were to increase up to $y'' > y'$, as indicated by the solid horizontal arrow in the figure. Since this change would raise the consumer's utility level, an adjustment in the housing price is required to cancel the gain, so as to keep utility constant at $\bar{u}$. Since utility decreases with p, the required adjustment in the housing price is upward, with p rising from p' to p''. This movement, which reduces utility back to $\bar{u}$, is represented by the solid vertical arrow in the figure. Since the higher y thus must be accompanied by a higher p, the indifference curve is upward sloping.

The second, higher indifference curve in figure 11.1 corresponds to an amenity level a_1, which is higher than a_0. To understand why this curve lies above the a_0 curve, start again with a situation where $a = a_0$, $p = p'$, and $y = y''$. Then let the amenity level increase to a_1. Since this change will raise the utility level above $\bar{u}$, adjustments in p or y are needed to cancel the gain. If p alone were to adjust, the required change is in the positive direction, with the increase in p canceling the utility gain from the higher a. This adjustment is represented by the dashed vertical arrow in the figure. Since this argument applies for any starting point, it follows that the indifference curve with $a = a_1$ lies above the curve with $a = a_0$.

11.2.2   Firm analysis

As was explained above, compensating differentials must also ensure that firm profits are equal across locations. To formalize this notion, suppose that firms in the economy produce bread, the non-housing commodity. As inputs, these firms use labor and "real estate," which corresponds to the floor space contained in factories and offices. Other inputs could be used as well, but as long as their prices are the same in all regions, these inputs can be ignored.

Although consumers were portrayed as consuming housing, it is useful to think of this commodity more generally as real estate, matching the nature of the firm's input. Thus, the analysis will portray both firms and individuals as consuming real estate, with the difference between residential and business real estate ignored for simplicity. As a result, the price p should now be viewed as the price per square foot of real estate, which is common across residential and business uses.

With firms using labor and real estate as inputs, their costs depend on the prices of these inputs, p and y. As was noted above, the consumer income y also represents the cost of labor to firms. If bread production occurs with constant returns to scale, then the cost per unit of output is the same no matter how much bread a firm produces, and it is given by the unit cost function $C(y, p, a)$. Since higher input prices raise costs, this cost function is increasing in both y and p.

The appearance of a in the cost function indicates that costs also may depend on amenities. To see how such a dependence may arise, consider crime (or its inverse, public safety) as an amenity. Consumers value public safety, but a safer city also reduces firm costs by reducing the need for security guards and other crime-prevention measures. In this case, the cost function would be decreasing in a, the level of public safety. Firm costs might also depend on climate amenities. For example, a firm located in a temperate climate could spend less on heating and cooling for its offices and factories, so that the cost function would again be decreasing in a, a measure of climate pleasantness. Although it is harder to visualize cases in which costs rise with amenities, some kinds of agricultural production might exhibit such a relationship. For example, certain crops that benefit from hot and humid conditions would be more expensive (or impossible) to grow in more temperate climates. A final possibility is that costs are entirely independent of amenities. For example, if the only relevant amenity were ocean access, then as long a firm doesn't rely on ocean shipping, there is no reason for costs to depend on the ocean amenity.

For firm profits to be the same (equal to zero) in all locations, the unit cost $C(y, p, a)$ must equal the price of a unit of the bread output. Since this price is normalized to 1, as in the urban model, the zero-profit condition is written $C(y, p, a) = 1$. This condition generates iso-profit curves, which are analogous to the consumer indifference curves from figure 11.1. An iso-profit curve shows, for a given amenity level, the combinations of y and p that yield zero profit.

Iso-profit curves are downward sloping, and figure 11.2 shows three such curves. To see the reason for their negative slope, consider the middle curve, which has $a = a_0$, and start at the point where $y = y'$ and $p = p'$. If y were to increase, then the firm's costs would rise, reducing profit below zero. To raise profit, canceling this change and restoring the zero profit level, the real-estate price p would have to fall. Since a higher y thus must be accompanied by a lower p, the iso-profit curve must be downward sloping.

Now consider how a change in the amenity level affects the position of the iso-profit curve. Suppose that costs fall as the amenity level rises,

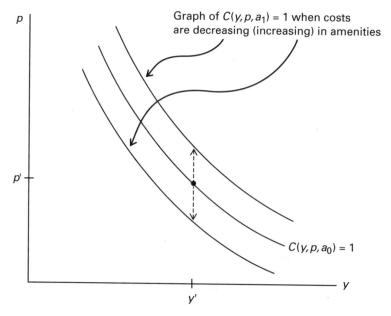

Figure 11.2
Iso-profit curves.

as in the first two examples above. Then, start again with a situation in which $a = a_0$, $p = p'$, and $y = y'$, and let the amenity level increase to $a_1 > a_0$. Since costs fall with a, the firm's profit level rises above zero. To cancel this change, restoring profit to zero, adjustments in p or y are needed, mirroring the consumer case. If the real-estate price alone were to adjust, an increase in p would be required to reduce profit, since costs are rising in p. This adjustment is represented by the dashed upward arrow in figure 11.2. Since the same argument applies for any starting point, it follows that the iso-profit curve with $a = a_1$ lies above the curve with $a = a_0$.

The positions of the curves are reversed, however, when costs are increasing in the amenity level. Then, starting with a situation in which $a = a_0$, $p = p'$, and $y = y'$, an increase in a up to a_1 *raises* costs, pushing profit below zero. To cancel this change, restoring profit to zero, p must fall, as indicated by the dashed downward arrow in figure 11.2. Thus, when costs are increasing in the amenity level, the iso-profit curve with $a = a_1$ lies below the curve with $a = a_0$.

Finally, suppose that firm costs are independent of the amenity level. Then, since an increase in a has no effect on profit, no offsetting change in p is needed to keep profit at zero. As a result, the iso-profit curve corresponding to the higher amenity level coincides with the curve for the lower amenity level. In other words, the same iso-profit curve is relevant, whatever the amenity level.

11.2.3   Comparing outcomes in high-amenity and low-amenity regions

Using the indifference curves and the iso-profit curves, the main question of interest can now be addressed: How do real-estate prices and incomes differ between high-amenity regions and low-amenity regions?

Consider first the case in which amenities have no effect on firm costs, which gives the most clear-cut answer. This case is illustrated in figure 11.3, which shows a single iso-profit curve (relevant for all amenity levels) and two indifference curves: one for the low-amenity region (with $a = a_0$) and one for the high-amenity region (with $a = a_1$).

In the low-amenity region, the real-estate price and the income level are given by the intersection point of the a_0 indifference curve and the iso-profit curve. This intersection point, which occurs at $p = p_0$ and $y = y_0$, simultaneously satisfies two requirements. First, when paying p_0 for real estate and earning y_0 in income, consumers enjoy utility level $\bar{u}$ since the point (p_0, y_0) lies on the a_0 indifference curve. Second, firms earn zero profit since the intersection point lies on the iso-profit curve.

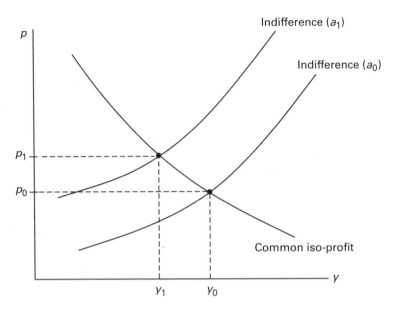

Figure 11.3
The case in which costs are independent of amenities.

Similarly, the intersection point between the iso-profit curve and the higher a_1 indifference curve gives the real-estate price and the income level in the high-amenity region. This point, denoted by (p_1, y_1), lies uphill from the low-amenity intersection on the iso-profit curve. This uphill location generates the crucial comparison between regions: the high-amenity region has a higher real-estate price than the low-amenity region $(p_1 > p_0)$ and a lower income level $(y_1 < y_0)$. Thus, when firm costs are independent of amenities, better amenities lead to higher real-estate prices and lower incomes.

This conclusion is intuitively appealing because it mirrors the separate compensating differentials in prices and incomes that would be required on the consumer side to equate utilities between the regions. In other words, if real-estate prices had to do all the work in equating utilities, then p_1 would have to be greater than p_0, whereas if incomes had to do all the work, y_1 would have to be less than y_0. When firm costs are independent of amenities, both adjustments happen together.

Now suppose that, instead of being independent of amenities, firm costs are decreasing in amenities. Then, instead of having a single iso-profit curve, the relevant diagram must have *two* iso-profit curves, with the higher one corresponding to the high-amenity region (recall figure

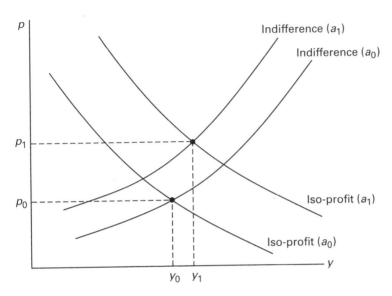

Figure 11.4
The case in which costs are decreasing in amenities.

11.2). Figure 11.4 illustrates this case. Once again, two intersection points are relevant, but now these are the intersection of the low indifference curve and the low iso-profit curve and the intersection of the high indifference curve and the high iso-profit curve. In the situation illustrated in figure 11.4, the high-amenity intersection point, (p_1, y_1), lies above and to the right of the low-amenity intersection point, (p_0, y_0). As a result, p_1 is greater than p_0, indicating that the higher-amenity region has the higher real-estate price. But y_1 is also greater than y_0, indicating that income is also higher in the high-amenity region, in contrast to the outcome in figure 11.3.

It is easy to see that this income comparison could be reversed if the diagram were drawn differently. In particular, suppose that the high-amenity iso-profit curve were not as high as the one shown, being closer to the low-amenity curve. Then, the intersection point (p_1, y_1) would move downhill on the a_1 indifference curve, and it could end up lying to the left of (p_0, y_0) while still being above it. In this case, the comparison would match that in figure 11.3: the high-amenity region would have a higher real-estate price and a lower income than the low-amenity region. This case, in which the shift in the iso-profit curve is modest, corresponds to a situation in which the cost reduction from amenities is small (requiring only a small increase in p to offset it). To

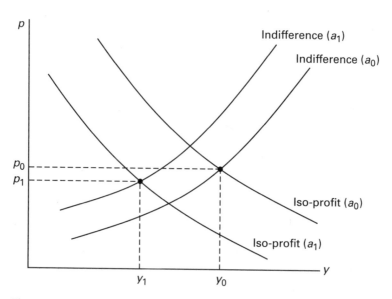

Figure 11.5
The case in which costs are increasing in amenities.

summarize, the conclusion to be drawn from figure 11.4 is as follows: When firm costs are decreasing in amenities, better amenities lead to higher real-estate prices but have an ambiguous effect on incomes. But if the amenity-related cost reduction is small, this ambiguity is dispelled, and better amenities lead to lower incomes.

Finally, consider the case in which firm costs are increasing in amenities, as illustrated in figure 11.5. Now the high-amenity region has a *lower* iso-profit curve, not a higher one. Thus, the high-amenity case corresponds to the intersection between the higher indifference curve and the lower iso-profit curve. In the situation depicted in the figure, this intersection point, (p_1, y_1), lies to the left of (p_0, y_0), the low-amenity intersection point, while also lying below it. As a result, y_1 is less than y_0, so that incomes are lower in the high-amenity region, but real-estate prices are lower too, with $p_1 < p_0$. This pattern again fails to match the one in figure 11.3.

As in the case of figure 11.4, the outcome could be different if the iso-profit shift were smaller, indicating that the cost increase from amenities is small. In particular, if the high-amenity curve were closer to the low-amenity curve, then (p_1, y_1) would move uphill along the a_1 indifference curve, perhaps ending up above (p_0, y_0). In this case, the comparison would again match that in figure 11.3: the high-amenity region would have a higher real-estate price and a lower income than the low-amenity region. In summary, the conclusion to be drawn from figure 11.5 is as follows: When firm costs are increasing in amenities, better amenities lead to lower incomes but have an ambiguous effect on real-estate prices. But if the amenity-related cost increase is small, better amenities lead to higher real-estate prices.

When the three cost cases are integrated, an overall conclusion can be stated: *If the effect of amenities on firm costs (which can be either negative, positive, or zero) is sufficiently small in magnitude, then higher amenities in a region lead to higher real-estate prices and lower incomes.* Thus, when the amenity cost effect is small, the outcome will be "close" to the one shown in figure 11.3, where cost effects are entirely absent. Better amenities will then lead to a higher p and a lower y.[2]

11.3   Measuring Urban Quality of Life

When amenities have little or no effect on firm costs, either real-estate prices or incomes can be used as an indicator of quality of life from the consumer's point of view. High real-estate prices would indicate the places that are nicest to live, as would low incomes. But since the connections between quality of life and real-estate prices and incomes can be ambiguous when firm costs are strongly linked to amenities, neither of these variables can be generally used with confidence as an unambiguous indicator of quality of life. How, then, can market data be used to identify the most desirable regions from the point of view of consumers?

Roback (1982) shows how, and her method is used by Blomquist et al. (1988) and other researchers to measure urban quality of life. The method first recognizes that consumers care about many kinds of amenities. The above model abstracted from this fact, but incorporating multiple amenities has no effect on the preceding analysis. Next, Roback's method assumes that amenities enter consumer utility in a simple linear fashion. The utility function thus includes the expression $\sum_{i=1}^{m} \beta_i a_i$, where a_i is the level of amenity i, β_i is the marginal valuation of that amenity, and m is the total number of different amenities. This weighted sum captures the contribution of amenities to consumer utility, and it therefore constitutes a measure of quality of life.

---

2. Exercise 11.1 offers an algebraic version of the analysis presented in figures 11.3–11.5.

If the marginal valuations of amenities could be estimated empirically, the qualities of life in different regions could be computed directly. In other words, if $\hat{\beta}_i$ denotes the estimated marginal valuation for amenity i, the quality of life in region k would be given by $\sum_{i=1}^{m} \hat{\beta}_i a_i^k$, with a_i^k denoting the level of amenity i in region k. This expression is just a weighted sum of actual amenity levels in region k, with the weights equal to the estimated marginal valuations.

The procedure for estimating the marginal valuations of amenities is, unfortunately, somewhat complicated. The first step is to run two regressions, the first of which relates housing prices in different regions to regional amenity levels as well as to housing characteristics. This is just a hedonic price regression like those discussed in chapter 6.[3] The second regression, known as a "hedonic wage equation," relates incomes for individual workers to the characteristics of the workers (age, education, experience, and so on) and to the amenity levels in the regions where they live. Note that, because the first regression shows the connection between real-estate prices and amenities and the second shows the connection between incomes and amenities, the regressions capture the kinds of patterns illustrated in figures 11.3–11.5. Also, since the hedonic wage regression includes personal characteristics, it realistically recognizes that workers in a region aren't all identical and will thus earn different incomes, in contrast to model's assumption of a common y. The second and final step in the procedure is to plug the estimated amenity coefficients from these two regressions into a particular formula, which then gives the $\hat{\beta}_i$ values.

The empirical analysis of Blomquist et al. (1988) uses 16 different amenity variables, including precipitation, temperature measures, sunshine, coastal access, crime, air and water pollution, and other variables. Their data are from 1980. In the housing-price regression, almost all the amenity variables show effects consistent with figure 11.3, with better amenities leading to higher prices. Better public safety (lower crime), though, has the opposite effect, leading to lower rather than higher housing prices.

The hedonic wage regression yields some additional contradictions of the pattern shown in figure 11.3, with worse amenities sometimes leading to lower rather than higher incomes. For example, more precipitation reduces rather than increases income, as do extreme temperature and higher particulate pollution (note that each of these variables

3. Note that the dependent variable for the regression is the value of the house, not the price per square foot (p).

Table 11.1
Quality-of-life rankings of metropolitan areas.

	1980 (Blomquist et al. 1988)	1980 (*Places Rated Almanac*, 1981)	1977–1995 (Gabriel and Rosenthal 2004)
1	Pueblo, Colorado	Atlanta, Georgia	Miami, Florida
2	Norfolk, Virginia	Washington, D.C.	San Diego, California
3	Denver, Colorado	Greensboro, North Carolina	Los Angeles, California
4	Macon, Georgia	Pittsburgh, Pennsylvania	San Francisco, California
5	Reno, Nevada	Seattle, Washington	Tampa, Florida
6	Binghamton, New York	Philadelphia, Pennsylvania	New York, New York
7	Newport News, Virginia	Syracuse, New York	Albany, New York
8	Sarasota, Florida	Portland, Oregon	Greensboro, North Carolina
9	West Palm Beach, Florida	Raleigh-Durham, North Carolina	Sacramento, California
10	Tucson, Arizona	Dallas–Fort Worth, Texas	Norfolk, Virginia

is an inverse amenity measure). Recall from figure 11.4, however, that such reverse effects are theoretically possible.

Using the results from these regressions, Blomquist et al. (1988) computed quality-of-life rankings for urban counties and their metropolitan areas for the year 1980. The first column in table 11.1 lists the top ten metropolitan areas on the resulting list. The second column gives a contemporaneous ranking from the *Places Rated Almanac* (Boyer and Savageau 1981), a non-academic source that also offers quality-of-life information.[4] Boyer and Savageau's approach differs from that of Blomquist et al. in that the marginal valuations of amenities (the $\hat{\beta}_i$ values) are chosen arbitrarily rather than through an empirical procedure based on economic theory. In other words, the valuations are based on the opinions of the almanac's staff members as to how amenities should be weighted.

The third column of table 11.1 lists the top ten metropolitan areas according to Stuart Gabriel and Stuart Rosenthal's (2004) quality-of-life ranking. The methodology of Gabriel and Rosenthal is conceptually equivalent to that of Blomquist et al. (1988), although urban amenities

---

4. These rankings are as reported in Berger, Blomquist, and Waldner 1987.

are captured by dummy variables for different cities (metropolitan-area "fixed effects") rather than by explicit amenity measures. This approach, which is made possible by the use of data spanning multiple years (from 1977 to 1995), generates a ranking for each year, and these rankings are then averaged to produce the list reproduced in table 11.1.

As can be seen from the table, the *Places Rated Almanac*'s ranking has no cities in common with the ranking of Blomquist et al. Moreover, only two West Coast cities appear in the rankings (Seattle and Portland, in the almanac's ranking), contrary to the apparent popular perceptions of the quality of life in that region. However, Gabriel and Rosenthal's ranking, which relies on more years of data, includes many of the obvious candidates while also diverging from the other two rankings in additional ways.[5] Although these differences show that the quality-of-life rankings need not agree and need not always match up with popular perceptions, the economic approach to generating these rankings is an important conceptual contribution.

11.4   Additional Issues

11.4.1   Firms' valuations of amenities

The empirical procedure outlined above reveals consumer valuations of amenities and generates quality-of-life rankings. But, amenities may also affect firm profits, and these effects could be used to generate an analogous ranking of metropolitan areas from the perspective of firms.

The procedure differs from the procedure for determining consumer valuations only in the second step. The first step again involves running a hedonic wage regression and a hedonic regression of real-estate prices, with the prices of business properties, rather than houses, now the dependent variable. The estimated amenity coefficients from these regressions are again plugged into a formula, although a different one than in the consumer case. The results give the marginal valuation of amenities from the firm's point of view (that is, the effect of amenities on profits). By applying these marginal valuations to existing amenity levels, metropolitan areas can then be ranked from the perspective of firms.

In addition to generating quality-of-life rankings, Rosenthal and Gabriel (2004) carry out an empirical exercise that is effectively equiva-

---

5. In addition to capturing amenities, Gabriel and Rosenthal's fixed effects capture additional unmeasured city characteristics that may account for the difference between their ranking and that of Blomquist et al. (1988).

lent to the procedure just explained, and they find that the ranking of metropolitan areas by firms is very different from the ranking by consumers (reproduced here in table 11.1). This finding suggests that the effects of amenities on consumer utilities and firm profits are often not in the same direction.

11.4.2   Amenities and migration

The model considered so far is an equilibrium model. It assumes that consumer utilities and firm profits are equalized in all locations. This assumption may not be true in the real-world economy, which could be in a disequilibrium state, with utilities or profits higher in some locations than in others. In such a situation, the economy will tend to move toward equilibrium, with economic agents migrating toward those locations that offer superior prospects. Consumer migration, in particular, could lead to population flows toward high-amenity regions, where housing prices and incomes may not yet have adjusted so as to cancel their amenity advantages. From studying regional population growth in the period 1970–2000, Jordan Rappaport (2007) concludes that migration did indeed flow toward regions with nice weather.

11.5   Summary

Housing prices are often viewed as an indicator of a region's quality of life, but compensating differentials can also work along the income dimension, with both prices and incomes varying to make consumers equally well off in all locations. Once this additional dimension is recognized, an additional equilibrium condition (equal profits for firms) must be introduced to pin down the possible patterns of housing prices and incomes across regions with different amenities. If the effect of amenities on firm costs is small, then regions with desirable amenities will have both high housing prices and low incomes. The empirical link between amenities, prices, and incomes can be used to estimate consumer valuations of amenities, and these valuations can then be used to produce quality-of-life rankings. A similar procedure allows regions to be ranked from the perspective of firms.

Exercises

Chapter 1

Exercise 1.1

Suppose that chemical X is manufactured using a raw material B that is available from a location called the "mine." Production of one ton of X requires 1/3 of a ton of B. A firm called X Enterprises, which has a contract to deliver 30 tons of X to a location called the "market," is trying to decide where to locate its plant. The mine and the market are 50 miles apart. Overland shipment of both X and B costs $2 per ton per mile shipped. However, additional costs must be incurred because a river passes between the mine and the market, and the river has no bridge. Goods must be loaded onto barges to cross the river, which is located 16 miles from the mine. Barge operators charge $1 per ton of X shipped across the river. However, since the input B is highly toxic when mixed with water, barge operators must charge an extremely high price to transport B across the river. This price defrays the cost of insurance that the operators must carry to meet liability claims should they accidentally pollute the river with their cargo. The cost of shipping one ton of B across the river is $195.

(a) Using the above information, find the transport-cost-minimizing location for X Enterprises. The answer can be found by computing transport costs at four locations: mine, market, mine side of the river, and market side of river. Assume that the width of the river is negligible, so that it can be ignored. Show your work.

(b) Illustrate your results in a carefully drawn diagram like that presented in figure 1.6 (use graph paper). Plot the input shipping-cost curve by plotting the input shipping costs at the same four locations as in (a) and then connecting the dots (the curve is drawn backward). Similarly, plot the output shipping cost at the four locations, and then connect the dots to generate the output shipping-cost curve. Then, plot the total shipping-cost curve by adding the input and output shipping costs at each of the four locations, plotting the points and connecting the dots. Using the diagram, identifying the best location for X Enterprises, which should be the same as your answer in (a). Note that the shipping-cost curves for this problem are straight lines with jumps at the river.

(c) Explain your results intuitively.

(d) Suppose that a bridge were built across the river, which would eliminate the cost of crossing it. Repeat (a), (b), and (c) under this assumption.

Exercise 1.2
Consider four cities, A, B, C, and D, located as follows:

A

D

B   C

Suppose that the residents of these cities consume widgets, with consumption in each city equaling 100 widgets (see the map below). The firm that produces widgets must decide how to arrange its production. It could set up four factories, one in each city, with each factory producing 100 widgets. In this case, the firm incurs no cost for shipping its output. Or the firm could locate its factory in the centrally located city, D. The single factory must then produce 400 widgets, 300 of which are shipped to cities A, B, and C. The shipping cost per widget is $2. A final assumption is that widget production exhibits economies of scale, with the cost per widget in a factory falling as output rises.

(a) Suppose the cost per widget varies with output as follows: cost is $4 if factory output is 100 widgets; cost is $1 if factory output is 400 widgets. In this situation, find the best arrangement of production for the firm (i.e., one central factory or four separate factories). The best arrangement leads to the lowest total cost for the firm, where the total is the sum of production and shipping cost.

(b) Repeat (a) if the cost per widget varies with output as follows: cost is $4 if factory output is 100 widgets; cost is $3 if factory output is 400 widgets.

(c) Explain intuitively any difference in the answers to (a) and (b).

(d) Suppose production costs are those given in (a), and let shipping cost per widget be given by t. Although $t = 2$ in (a), what value of t would make the two arrangements for production (centralized vs. separate factories) equivalent in terms of cost?

Exercise 1.3
Suppose that a developer is choosing tenants for a shopping center. There are four possible tenants: a department store, a toy store, a shoe store, and a hardware store. If each store were to be located in isolation outside a shopping center it would earn a certain level of gross profit per period (this is the level of profit before subtracting out space rent). In addition, each store requires a certain number of square feet of floor space, which is the same regardless of whether or not it locates in a shopping center. The relevant values for each store type are as follows:

	Gross profit in isolation	Required square footage
Department store	$100,000	9,000
Toy store	$11,200	1,000
Shoe store	$7,800	800
Hardware store	$7,000	1,100

When the stores are located together, each store earns a greater gross profit from the additional customer traffic generated by the nearby locations of other stores. The increase in gross profit for each store type ("affected store type") resulting from the presence of other store types ("added store type") is as follows:

Affected store type	Added store type Department	Toy	Shoe	Hardware
Department	—	$6,000	$8,000	$1,000
Toy	$2,000	—	$600	$300
Shoe	$2,000	$500	—	$200
Hardware	$1,000	$400	$200	—

Suppose that the shopping center developer charges a rent equal to each store's gross profit, leaving the store with a net profit of exactly zero. Total rent from the shopping center is then equal to the total gross profit of all its stores. The developer's profit is thus equal to total gross profit of all stores in the center minus the cost of providing space to the stores (that is, total rent minus the cost of providing space). Finally, suppose that, owing to high-quality construction and the need to provide common space around the stores, the construction cost for shopping center space is high. In particular, suppose that the cost per period per square foot of store floor space is $10.

(a) Give an intuitive explanation for the pattern of incremental profits from the presence of other stores in the second table above.

(b) Suppose the developer were to construct a single-store shopping center (a contradiction in terms, perhaps). There are four types of such centers (a department store alone, a toy store alone, and so on). Using the information above, compute the developer's profit from each of these four types of centers.

(c) Next compute the developer's profit from the various types of two-store shopping centers (i.e., department store plus shoe store, department store plus toy store, and so on; how many possibilities are there?)

(d) Finally, compute profits from the various types of three-store centers and from the single type of four-store center.

(e) Comparing your answers from (b), (c), and (d), identify the optimal shopping center (the one yielding the highest profit to the developer). Explain intuitively why this particular collection of stores is optimal.

Chapter 2

Exercise 2.1
In this exercise, you will analyze the supply-demand equilibrium of a city under some special simplifying assumptions about land use. The assumptions are: (i) all dwellings must contain exactly 1,500 square feet of floor space, regardless of location, and (ii) apartment complexes must contain exactly 15,000 square feet of floor space per square block of land area. These land-use restrictions, which are imposed by a zoning authority, mean that dwelling sizes and building heights do not vary with distance to the central business district, as in the model from chapter 2. Distance is measured in blocks.

Suppose that income per household equals $25,000 per year. It is convenient to measure money amounts in thousands of dollars, so this means that $y = 25$, where y is income. Next suppose that the commuting cost parameter t equals 0.01. This means that a person living ten blocks from the CBD will spend $0.01 \times 10 = 0.1$ per year (in other words, $100) getting to work.

The consumer's budget constraint is $c + pq = y - tx$, which reduces to $c + 1{,}500p = 25 - 0.01x$ under the above assumptions. Since housing consumption is fixed at 1,500, the only way that utilities can be equal for all urban residents is for bread consumption c to be the same at all locations. The consumption bundle (the bread, housing combination) will then be the same at all locations, yielding equal utilities.

For c to be constant across locations, the price per square foot of housing must vary with x in a way that allows the consumer to afford a fixed amount of bread after paying his rent and his commuting cost. Let c^* denote this constant level of bread consumption for each urban resident. For the moment, c^* is taken as given. We'll see below, however, that c^* must take on just the right value or else the city will not be in equilibrium.

(a) Substituting c^* in place of c in the budget constraint $c + 1{,}500p = 25 - 0.01x$, solve for p in terms of c^* and x. The solution tells what the price per square foot must be at a given location in order for the household to be able to afford exactly c^* worth of bread. How does p vary with location?

Recall that the zoning law says that each developed block must contain 15,000 square feet of floor space. Suppose that annualized cost of the building materials needed to construct this much housing is 90 (that is, $90,000).

(b) Profit per square block for the housing developer is equal to $15{,}000p - 90 - r$, where r is land rent per square block. In equilibrium, land rent adjusts so that this profit is identically zero. Set profit equal to zero, and solve for land rent in terms of p. Then substitute your p solution from (a) in the resulting equation. The result gives land rent r as a function of x and c^*. How does land rent vary with location?

Since each square block contains 15,000 square feet of housing and each apartment has 1,500 square feet, each square block of the city has 10 households living on it. As a result, a city with a radius of $\bar{x}$ blocks can accommodate $10\pi\bar{x}^2$ households ($\pi\bar{x}^2$ is the area of the city in square blocks).

(c) Suppose the city has a population of 200,000 households. How big must its radius $\bar{x}$ be in order to fit this population? Use a calculator and round off to the nearest block.

(d) In order for the city to be in equilibrium, housing developers must bid away enough land from farmers to house the population. Suppose that $c^* = 15.5$, which means that each household in the city consumes $15,500 worth of bread. Suppose also that farmers offer a yearly rent of $2,000 per square block of land, so that $r_A = 2$. Substitute $c^* = 15.5$ into the land rent function from (b), and compute the implied boundary of the city. Using your answer to (c), decide whether the city is big enough to house its population. If not, adjust c^* until you find a value that leads the city to have just the right radius.

(e) Using the equilibrium c^* from (d) and the results of (a) and (b), write down the equation for the equilibrium land rent function. What is the rent per square block at the CBD ($x = 0$) and at the edge of the city? Plot the land rent function. How much does a household living at the edge of the city spend on commuting?

(f) Suppose that the population of the city grows to 255,000. Repeat (c), (d), and (e) for this case (but don't repeat the calculation involving $c^* = 15.5$). Explain your findings. How does population growth affect the utility level of people in the city? The answer comes from looking at the change in c^* (since housing consumption is fixed at 1,500 square feet, the utility change can be inferred by simply looking at the change in bread consumption). Note that because they are fixed, housing consumption doesn't fall and building heights don't rise as population increases, as happened in the model in chapter 2. Are the effects on r and $\bar{x}$ the same?

(g) Now suppose that population is back at 200,000 (as in (c)) but that r_A rises to 3 (that is, farmers now offer $3,000 rent per square block). Note that, unlike in the chapter, the $\bar{x}$ value can't change as r_A rises (what is the reason?). Repeat (d), (e) for this case. Compare your answers with those in (f).

(h) Now suppose that instead of being located on a flat featureless plain, the CBD is located on the ocean (where the coast is perfectly straight). This means that only a half-circle of land around the CBD is available for housing. How large must be the radius of this half-circle be to fit the population of 200,000 residents? Using your answer, repeat (d) and (e), assuming that all parameters are back at their original values. Are people in this coastal city better or worse off than people in the inland city of (c) and (d)? (Assume unrealistically that people don't value the beach!) Can you give an intuitive explanation for your answer?

(i) Finally, focus again on the inland city, and suppose that the zoning authority imposes a building height restriction. This restriction limits housing square footage per block to 7,500, half the previous amount. The cost of building materials per square block falls from 90 to 43 (note that the cost is less than half as much because of diminishing returns). Find the new value of $\bar{x}$ (compare the answer in (h)), and repeat (d) and (e). How does the height restriction affect the utility of urban residents? Explain intuitively why this effect emerge. Does the restriction seem to be a good policy?

Chapter 3

Exercise 3.1
In this exercise, you will analyze building height variation in a city where buildings of different ages coexist. As in the example in chapter 3, suppose that the city grows outward by one block each year. Block 0 is built in year 0, block 1 is built in year 1, block 2 is built in year 2, and so on. Suppose also that buildings are torn down and replaced after standing for 4 years. Buildings built in year 0 are replaced in year 4, buildings built in year 1 are replaced in year 5, and so on.

(a) Derive the city's building-age pattern in year 11, when it has a radius of 12 blocks (0–11). Once the age pattern is derived, write down the year in which buildings in each block were built.

(b) Suppose that the height of buildings depends on their location and their construction date. For a given construction date, buildings farther from the CBD are shorter. At a given location, buildings built later in time are taller. Let S equal the height of a building measured in stories, and suppose that $S = 5T - 2x$, where T is the construction date (the number of the year in which the building was built) and x is the number of the block in which the building is located. Using this formula and the results of (a), compute building heights in each block of the city in year 11. Plot your results.

(c) Now suppose that building heights are determined by a different formula: $S = 5T - 5x + 10$. Repeat (b) for this case.

(d) Contrast the patterns shown in your plots to the building-height pattern predicted by the model from chapter 2, where building height is continually adjusted in response to changing conditions.

Exercise 3.2

In this problem, you will solve for the equilibrium population of an idealized city experiencing rural–urban migration, following the augmented Harris-Todaro model from chapter 3. The incomes earned in urban employment and in the rural area are y and y_A, respectively, and t is commuting cost per mile. J is the number of available urban jobs.

(a) Suppose the city is on an island and is a rectangle 10 blocks wide with the employment center at one end. The city spreads out along the length of the island to accommodate its population, with its edge located $\bar{x}$ blocks from the employment center. Compute the city's land area in square blocks as a function of $\bar{x}$. Assuming that each urban resident consumes 0.001 square block of land, compute the amount of land needed to house the city's population L. Set the resulting expression equal to the city's land area, and solve for $\bar{x}$ in terms of L.

(b) With J jobs in the city, the chance of a resident getting one of the jobs is J/L, which makes the expected income of a city resident equal to $y(J/L)$. The expected disposable income net of a commuting cost for a resident living at the city's boundary is then $y(J/L) - t\bar{x}$. The rural–urban migration equilibrium is achieved when this disposable income equals the rural income, as was explained in chapter 3. Write down this equation, and substitute your solution for $\bar{x}$ in terms of L from (a). Then multiply through by L to get a quadratic equation that determines L.

(c) Suppose that $y = 10,000$, $y_A = 2,000$, $t = 100$, and $J = 30,000$. Substitute these values into your equation from (b), and use the quadratic formula to solve for L (it's the positive root). The answer gives the city's equilibrium population.

(d) In equilibrium, what is the chance of getting an urban job? What is the implied unemployment rate in the city?

(e) What is the distance to the edge of the city? How much does a resident living at the edge spend on commuting?

(f) Suppose that y rises to 12,000. Repeat (c), (d), and (e). Give an intuitive explanation of the changes in your answers to (c) and (d).

Chapter 4

Exercise 4.1

Suppose that landowners have the power to restrict $\bar{x}$, the distance to the edge of the city, in order to increase the land rent they earn. Suppose that, with no restriction, the urban land rent function is given by $r = 100 - x$, where x is distance in blocks to the CBD. Suppose that agricultural land rent r_A is equal to 20.

(a) Compute $\bar{x}$ in the absence of any restriction by landowners, and illustrate your result in a diagram.

Now suppose that landowners can restrict $\bar{x}$ to a value of 65 blocks. When they impose this restriction, the urban land-rent curve shifts up, with the new rent function given by $r = 105 - x$.

(b) Show the new land-rent curve in your diagram, and indicate the area corresponding to the land-rent loss resulting from the restriction, as well as the additional area showing the land-rent gain.

(c) Compute the sizes of these areas, and compute the net gain or loss in land rent from imposing the $\bar{x}$ restriction. Is the restriction beneficial to the landlords? Will it be imposed? (Hint: The area corresponding to the land rent gain is a parallelogram, but instead of using the area formula for that type of shape, the area can be computed more easily by multiplying the horizontal length of the parallelogram (65 blocks) by its height.)

Now suppose that the landowners can impose a further restriction, with $\bar{x}$ set equal to 50 blocks. When this restriction is imposed, the urban land-rent curve shifts up more, with the new rent function given by $r = 110 - x$.

(d) Repeat (b) and (c). Relative to the original $\bar{x}$ restriction of 65, is this further restriction beneficial to the landlords? Will it be imposed?

(e) If your answer is different from before, explain intuitively why a difference emerges.

Chapter 5

Exercise 5.1

Suppose there are three potential users of a freeway: Mr. 1, Mr. 2, and Mr. 3. The cost of the best alternative route for each commuter is as follows:

Commuter	Alternate cost
Mr. 1	$7
Mr. 2	$5
Mr. 3	$3

The average cost AC of using the freeway (i.e., the cost per car) as a function of traffic volume T is as follows:

T	AC
1	$2
2	$5
3	$9

Using this information, answer the following questions:

(a) Find the equilibrium allocation of traffic between the freeway and alternate routes.

(b) Compute the total commuting cost for *all* commuters for the following four allocations of traffic. Total cost is the cost incurred by freeway users *plus* the cost incurred by commuters who use their alternate routes.

On freeway	On alternate routes
No one	Mr. 1, Mr. 2, Mr. 3
Mr. 1	Mr. 2, Mr. 3
Mr. 1, Mr. 2	Mr. 3
Mr. 1, Mr. 2, Mr. 3	No one

(Hint: Remember the definition of AC.)

(c) Remember that the socially optimal allocation of traffic between the freeway and alternate routes is the one that minimizes total commuting cost for all commuters. On the basis of your answer to (b), which allocation is socially optimal? How does total cost at the optimum compare with the total cost at the equilibrium? (Note that you don't have to use an MC curve to get the answer to this question.)

Exercise 5.2

Adam and his friends Brigit, Cheryl, David, Emily, Frank, Gail, Henry, Ivan, and Juliet have two choices for weekend activities. They can either go to the local park or get together in Adam's hot tub. The local park isn't much fun, which means that the benefits from being there are low on the friends' common utility scale. In fact, each of the friends receives a benefit equal to 3 "utils" from being at the park. This benefit doesn't depend on how many of the friends go to the park. Adam's hot tub, on the other hand, can be fun, but the benefits of using it depend on how many of the friends are present. When the tub isn't too crowded, it's quite enjoyable. When lots of people show up, however, the tub is decidedly less pleasant. The relationship between benefit per person (measured in utils) and the number of people in the hot tub (denoted by T) is $AB = 2 + 8T - T^2$, where AB denotes "average benefit."

(a) Using the above formula, compute AB for $T = 1, 2, 3, \ldots, 10$. Next compute total benefit from use of the hot tub for the above T values as well as $T = 0$. Total benefit is just T times AB. Finally, compute marginal benefit (MB), which equals the change in total benefit from adding a person to the hot tub. To do so, adopt the following convention: define MB at $T = T'$ to be the change in total benefit when T is increased from $T' - 1$ to T' (in other words, MB gives the change in total benefits from entry of the "last" person). Deviation from this convention will lead to inappropriate answers. For example, computation of MB using calculus will lead you astray, since we are dealing with a discrete problem rather than a continuous one.

(b) Recalling that the park yields 3 utils in benefits to each person, find the equilibrium size of the group using the hot tub. Show that (aside from the owner Adam), we can't be sure of the identities of the other hot tub users. (Hint: In contrast to the freeway case, the relevant benefit number will not exactly equal 3 at the equilibrium, with a similar outcome occurring in the other cases considered below.)

(c) Find the optimal size of the hot tub group, and give an explanation of why it differs from the equilibrium size. Next compute the grand total of benefits for all the friends, which is the sum of total benefits for the hot tub group and total benefits for those using the park. Perform this computation for both the equilibrium and the optimal group sizes. What do your results show?

Now suppose that a new video game arcade opens in the friends' town. While all the friends prefer playing video games to going to the park, some friends like video games more than others. The utils received from playing video games are as follows for the friends:

Adam	8
Brigit	13
Cheryl	18
David	20
Emily	27
Frank	30
Gail	31
Henry	34
Ivan	36
Juliet	37

(d) Using the above information, identify the equilibrium group of hot tub users. Then identify the optimal group of hot tub users. Why do the groups differ? Compute the grand total of benefits for hot tub users and video game players in both situations.

(e) Compute the toll/subsidy schedule required to support the optimum. Recall that in the freeway case, the toll at a given T is equal to the difference between MC and AC at that T. In the present case, the toll (or subsidy) is given by AB minus MB. Show that when this toll/subsidy schedule is used, the equilibrium coincides with the optimum. Find the toll charged (or subsidy paid) in the new equilibrium in both the park case and the video games case.

Chapter 6

Exercise 6.1

Assume that the parameter values in the model of housing tenure choice are as follows:

$i = 0.03$ (mortgage interest rate),

$h = 0.02$ (property tax rate),

$d = 0.02$ (depreciation rate),

$g = 0.04$ (housing appreciation rate),

$e = 0.02$ (rate of excess depreciation),

$\lambda = 0.35$ (landlord's tax rate).

(a) Using this information, compute $\hat{\tau}$, the critical consumer income-tax rate that separates renters and owner-occupiers. Note that in this computation, you are finding the intersection point of the flat rent line and the downward-sloping line corresponding to the owner-occupier's cost.

(b) Suppose λ increases to 0.40, and compute the new $\hat{\tau}$. How do the relative sizes of the renter and owner groups change? Give an intuitive explanation for your answer, and illustrate your answer in a diagram.

(c) Suppose λ is back at 0.35 but that h increases to 0.03, and compute the new $\hat{\tau}$. How do the relative sizes of the renter and owner groups change? Give an intuitive explanation for your answer, and illustrate it in a diagram (note that this diagram isn't as simple as that in (b)).

Exercise 6.2
Using a two-period model, this problem investigates tenure choice in the presence of a down-payment requirement along with the incentives for mortgage default. Consumer utility depends on non-housing consumption in each period, which equals what is left after paying housing costs. With c_1 and c_2 denoting consumption in periods 1 and 2, utility is equal to $c_1 + \delta c_2$, where δ is the discount factor. A high value of δ indicates that the consumer is "patient," placing a relatively high value on second-period consumption relative to first-period consumption.

Everyone is a renter in the first period. To become an owner-occupier, which happens in the second period, the consumer must accumulate a down payment D while renting. At the end of the first period, the consumer purchases a house, which costs V, using the down payment D along with a mortgage equal to $M = V - D$. The consumer moves in at the beginning of the second period, paying the user cost during that period, and the house is sold at the end of the period. When the house is sold, the mortgage is paid off, and the consumer gets back the down payment. If the consumer instead remains a renter in the second period, there's no need to accumulate a down payment, and housing cost in the second period just equals rent.

Using the previous information, the non-housing consumption levels for an owner-occupier are as follows:

c_1 = income − rent − down payment

and

c_2 = income – owner-occupier's user cost + down payment.

For a renter,

c_1 = income – rent

and

c_2 = income – rent.

Suppose that the simple model of subsection 6.3.5 (where $e = 0$) applies, and that property taxes, depreciation, and capital gains are all 0 ($h = d = g = 0$). But the mortgage interest rate equals 5 percent, so that $i = 0.05$, and the consumer's income tax rate is $\tau = 0.3$. In addition, $V = 200$ and income = 40 (dollar amounts are measured in thousands, so that the house's value is \$200,000). The required downpayment equals 10 percent of the house's value, so $D = 0.1V$. For simplicity, let the house size be fixed at $q = 1$, so that $V = v$ (house value and value per unit are then the same). With this assumption, V can be used in place of v in the user-cost and rent formulas in subsection 6.3.5.

(a) Using this information, compute D along with rent R and the owner-occupier's user cost. Note that the user cost is given by the usual formula, even though a down payment is present.

Your answer should show that the owner-occupier's user cost is less than rent. Note that, to benefit from this lower second-period housing cost, the consumer must save funds for a down payment in the first period. Whether the lower housing cost makes it worthwhile to undertake this saving depends on the consumer's patience, as you will see below.

(b) Using the formulas above, compute c_1 and c_2 for an owner-occupier.

(c) Compute c_1 and c_2 for a renter.

(d) Plug the results of parts (b) and (c) into the utility formula $c_1 + \delta c_2$ to get the utilities of an owner-occupier and a renter as functions of the discount factor δ.

(e) Compute the value of δ that makes the consumer indifferent between being a renter and an owner-occupier. Let this value be denoted by δ^*.

(f) Pick a δ value larger than your δ^* (but less than 1) and compare the utilities of the renter and the owner-occupier for this value. Then pick a δ value smaller than your δ^* (but greater than 0) and compare the utilities of the renter and the owner-occupier.

(g) What do your results say about the effect of consumer patience on the rent-own decision? Recall that a higher δ means greater patience. Give an intuitive explanation of your conclusion.

Suppose now that, once the second period is reached, the value of the house drops unexpectedly. Instead of staying at 200, V drops to 190. This drop occurs *after* the owner-occupier has made the mortgage-interest payment (so that the user cost is already paid).

(h) Under the previous numerical assumptions, what is the size (M) of the consumer's mortgage? Are the proceeds from sale of the house enough to payoff the mortgage? Does the consumer get all of his down payment back?

(i) Suppose that V were instead to drop to 170. Are the proceeds from sale of the house enough to pay off the mortgage?

If the answer to part (i) is No, the consumer has two options. The first is to default on the mortgage, which means handing the house over to the bank rather than paying off the loan. The second option is to pay off the mortgage, which means paying the bank an additional amount beyond the proceeds from selling the house in order to retire the loan.

(j) Suppose that default is costless, so that the default cost C is 0. In the situation from part (i), which option (default or paying off the mortgage) is better? In other words, which option imposes a lower cost on the consumer?

(k) Suppose instead that consumer incurs $5,000 worth of default costs (the future cost of impaired credit, the psychic cost of guilt, and so on), so that $C = 5$. Which of the options from part (j) is best?

(l) Suppose instead that $C = 12$. Which option is best?

Chapter 7

Exercise 7.1
Although adjustment to the equilibrium may take a long time in a stock-flow housing model, adjustment is fast under some circumstances, which makes for an easy analysis. This problem considers such a case and illustrates the effect of rent control. Suppose that the initial demand curve for housing is given by $p = 3 - H$, where p is the rental price per square foot of housing and H is the size of the stock in square

feet. Note that this equation gives the height up to the demand curve at any H. The flow supply curve for housing is given by $p = \Delta H + 2$, where ΔH is the change in the stock. Again, this equation gives the height up to the flow supply curve at any value of ΔH. Note that the slopes of the two curves are -1 and 1, respectively, a fact that allows simple answers to be derived below.

(a) Compute the equilibrium price p_e (the price at which $\Delta H = 0$).

(b) Suppose that prior to the demand shock, the housing market is in equilibrium, with a stock of size $H = 1$. Verify that the price in the market equals p_e when the stock is this size.

    After the demand shock (e.g., arrival of the Cuban refugees), demand increases to $p = 8 - H$.

(c) With the new higher demand, the price in the market shoots up to a higher value, denoted by p'. Compute p'.

(d) Next, compute the change in the housing stock that occurs as developers respond to this new price (compute ΔH). Then, compute the new size for the housing stock, which equals the original stock plus ΔH.

(e) Compute the price that prevails in the market after this increase in the housing stock. Is further adjustment of the stock required to reach equilibrium? How many periods does it take for the market to reach the new equilibrium?

    Instead of following the sequence you have just analyzed, now suppose that rent control is imposed immediately after the demand shock, with the controlled price set at $p_c = 3$.

(f) Compute H', the stock size at which rent control ceases to have an effect (in other words, the stock size where the equilibrium price is equal to p_c). How many periods does it take for the stock to reach H' under rent control?

(g) How many periods does it take for the market to reach the new equilibrium, where $p = p_e$?

(h) Illustrate your entire analysis in a diagram.

(i) On the basis of your analysis, does rent control seem like a good response to a demand shock?

Exercise 7.2
This problem illustrates a consumer's decision to be homeless in the presence of a minimum housing-consumption constraint, imposed through misguided government regulation. Let c denote "bread" con-

sumption and q denote housing consumption in square feet of floor space. Suppose that a unit of bread costs \$1 and that q rents for \$1 per square foot. The consumer's budget constraint is then $c + q = y$, where y is income, which equals \$1,000 per month.

(a) Plot the budget line, putting q on the vertical axis and c on the horizontal axis. What is the budget line's slope?

(b) Suppose that minimum housing-consumption constraint says that q must be 500 square feet or larger. Show the portion of the budget line that is inaccessible to the consumer under this constraint. Assuming the consumer rents the smallest possible dwelling, with $q = 500$, what is the resulting level of bread consumption?

Assume that the consumer's utility function is given by $U(c, q) = c + \alpha \ln(q + 1)$, where ln is the natural log function (available on your calculator). Using calculus, it can be shown that the slope of the indifference curve at a given point (c, q) in the consumption space is equal to $-(q + 1)/\alpha$.

(c) Assume that $\alpha = 101$. Supposing for a moment that the minimum housing-consumption constraint were absent, how large a dwelling would the consumer rent? The answer is found by setting the indifference-curve slope expression equal to the slope of the budget line from (a) and solving for q. Note that this solution gives the tangency point between an indifference curve and the budget line. Is the chosen q smaller than 500? Illustrate the solution graphically. Compute the associated c value from the budget constraint, and substitute c and q into the utility function to compute the consumer's utility level.

(d) Now reintroduce the housing-consumption constraint, and consider the consumer's choices. The consumer could choose either to be homeless, setting $q = 0$, or to consume the smallest possible dwelling, setting $q = 500$. Compute the utility level associated with each option, and indicate which one the consumer chooses. Compute the utility loss relative to the case with no housing-consumption constraint. Illustrate the solution graphically, showing the indifference curves passing through the two possible consumption points.

(e) Now assume that $\alpha = 61$. Repeat (c) for this case.

(f) Repeat (d).

(g) Give an intuitive explanation for why the outcomes in the two cases are different.

Chapter 8

Exercise 8.1

In this problem, you will compare the level of a public good chosen under majority voting with the socially optimal level under three different sets of circumstances. Suppose first that individual i's demand curve for z is given by α_i/z, where α_i is a positive parameter. Instead of being linear, this demand curve is a hyperbola. Suppose further that z costs \$1 per unit to produce ($c = 1$) and that this cost is shared equally among consumers. Therefore, cost per person is $1/n$ per unit of z. Then consider the three sets of circumstances listed below. Each situation has a different number of consumers in the economy and different collections of α values for the consumers. The number of consumers is denoted by n and the vector of α values by $A = (\alpha_1, \alpha_2, \dots, \alpha_{n-1}, \alpha_n)$.

Case 1: $n = 7$, $A = (4, 2, 12, 4, 5, 13, 8)$.

Case 2: $n = 5$, $A = (10, 6, 11, 14, 8)$.

Case 3: $n = 9$, $A = (6, 9, 10, 4.5, 12, 7, 13.5, 8, 11)$.

Using this information, do the following:

(a) For each case, compute the preferred z level for each voter. Identify the median voter, and indicate the z level chosen under majority voting.

(b) For each case, compute the D_Σ curve, and find the socially optimal level of z.

(c) For each case, compare the z level under majority voting with the socially optimal z. Explain the difference (if any) between the two z values.

Exercise 8.2

Consider two homogeneous jurisdictions, one of which contains rich consumers (type 1), who are high demanders of the public good z, while the other contains poor consumers (type 2), who are low demanders. The demand curves for the types are given by $D_1 = 6 - z$ and $D_2 = 4 - z$. The public good is financed by a property tax in each jurisdiction, but since the jurisdictions are homogeneous, the property tax is equivalent to a head tax. The level of z is decided by majority vote. Suppose that $c(n)/n$, the per capita cost of a unit of z, equals 3 in each jurisdiction.

(a) Find the public good level in each jurisdiction, and illustrate the levels in a diagram. Show the surplus levels for both types of consumers.

Now consider what happens if one poor consumer moves into the rich jurisdiction. Because the poor consumer buys a small house, his cost per unit of z is lower than 3. Using some algebra, it can be shown that the cost per unit of z for the poor consumer equals $3q_2/q_1$, where q_2 gives the size of a poor consumer's house and q_1 gives the size of a rich consumer's house. Since $q_2 < q_1$, this cost is smaller than 3. In contrast, the cost per unit of z for a rich consumer remains at 3 (this outcome requires that just one poor person moves into the jurisdiction).

(b) Suppose that $q_2/q_1 = 1/3$, so that a poor consumer's house is only one-third as large as a rich consumer's house. Using the above formula, compute the cost per unit of z for the poor household. Remembering that majority rule prevails, compute the change in surplus for the poor consumer if he moves into the rich jurisdiction. Illustrate your calculation in a diagram. On the basis of your answer, will the poor consumer relocate?

(c) Repeat (b) under the assumption that $q_2/q_1 = 2/3$.

(d) Repeat (b) under the assumption that $q_2/q_1 = 5/6$.

(e) Provide an intuitive explanation of your results.

Exercise 8.3

Consider a city with three consumers: 1, 2, and 3. The city provides park land for the enjoyment of its residents. Parks are a public good, and the amount of park land (which is measured in acres) is denoted by z. The demands for park land for the three consumers are as follows:

$D_1 = 40 - z$,

$D_2 = 30 - z$,

$D_3 = 20 - z$.

These formulas give the height of each consumer's demand curve at a given level of z. Note that each demand curve cuts the horizontal axis, eventually becoming negative. For the problem to work out right, you must use this feature of the curves in deriving D_Σ. In other words, don't assume that the curves become horizontal once they hit the axis.

(a) The height of the D_Σ curve at a given z is just the sum of the heights of the individual demands at that z. Using this fact, compute the expression that gives the height up to the D_Σ curve at each z.

(b) The cost of park land per acre, denoted by c, is 9 (like the demand intercepts, you can think of this cost as measured in thousands of dollars). Given the cost of park land, compute the socially optimal number of acres of park land in the city.

(c) Compute the level of social welfare at the optimal z. This is just the area of the surplus triangle between D_Σ and the cost line.

(d) Suppose there are two other jurisdictions, each with three consumers, just like the given jurisdiction. Compute total social welfare in the three jurisdictions, assuming each chooses the same amount of park acres as the first jurisdiction.

(e) Now suppose the population is reorganized into three homogeneous jurisdictions. The first has three type-1 consumers (i.e., high demanders). The second has three type-2 consumers (medium demanders), and the third has three type-3 consumers (low demanders). Repeat (a), (b), and (c) for each jurisdiction, finding the D_Σ curve, the optimal number of park acres, and social welfare in each jurisdiction.

(f) Compute total social welfare by summing the social welfare results from (e) across jurisdictions. How does the answer compare with social welfare from (d)? On the basis of your answer, are homogeneous jurisdictions superior to the original mixed jurisdictions?

Exercise 8.4

Suppose that the cost function for a particular public good is given by

$c(n)z = (40n - 12n^2 + n^3)z$.

(a) Using this formula, derive the formula for the cost per unit of z per capita, or $c(n)/n$.

(b) The best jurisdiction size is where $c(n)/n$ is as small as possible. Using the results of (a), compute this per capita cost for $n = 1, 2, 3, \ldots,$ 10. What jurisdiction size minimizes unit cost per capita? What is the resulting level of the unit cost?

(c) Suppose that all consumers in the economy are identical, and each consumer's demand for z is given by $D = 20 - z$. Using the results of (b), compute the D_Σ curve for an optimal-size jurisdiction (this is a jurisdiction of the size found in (b)). This computation is done by adding up as many individual D's as there are people in the optimal jurisdiction.

(d) Using the unit cost figure from (b), find the optimal level of z in the optimal-size jurisdiction. Also, compute social welfare in the optimal-size jurisdiction.

(e) Suppose the economy consists of 18 people. How many optimal-size jurisdictions can be created out of this population? Using the results of (d), what is total social welfare in the economy?

(f) Now suppose that instead of being divided into optimal-size juris-dictions, the population is divided into two jurisdictions of size 9. Using the previous results, find the unit cost of z per capita in these jurisdictions. Then find the optimal level of z in each jurisdiction, as well as social welfare in each jurisdiction.

(g) Compute social welfare in the whole economy when there are two 9-person jurisdictions. Compare your answer with that from (e). How big is the loss resulting from non-optimal jurisdiction sizes?

Chapter 9

Exercise 9.1
Suppose there are two polluting factories, surrounded by identical residential neighborhoods. The marginal damage curves are identical for the two neighborhoods, and they are given by $MD_1 = P$ and $MD_2 = P$, where P is the level of pollution. The marginal benefit curves for the factories, however, are different. The marginal benefit curve for the first factory is $MB_1 = 8 - P$, while the curve for the second factory, which uses a cleaner production process, is given by $MB_2 = 4 - P$ (both curves become zero once they hit the horizontal axis).

(a) Illustrate the curves for the two neighborhoods in two diagrams, and identify the pollution levels chosen by the firms in the absence of government intervention. Find the level of social surplus achieved in this case.

(b) Find the socially optimal pollution levels in the two neighbor-hoods. Why do they differ? Compute social welfare in each neighbor-hood, and sum the values across the two neighborhoods to get total surplus. This is the surplus level that would result from imposition of separate pollution standards in the two neighborhoods.

(c) Suppose the government institutes a common pollution standard, which applies to both neighborhoods. This standard restricts pollution from any factory to a maximum value of three units. Under this standard, how much does each factory pollute? Compute the resulting level of social surplus in each neighborhood, and add the values.

(d) Considering the social surplus from (a), (b), and (c), comment on the wisdom of using a common pollution standard. How does the standard compare with separate pollution standards, and with the case in which the government doesn't intervene at all?

Exercise 9.2

Suppose the marginal damage and marginal benefit curves in a polluted neighborhood are $MD = P/3$ and $MB = 4 - P$. Also, suppose that transactions costs are low, so that the neighborhood residents and the firm can bargain. We saw that in this case, the socially optimal level of pollution is achieved. Start by computing the socially optimal P. Then, for each of the following cases, compute the amount of money transferred through the bargaining process, and indicate who pays whom (i.e., whether consumers pay the firm, or vice versa). Also, compute the gains to each party relative to the status quo (i.e., the starting point of the bargaining process).

(a) Residents have the right to clean air; firm is dominant in the bargaining process.

(b) Residents have the right to clean air; residents are dominant in the bargaining process.

(c) Firm has the right to pollute; firm is dominant in the bargaining process.

(d) Firm has the right to pollute; residents are dominant in the bargaining process.

Exercise 9.3

Suppose that pollution in a neighborhood comes from *two* factories, with marginal benefit curves given by $MB_1 = 12 - P_1$ and $MB_2 = 8 - P_2$. The level of pollution in the neighborhood is given by $P = P_1 + P_2$. The government wants to limit pollution by instituting a pollution-rights market. The government's desired level of P is 10, so it prints 10 pollution rights and offers them for sale to the firms.

(a) Find the equilibrium selling price of a pollution right, as well as the allocation of rights (and hence pollution levels) across the two factories.

(b) Repeat (a) for the case in which the government's desired level of pollution equals 14.

(c) Comment on the usefulness of a pollution rights market in achieving efficient levels of pollution abatement.

Chapter 10

Exercise 10.1

Suppose that a city operates two neighborhood schools, one in the rich neighborhood and one in the poor neighborhood. The schools are equal in size and currently have equal budgets. The city receives $10 million in federal grant money that can be used to supplement the budgets of the two schools, which are initially identical. For each school, the average score on a standardized achievement test depends on how many dollars are allocated to the school. Letting S denote the average test score and X denote additional spending in millions of dollars, the relationships between scores and additional spending for the two schools are as follows:

$$S_{poor} = 40 + X_{poor},$$

$$S_{rich} = 45 + 3X_{rich}.$$

(a) Plot the above relationships and interpret the differences between the slopes and intercepts in intuitive terms. Do you think that the difference in the "productivity" of additional educational spending between rich and poor reflected in the above formulas is realistic? (To answer, you might focus on the differences in home life for the groups and differences in the availability of extra-curricular enrichment activities.)

(b) Derive and plot the community's transformation curve between S_{rich} and S_{poor}, remembering that X_{poor} and X_{rich} must sum to 10. Because of the linear relationship between S and X for each group, the transformation curve is a straight line. (Hint: You should be able to find the transformation curve solely by locating its endpoints.)

(c) Find and plot the test scores that would result if the city divided the grant money equally between the schools.

(d) Find and plot the test scores that would result if the city allocated the grant money to equalize the scores across schools.

(e) Finally, consider the case in which the community's goal is to maximize its overall average test score, which equals $(S_{poor} + S_{rich})/2$? How should it allocate the grant money? Find the answer by using a diagram that extends the iso-crime line approach from the chapter. (You will not get full credit for finding the answer by trial-and-error number crunching, although you are welcome to include such numbers along with your diagram). Using the results of (a), explain why your answer comes out the way it does.

(f) What if the coefficient of X_{poor} in the above formula had been equal to 2 and the coefficient of X_{rich} had been equal to 1.5? Without drawing any diagrams or doing any computations, you should be able to tell how the community would allocate the grant money if its goal were to maximize the average score. What allocation would it choose?

(g) Suppose the community's social welfare function is $(1/5)S_{poor} + \sqrt{S_{rich}}$. How should the grant money be allocated to maximize this function? (here, you can crunch some numbers, or use calculus if you like). Show the solution in your plot and contrast it to that from (c).

Chapter 11

Exercise 11.1
In this question, you will carry out the algebraic equivalent to the diagrammatic analysis investigating the effect of amenities on incomes and real-estate prices. To start, let the consumer utility function be given by $q^{1/2}c^{1/2}a^{1/2}$, where c is consumption of "bread" (a catch-all commodity), q is real estate (housing), and a is amenities, which are valued by the consumer given that a's exponent is positive. Letting y denote income, it can be shown that the consumer demand functions for bread and housing are given by $c = y/2$ and $q = y/(2p)$, where p is the price per unit of real estate.

(a) Substitute the above demand functions into the utility function to get what is known as the "indirect" utility function, which gives utility as a function of income, prices, and amenities.

(b) Using your answer from (a), how does utility change when income y rises? When the real-estate price p rises? How does utility change when amenities increase?

   With free mobility, everyone must enjoy the same utility level regardless of where they live. Let this constant utility level be denoted by $\bar{u}$.

(c) Set the utility expression from (a) equal to $\bar{u}$. The resulting equation shows how y and p must vary with amenities a in order for everyone to enjoy utility $\bar{u}$. To see one implication of the equation, solve it to yield p as a function of the other variables. According to your solution, how must p change when amenities rise, with y held constant? Given an intuitive explanation of your answer. How must p change if y were to rise, with amenities held constant? Again, explain your answer.

As was explained in the chapter, another condition is needed to pin down an explicit solution that tells how y and p vary as amenities change. That condition comes from requiring that the production cost of firms be constant across locations. To generate this condition, let the production function for bread be given by $Dq^{1/2}L^{1/2}a^{\theta}$, where q now represents the firm's real-estate input, L is labor input and a again is amenities (D is a constant). The exponent θ could be either positive or negative, indicating that an increase in a could either raise or lower output. Recalling that p is the price of real estate and y is the price of labor, it can be shown that the cost per unit of bread output is equal to $p^{1/2}y^{1/2}a^{-\theta}$.

(d) This function shows that an increase in p or y raises unit cost, but that an increase in a could either raise or lower costs. Give an example for each possibility, identifying an amenity a valued by consumers that could alternatively raise, or lower, production costs for particular goods.

(e) The condition ensuring that costs are constant across locations can be written as $p^{1/2}y^{1/2}a^{-\theta} = 1$. Suppose that $\theta > 0$, so that higher amenities reduce costs. What must happen to p as a increases to keep costs constant, with y held fixed? Give an intuitive explanation for your answer.

(f) To generate an explicit solution for y in terms of amenities, take the p solution from (c) and substitute it into the constant-cost condition from (e). The resulting equation just involves y, and use it to solve for y as a function of a.

(g) Suppose that θ is negative. Using your solution from (f), how does y change when a increases? Suppose instead that θ is positive but that its magnitude is unknown. Can you say how y responds to an increase in a? How about if θ is positive and small? How about if θ is positive and large? How about if θ is zero?

(h) Now take the y solution from (f) and use it to eliminate y from the p solution in (c). Solve the resulting equation for p as a function of a. Suppose that θ is positive. How does p change when a increases?

Suppose instead that θ is negative but that its magnitude is unknown. Can you say how p responds to an increase in a? How about if θ is negative but close to zero? How about if θ is negative and far from zero? How about if θ equals zero?

(i) Summarize your conclusions about how amenities affect incomes and real-estate prices. Although some conclusions are ambiguous, it is possible to offer a clear-cut statement when the effect of amenities on production is "small," either positive or negative (with θ close to zero). What conclusion can be stated in this case?

(j) Relate your answer from (i) to the diagrammatic analysis from the chapter.

References

Aaronson, Daniel. 1998. Using Sibling Data to Estimate the Impact of Neighborhoods on Children's Educational Outcomes. *Journal of Human Resources* 33: 915–946.

Alonso, William. 1964. *Location and Land Use*. Harvard University Press.

Anas, Alex, Richard Arnott, and Kenneth A. Small. 1994. Urban Spatial Structure. *Journal of Economic Literature* 36: 1426–1464.

Arnott, Richard. 1995. Time for Revisionism on Rent Control? *Journal of Economic Perspectives* 9: 99–120.

Artle, Roland, and Pravin Varaiya. 1978. Life Cycle Consumption and Homeownership. *Journal of Economic Theory* 18: 38–58.

Ballester, Coralio, Antoni Calvó-Armengol, and Yves Zenou. 2006. Who's Who in Networks. Wanted: The Key Player. *Econometrica* 74: 1403–1417.

Baum-Snow, Nathaniel. 2007. Did Highways Cause Suburbanization? *Quarterly Journal of Economics* 122: 775–805.

Becker, Gary. 1968. Crime and Punishment: An Economic Approach. *Journal of Political Economy* 76: 169–217.

Behrman, Jere R., and Steven G. Craig. 1987. The Distribution of Public Services: An Exploration of Local Government Preferences. *American Economic Review* 77: 37–49.

Benabou, Roland. 1993. Workings of a City: Location, Education, and Production. *Quarterly Journal of Economics* 108: 619–652.

Berger, Mark C., Glenn C. Blomquist, and Werner Waldner. 1987. A Revealed-Preference Ranking of Quality of Life for Metropolitan Areas. *Social Science Quarterly* 68: 761–778.

Bergstrom, Ted C. 1979. When Does Majority Rule Supply Public Goods Efficiently? *Scandinavian Journal of Economics* 81: 216–226.

Bertaud, Alain, and Jan K. Brueckner. 2005. Analyzing Building-Height Restrictions: Predicted Impacts and Welfare Costs. *Regional Science and Urban Economics* 35: 109–125.

Blomquist, Glenn C. 2006. Measuring Quality of Life. In *A Companion to Urban Economics*, ed. R. J. Arnott and D. L. McMillen. Blackwell.

Blomquist, Glenn C., Mark C. Berger, and John P. Hoehn. 1988. New Estimates of the Quality of Life in Urban Areas. *American Economic Review* 78: 89–107.

Boyer, Richard, and David Savageau. 1981. *Places Rated Almanac: Your Guide to Finding the Best Places to Live in America*. Rand McNally.

Bradford, David F., and Harry H. Kelejian. 1973. An Econometric Model of the Flight to the Suburbs. *Journal of Political Economy* 81: 566–589.

Brueckner, Jan K. 1981. Congested Public Goods: The Case of Fire Protection. *Journal of Public Economics* 15: 45–58.

Brueckner, Jan K. 1982. A Test for Allocative Efficiency in the Local Public Sector. *Journal of Public Economics* 19: 311–331.

Brueckner, Jan K. 1986. The Downpayment Constraint and Housing Tenure Choice: A Simplified Exposition. *Regional Science and Urban Economics* 16: 519–525.

Brueckner, Jan K. 1987. The Structure of Urban Equilibria: A Unified Treatment of the Muth-Mills Model. In *Handbook of Regional and Urban Economics*. vol. II. ed. E. S. Mills. North-Holland.

Brueckner, Jan K. 1993. Inter-Store Externalities and Space Allocation in Shopping Centers. *Journal of Real Estate Finance and Economics* 7: 5–16.

Brueckner, Jan K. 1999. Modeling Urban Growth Controls. In *Environmental and Public Economics: Essays in Honor of Wallace E. Oates*, ed. A. Panagariya, P. Portney, and R. M. Schwab. Edward Elgar.

Brueckner, Jan K. 2000a. Urban Growth Models with Durable Housing: An Overview. In *Economics of Cities*, ed. J.-F. Thisse and J.-M. Huriot. Cambridge University Press.

Brueckner, Jan K. 2000b. Urban Sprawl: Diagnosis and Remedies. *International Regional Science Review* 23: 160–171.

Brueckner, Jan K. 2000c. Welfare Reform and the Race to the Bottom: Theory and Evidence. *Southern Economic Journal* 66: 505–525.

Brueckner, Jan K. 2002. Internalization of Airport Congestion. *Journal of Air Transport Management* 8: 141–147.

Brueckner, Jan K. 2004. Fiscal Decentralization with Distortionary Taxation: Tiebout vs. Tax Competition. *International Tax and Public Finance* 11: 133–153.

Brueckner, Jan K. 2007. Urban Growth Boundaries: An Effective Second-Best Remedy for Unpriced Traffic Congestion? *Journal of Housing Economics* 16: 263–273.

Brueckner, Jan K., and David Fansler. 1983. The Economics of Urban Sprawl: Theory and Evidence on the Spatial Sizes of Cities. *Review of Economics and Statistics* 55: 479–482.

Brueckner, Jan K., and Robert W. Helsley. 2011. Sprawl and Blight. *Journal of Urban Economics* 69: 205–213.

Brueckner, Jan K., and Hyun-A Kim. 2001. Land Markets in the Harris-Todaro Model: A New Factor Equilibrating Rural-Urban Migration. *Journal of Regional Science* 41: 507–520.

Brueckner, Jan K., and Fu-Chuan Lai. 1996. Urban Growth Controls with Resident Landowners. *Regional Science and Urban Economics* 26: 125–144.

Brueckner, Jan K., and Ann G. Largey. 2008. Social Interaction and Urban Sprawl. *Journal of Urban Economics* 65: 18–34.

Brueckner, Jan K., and Stuart S. Rosenthal. 2009. Gentrification and Neighborhood Housing Cycles: Will America's Future Downtowns Be Rich? *Review of Economics and Statistics* 91: 725–743.

Brueckner, Jan K., Jacques-François Thisse, and Yves Zenou. 1999. Why Is Central Paris Rich and Downtown Detroit Poor? An Amenity-Based Theory. *European Economic Review* 43: 91–107.

Bruegmann, Robert. 2005. *Sprawl: A Compact History*. University of Chicago Press.

Burchfield, Marcy, Henry G. Overman, Diego Puga, and Matthew A. Turner. 2006. Causes of Sprawl: A Portrait from Space. *Quarterly Journal of Economics* 121: 587–633.

Carlino, Gerald A., Satyajit Chatterjee, and Robert M. Hunt. 2007. Urban Density and the Rate of Invention. *Journal of Urban Economics* 61: 389–419.

Chay, Kenneth, and Michael Greenstone. 2005. Does Air Quality Matter? Evidence from the Housing Market. *Journal of Political Economy* 113: 376–424.

Ciccone, Antonio, and Robert E. Hall. 1996. Productivity and the Density of Economic Activity. *American Economic Review* 86: 54–70.

Coase, Ronald H. 1960. The Problem of Social Cost. *Journal of Law & Economics* 3: 1–44.

Colwell, Peter F., and Joseph W. Trefzger, 1992. "Homelessness: A Fresh Look." Office of Real Estate Research Letter, University of Illinois, 1992.

Conley, John P., and Ping Wang. 2006. Crime and Ethics. *Journal of Urban Economics* 60: 107–123.

Coulson, Edward N. 1991. Really Useful Tests of the Monocentric City Model. *Land Economics* 67: 299–307.

Crane, Randall. 1996. The Influence of Uncertain Job Location on Urban Form and the Journey to Work. *Journal of Urban Economics* 39: 342–356.

Davidoff, T. 2006. Labor Income, Housing Prices, and Homeownership. *Journal of Urban Economics* 59: 209–235.

De Bartolome, Charles. 1990. Equilibrium and Inefficiency in a Community Model with Peer Group Effects. *Journal of Political Economy* 98: 110–133.

Dietz, Robert, and Donald R. Haurin. 2003. The Private and Social Micro-Level Consequences of Homeownership. *Journal of Urban Economics* 54: 401–450.

Downs, Anthony. 1988. *Residential Rent Controls: An Evaluation*. Urban Land Institute.

Eberts, Randall W. 1981. An Empirical Investigation of Intraurban Wage Gradients. *Journal of Urban Economics* 10: 50–60.

Eid, Jean, Henry G. Overman, Diego Puga, and Matthew A. Turner. 2008. Fat city: Questioning the Relationship between Urban Sprawl and Obesity. *Journal of Urban Economics* 63: 385–404.

Fischel, William A. 1985. *The Economics of Zoning Laws: A Property Rights Approach to American Land Use Controls*. Johns Hopkins University Press.

Foote, Christopher L., Kristopher Gerardi, and Paul S. Willen. 2008. Negative Equity and Foreclosure: Theory and Evidence. *Journal of Urban Economics* 64: 234–245.

Freeman, Scott, Jeffrey Grogger, and Jon Sonstelie. 1996. The Spatial Concentration of Crime. *Journal of Urban Economics* 40: 216–231.

Fujita, Masahisa. 1989. *Urban Economic Theory*. Cambridge University Press.

Fujita, Masahisa, and H. Ogawa. 1982. Multiple Equilibria and Structural Transition of Non-Monocentric Urban Configurations. *Regional Science and Urban Economics* 18: 161–196.

Fujita, Masahisa, and Jacques-François Thisse. 2002. *Economics of Agglomeration: Cities, Industrial Location and Regional Growth*. Cambridge University Press.

Gabriel, Stuart A., and Stuart S. Rosenthal. 2004. Quality of the Business Environment versus Quality of Life: Do Firms and Households Like the Same Cities? *Review of Economics and Statistics* 86: 438–444.

Giuliano, Genevieve, and Kenneth A. Small. 1991. Subcenters in the Los Angeles Region. *Regional Science and Urban Economics* 21: 163–182.

Glaeser, Edward L. 1999. "An Overview of Crime and Punishment." Unpublished paper, Harvard University.

Glaeser, Edward L. 2008. *Cities, Agglomeration and Spatial Equilibrium*. Oxford University Press.

Glaeser, Edward L., Joseph Gyourko, and Raven Saks. 2005. Why Is Manhattan So Expensive? Regulation and the Rise in Housing Prices. *Journal of Law & Economics* 48: 331–370.

Glaeser, Edward L., Hedi D. Kallal, José A. Scheinkman, and Andrei Shleifer. 1992. Growth in Cities. *Journal of Political Economy* 100: 1126–1152.

Glaeser, Edward L., and Matthew E. Kahn. 2004. Sprawl and Urban Growth. In *Handbook of Regional and Urban Economics*, volume IV, ed. J. V. Henderson and J.-F. Thisse. Elsevier.

Glaeser, Edward L., Matthew E. Kahn, and Jordan Rappaport. 2008. Why Do the Poor Live in Cities? *Journal of Urban Economics* 63: 1–24.

Glaeser, Edward L., Bruce Sacerdote, and José A. Scheinkman. 1996. Crime and Social Interactions. *Quarterly Journal of Economics* 111: 508–548.

Gobillon, Laurent, Harris Selod, and Yves Zenou. 2007. The mechanisms of spatial mismatch. *Urban Studies* 44: 2401–2427.

Goodman, Allen C. 1988. An Econometric Model of Housing Price, Permanent Income, Tenure Choice and Housing Demand. *Journal of Urban Economics* 23: 327–353.

Grether, D.M., and Peter Mieszkowski. 1974. The Determinants of Real Estate Values. *Journal of Urban Economics* 1: 127–146.

Gyourko, Joseph, and Peter Linneman. 1989. Equity and Efficiency Aspects of Rent Control: An Empirical Study of New York City. *Journal of Urban Economics* 26: 54–74.

Gyourko, Joseph, and Peter Linneman. 1990. Rent Controls and Rental Housing Quality: A Note on the Effect of New York City's Old Controls. *Journal of Urban Economics* 27: 398–409.

Hamilton, Bruce. 1982. Wasteful Commuting. *Journal of Political Economy* 90: 1035–1053.

Hanushek, Eric A., John F. Kain, Jacob M. Markman, and Steven G. Rivkin. 2003. Does peer ability affect student achievement? *Journal of Applied Econometrics* 18: 527–544.

Harris, John R., and Michael P. Todaro. 1970. Migration, Unemployment and Development: A Two-Sector Analysis. *American Economic Review* 60: 126–142.

Haurin, Donald R., and H. Leroy Gill. 2002. The Impact of Transaction Costs and the Expected Length of Stay on Homeownership. *Journal of Urban Economics* 51: 563–584.

Henderson, J. Vernon. 1986. Efficiency of Resource Usage and City Size. *Journal of Urban Economics* 18: 47–70.

Henderson, J. Vernon. 2003. Marshall's Scale Economies. *Journal of Urban Economics* 53: 1–28.

Hirsch, Werner Z. 1970. *The Economics of State and Local Government.* McGraw-Hill.

Honig, Majorie, and Randall Filer. 1993. Causes of Intercity Variation in Homelessness. *American Economic Review* 83: 248–255.

Hoxby, Caroline M. 2000. Does Competition Among Public Schools Benefit Students and Taxpayers? *American Economic Review* 90: 1209–1238.

Ihlanfeldt, Keith R. 2007. The Effect of Land Use Regulation on Housing and Land Prices. *Journal of Urban Economics* 61: 420–435.

Ihlanfeldt, Keith R., and David L. Sjoquist. 1998. The Spatial Mismatch Hypothesis: A Review of Recent Studies and their Implications for Welfare Reform. *Housing Policy Debate* 9: 849–892.

Jaffe, Adam, Manuel Trajtenberg, and Rebecca Henderson. 2003. Geographic Localization of Knowledge Spillovers as Evidenced by Patent Citations. *Quarterly Journal of Economics* 108: 577–598.

Kelley, Allen C., and Jeffrey G. Williamson. 1984. *What Drives Third World City Growth?* Princeton University Press.

Kling, Jeffrey R., Jeffrey B. Liebman, and Lawrence F. Katz. 2007. Experimental Analysis of Neighborhood Effects. *Econometrica* 75: 83–119.

Krol, Robert, and Shirley Svorny. 2005. The effect of rent control on commute times. *Journal of Urban Economics* 58: 421–436.

Krugman, Paul. 1992. *Geography and Trade.* MIT Press.

Leape, Jonathan. 2006. The London Congestion Charge. *Journal of Economic Perspectives* 20: 157–176.

Lee, Kangoh, and Santiago Pinto. 2009. Crime in a Multi-Jurisdictional Model with Public and Private Crime Prevention. *Journal of Regional Science* 49: 977–996.

LeRoy, Stephen F., and Jon Sonstelie. 1983. Paradise Lost and Regained: Transportation Innovation, Income, and Residential Location. *Journal of Urban Economics* 13: 67–89.

Levitt, Steven D. 1997. Using Electoral Cycles in Police Hiring to Estimate the Effect of Police on Crime. *American Economic Review* 87: 270–290.

Levitt, Steven D. 2004. Understanding Why Crime Fell in the 1990s: Four Factors that Explain the Decline and Six that Do Not. *Journal of Economic Perspectives* 18: 163–190.

Mayo, Stephen K. 1981. Theory and Estimation in the Economics of Housing Demand. *Journal of Urban Economics* 10: 95–116.

McDonald, John F. 1989. Econometric Studies of Urban Population Density: A Survey. *Journal of Urban Economics* 26: 361–385.

McGrath, Daniel T. 2005. More Evidence on the Spatial Scale of Cities. *Journal of Urban Economics* 58: 1–10.

McMillen, Daniel P. 1996. One Hundred Fifty Years of Land Values in Chicago: A Nonparametric Approach. *Journal of Urban Economics* 40: 100–124.

McMillen, Daniel P. 2006. Testing for Monocentricity. In *Companion to Urban Economics*, ed. R. Arnott and D. McMillen. Blackwell.

Mills, Edwin S. 1967. An Aggregative Model of Resource Allocation in a Metropolitan Area. *American Economic Review* 57: 197–210.

Muth, Richard F. 1969. *Cities and Housing*. University of Chicago Press.

Nechyba, Thomas J., and Randy Walsh. 2004. Urban Sprawl. *Journal of Economic Perspectives* 18: 177–200.

Ng, Chen Feng. 2008. Commuting Distances in a Household Location Choice Model with Amenities. *Journal of Urban Economics* 63: 116–129.

Oates, Wallace. 1969. The Effects of Property Taxes and Local Public Spending on Property Values: An Empirical Study of Tax Capitalization and the Tiebout Hypothesis. *Journal of Political Economy* 17: 957–971.

O'Flaherty, Brendan. 1996. *Making Room: The Economics of Homelessness*. Harvard University Press.

Oreopoulos, Philip. 2003. The Long-Run Consequences of Living in a Poor Neighborhood. *Quarterly Journal of Economics* 118: 1533–1575.

Pack, Janet R., and Howard Pack. 1978. Metropolitan Fragmentation and Local Public Expenditures. *National Tax Journal* 81: 349–362.

Papageorgiou, Yorgos, and David Pines. 1998. *An Essay on Urban Economic Theory*. Kluwer.

Quigley, John M. 1982. Nonlinear Budget Constraints and Consumer Demand: An Application to Public Programs for Residential Housing. *Journal of Urban Economics* 12: 177–201.

Quigley, John M., Steven Raphael, and Eugene Smolensky. 2001. Homeless in America, Homeless in California. *Review of Economics and Statistics* 83: 37–51.

Rappaport, Jordan. 2007. Moving to Nice Weather. *Regional Science and Urban Economics* 37: 375–398.

Rhee, Hyok-Joo. 2008. Home-based Telecommuting and Commuting Behavior. *Journal of Urban Economics* 63: 198–216.

Ridker, Ronald G., and John A. Henning. 1967. The Determinants of Residential Property Values with Special Reference to Air Pollution. *Review of Economics and Statistics* 49: 246–257.

Roback, Jennifer. 1982. Wages, Rents and the Quality of Life. *Journal of Political Economy* 90: 257–278.

Rosen, Sherwin. 1974. Hedonic Prices and Implicit Markets: Product Differentiation in Pure Competition. *Journal of Political Economy* 82: 34–55.

Rosenthal, Stuart S., and William C. Strange. 2003. Geography, Industrial Organization, and Agglomeration. *Review of Economics and Statistics* 85: 377–393.

Rosenthal, Stuart S., and William C. Strange. 2004. Evidence on the Nature and Sources of Agglomeration Economies. In *Handbook of Urban and Regional Economics*. vol. 4. ed. J. V. Henderson and J.-F. Thisse. Elsevier.

Scotchmer, Suzanne. 1994. Public Goods and the Invisible Hand. In *Modern Public Finance*, ed. J. Quigley and E. Smolensky. Harvard University Press.

Shoup, Carl S. 1964. Standards for Distributing a Free Government Service: Crime Protection. *Public Finance* 19: 383–392.

Shoup, Donald. 2005. *The High Cost of Free Parking*. Planners Press.

Sinai, Todd, and Nicholas S. Souleles. 2005. Owner-Occupied Housing as a Hedge Against Rent Risk. *Quarterly Journal of Economics* 120: 763–789.

Small, Kenneth A., and Erik T. Verhoef. 2007. *The Economics of Urban Transportation*. Routledge.

Smith, V. Kerry, and Ju-Chin Huang. 1995. Can Markets Value Air Quality? A Meta-Analysis of Hedonic Property Value Models. *Journal of Political Economy* 103: 209–227.

Sonstelie, Jon, and Andrew Narwold. 1984. State Income Taxes and Homeownership: A Test of the Tax Arbitrage Theory. *Journal of Urban Economics* 36: 249–277.

Strumpf, Koleman, and Paul Rhode. 2003. Assessing the Importance of the Tiebout Hypothesis: Local Heterogeneity from 1850 to 1990. *American Economic Review* 93: 1648–1677.

Ter-Minassian, T. 1997. *Fiscal Federalism in Theory and Practice*. International Monetary Fund.

Tiebout, Charles M. 1956. A Pure Theory of Local Expenditures. *Journal of Political Economy* 64: 416–424.

U.S. Environmental Protection Agency. 2009. *Acid Rain and Related Programs: 2007 Progress Report*. Government Printing Office.

Weitzman, Martin L. 1974. Prices vs. Quantities. *Review of Economic Studies* 41: 477–491.

Wheaton, William C. 1974. A Comparative Static Analysis of Urban Spatial Structure. *Journal of Economic Theory* 9: 223–237.

Wheaton, William C. 1977. Income and Urban Residence: An Analysis of Consumer Demand for Location. *American Economic Review* 67: 620–631.

Wheaton, William C. 1998. Land Use and Density in Cities with Congestion. *Journal of Urban Economics* 43: 258–272.

Wheaton, William C. 1993. Land Capitalization, Tiebout Mobility, and the Role of Zoning Regulations. *Journal of Urban Economics* 34: 102–117.

Wildasin, David E. 1986. *Urban Public Finance*. Harwood.

Williams, Joseph T. 1993. Agency and Ownership of Housing. *Journal of Real Estate Finance and Economics* 7: 83–97.

Wilson, John D. 1999. Theories of Tax Competition. *National Tax Journal* 52: 269–304.

Zenou, Yves. 2003. The Spatial Aspects of Crime. *Journal of the European Economic Association* 1: 459–467.

Index